HANDBOOK OF RESEARCH METHODS ON TRUST

CW00552148

Handbook of Research Methods on Trust

Edited by

Fergus Lyon

Professor of Enterprise and Organisation, Middlesex University Business School, UK

Guido Möllering

Associate Professor of Organization and Management, Jacobs University Bremen, Germany

Mark N.K. Saunders

Professor of Business Research Methods, Surrey Business School, University of Surrey, UK

Edward Elgar
Cheltenham, UK • Northampton, MA, USA

Published by
Edward Elgar Publishing Limited
The Lypiatts
15 Lansdown Road
Cheltenham
Glos GL50 2JA
UK

Edward Elgar Publishing, Inc.
William Pratt House
9 Dewey Court
Northampton
Massachusetts 01060
USA

A catalogue record for this book
is available from the British Library

Library of Congress Control Number: 2011928595

MIX
Paper from
responsible sources
FSC® C018575
www.fsc.org

ISBN 978 1 84844 767 7 (cased)

Typeset by Servis Filmsetting Ltd, Stockport, Cheshire
Printed and bound by MPG Books Group, UK

Contents

Figures and tables

FIGURES

TABLES

Editors

Fergus Lyon is Professor of Enterprise and Organizations in the Centre for Enterprise and Economic Development Research, Middlesex University. His research interests include trust and co-operation in networks and clusters, enterprise behaviour, social enterprise and entrepreneurship, market institutions, social enterprise and economic development policy. He has published widely, including in *Organization Studies, Cambridge Journal of Economics, Society and Space, World Development and Human Organisation*. He has carried out research in the UK, Ghana, Nigeria, India, Pakistan and Nepal. Recent work involves trust in business science relationships and he has established a five-year ESRC funded research programme on the Third Sector and Social Enterprises in the UK. This will involve research on trust in relationships between public, private and third sector organizations.

Guido Möllering is Associate Professor of Organization and Management at Jacobs University Bremen. He was previously a Senior Research Associate at the Max Planck Institute for the Study of Societies in Cologne, Germany. He received his doctorate in Management Studies from the University of Cambridge, UK, and his habilitation in Business Administration from Freie Universität Berlin, Germany. His research is mainly on trust and/or inter-organizational relationships. He has published widely in this area, with some articles in leading journals such as *Organization Science, Journal of International Business Studies* and *Sociology*. He serves on a number of editorial boards, for example as an Associate Editor of the *Journal of Trust Research*. He is the author of the book *Trust: Reason, Routine, Reflexivity* (Elsevier, 2006).

Mark N.K. Saunders is Professor in Business Research Methods at the University of Surrey, Surrey Business School. He was formerly Assistant Dean (Director of Research and Doctoral Programmes) and Professor of Business Research Methods at Oxford Brookes University Business School. He is a Visiting Professor at Newcastle Business School, Northumbria University and Worcester Business School, University of Worcester. His research interests include human resource aspects of the management of change, in particular trust, and research methods. He has published in management journals including *Personnel Review, European Journal of Work and Organisational Psychology, Journal of Personal*

Psychology, Service Industries Journal, Employee Relations, Management Learning and *International Journal of Public Sector Management.* He is a member of the editorial boards of *Personnel Review, Journal of Services Research* and the *Electronic Journal of Business Research.* Mark is co-editor (with Denise Skinner, Graham Dietz, Nicole Gillespie and Roy J. Lewicki) of *Organizational Trust: A Cultural Perspective* (Cambridge University Press, 2010) and lead author of *Research Methods for Business Students* (fifth edition, FT Prentice Hall, 2009), which has been translated into Chinese, Dutch and Russian. He has co-authored a range of other books, including *Strategic Human Resource Management* (FT Prentice Hall, 2007) and *Dealing with Statistics: What You Need to Know* (Open University Press McGraw Hill, 2008).

Contributors

Nadezhda Alex is a PhD Student at the University of Siegen. In 2006–8, she worked for the German research team of the EU-financed CBCED project on cross-border entrepreneurship, collecting and analysing data on trust and learning. Her thesis focuses on trust in cross-border co-operations between German and Bulgarian enterprises, considering different cultural contexts.

Melanie J. Ashleigh is a Senior Lecturer in the School of Management, University of Southampton. Her research interests cover a broad spectrum of disciplines, including trust in teams and technology, trust and transactive memory, trust and wellbeing and training and trust.

Reinhard Bachmann is Professor of Strategy at the University of Surrey. He has published widely in journals such as *Organization Studies*, *British Journal of Sociology* and the *Cambridge Journal of Economics*. Together with Christel Lane he edited *Trust Within and Between Organisations* (Oxford University Press, 1998/2000) and with Akbar Zaheer he edited the *Handbook of Trust Research* (Edward Elgar, 2006/2008) and the *Landmark Papers on Trust* (Edward Elgar, 2008). He is Deputy Editor-in-chief of the *Journal of Trust Research* and serves on the editorial board of *Organization Studies*. His work emphasizes the role of social mechanisms (trust, power, and so on) and societal influences (institutional arrangements, cultural traditions) on the structure and quality of organizational relationships and business strategies.

Davide Barrera is Assistant Professor in the Department of Social Sciences at the University of Turin. His areas of research interests include social mechanisms, behavioural game theory, co-operation problems and social networks. He has published on the effects of social networks in trust and co-operation problems.

Katinka M. Bijlsma-Frankema is Associate Professor of Organization Theory at VU University Amsterdam and Professor of Organization Sciences at the European Institute for Advanced Studies in Management. Her current research interests include trust, control and performance of teams. She is founder and past chair of the First International Network on Trust (FINT), in which 150 scholars from 29 countries participate, and chaired five international workshops on trust. She co-edited special issues on trust (and control), including *Group and Organization Management* (2007) and edited volumes on trust (Edward Elgar, 2005), and organizational control (Cambridge University Press, 2010).

Michelle C. Bligh is Associate Professor of Organizational Behavior at Claremont Graduate University. Her research interests include charismatic and political leadership, followership, interpersonal trust and gender issues. Her work has been published in the *Journal of Applied Psychology*, *Leadership Quarterly* and *Leadership*, and she serves on the editorial review boards of *Leadership Quarterly*, *Leadership* and the *European Journal of Work and Organizational Psychology*. Dr Bligh has helped a variety of public and private sector organizations assess and improve their effectiveness in the areas of leadership development, organizational culture and change management.

Boris F. Blumberg is Assistant Professor of Organization and Strategy at Maastricht University. He studied business economics at Mannheim and obtained a PhD in sociology from Utrecht University. Currently his research focuses on social networks, entrepreneurship and self-employment. Moreover, he has a keen interest in research methods and is author of *Business Research Methods* (McGraw-Hill, 2011), a leading textbook on business research methods.

Gerard Breeman is Assistant Professor at Wageningen University (Public Administration and Policy Group) and Research Fellow at the Montesquieu Institute in The Hague. His main research interests are policy agenda-setting, and trust and policy-making. He publishes in journals such as the *Journal of European Integration* and *Acta Politica*.

Chad Brinsfield is Assistant Professor of Management at the University of St Thomas, Opus College of Business, in Minneapolis. He received his MBA in Management and PhD in Labor and Human Resources from the Ohio State University, Fisher College of Business. He has extensive industry experience in manufacturing and logistics, including positions as a general manager for an international automotive parts supplier, and founder and president of a logistics services organization. He has researched and published in the areas of silence and voice in organizations, trust and commitment.

Calvin Burns is Lecturer in Organizational Behaviour at Strathclyde Business School, Glasgow. He is interested in the role of risk and trust in organizational safety culture. An emerging area of his work concerns automatic attitude activation about risk and trust and how this affects decision-making and risk-taking behaviour. Most of his work has been conducted in high-hazard industries such as construction, healthcare and oil and gas production. Currently, he is collaborating on a multi-disciplinary project about risk which is funded by the Canadian government. This will involve research on trust between different government agencies, and between government agencies and the general public.

Vincent Buskens is Professor of Theoretical Sociology in the Department of Sociology and the Interuniversity Center for Social Science Theory and Methodology (ICS) of Utrecht University, and Professor of Empirical Legal Studies at the Erasmus School of Law, Erasmus University, Rotterdam. His research focuses on social networks, trust and other social dilemma problems using experimental as well as survey methods. He is the author of *Social Networks and Trust* (Kluwer, 2002) and co-editor of the volume *eTrust: Forming Relationships in the Online World* (Russell Sage Foundation, 2009).

John S. Carroll is Morris A. Adelman Professor of Management at the MIT Sloan School of Management and Engineering Systems Division and Co-Director of the Lean Advancement Initiative. Dr Carroll conducts research on social-psychological and organizational factors that promote safety in high-hazard industries such as nuclear power and health care. He focuses on (1) safety culture as supported by communication, leadership, and systems thinking and (2) self-analysis and organizational learning. Dr Carroll is a Fellow of the American Psychological Society. He has published four books and numerous articles.

Stacey Conchie is Lecturer in Psychology at the University of Liverpool. She is interested in how trust affects risk communication, risk-taking, and safety in organizational settings. Most of her research has been conducted in high-risk or high-hazard industries such as construction, healthcare and oil and gas production. An emerging area of her work concerns automatic attitude activation about trust, or implicit trust.

Donald L. Ferrin is Associate Professor of Organizational Behavior at the Lee Kong Chian School of Business, Singapore Management University. His research focuses on many different aspects of trust in the workplace, including the nature of trust, determinants of trust and trust-formation processes, benefits and functions of trust, trust networks within organizations and trust repair after a violation. His recent work focuses on non-verbal and intuitive sources of trust, the dynamics of trust in the context of negotiation and corporate- and governmental-level trust repair strategies. His research has appeared in various scholarly journals such as the *Journal of Applied Psychology*, *Organizational Behavior and Human Decision Processes* and *Organization Science*.

Nicole Gillespie is Senior Lecturer in Management at the University of Queensland. She has held faculty and research positions at Warwick Business School, Melbourne Business School and the University of Melbourne. Her research interests include trust in organizational contexts (particularly building and repairing trust, developing trust across cultures and trust measurement), as well as leadership, team processes, stress and wellbeing and organizational change. Dr Gillespie's research appears in leading journals, including *Academy of Management Review*, *Journal of Management* and *Work and Stress*, as well as books and chapters (she is co-editor of *Organisational Trust: A Cultural Perspective*, Cambridge University Press, 2010).

Christine Goodall completed her doctorate at Staffordshire University in 2007 and since then has conducted independent research while continuing to work professionally in management within the voluntary sector. She also teaches management and social science subjects for Staffordshire University and has worked with the Department for Voluntary Sector Studies at the University of Wales, Lampeter.

Jeffrey C. Kohles is an Associate Professor of Management and Organizational Behaviour in the College of Business Administration, as well as Director and founding member of the Center for Leadership Innovation and Mentorship Building (CLIMB) at California State University, San Marcos. He was previously a Research Fellow at the Center for International Leadership in Buffalo, New York, as well as a Research Associate at the Kravis Leadership Institute in Claremont, California. His research interests include leadership, organizational communication, and the implementation of organization-level vision and strategy at the individual level. His research has been published in the *Academy of Management Review*, *Journal of Applied Psychology*, *Organizational Behaviour and Human Decision Processes*, *Leadership Quarterly*, *Leadership*, *Group and Organization Management*, *Journal of Managerial Psychology*, *Applied Psychology: An International Review*, *Academy of Management Best Papers Proceedings*, *European Business Forum* and *European Journal of Social Psychology*. He has also helped a variety of public and private sector organizations assess and improve their effectiveness in the areas of leadership development, organizational culture, strategy implementation and general product and service assessment methodology.

Roderick M. Kramer is the William R. Kimball Professor of Organizational Behavior at the Stanford University Graduate School of Business. He is the author of more than 100 scholarly articles, and his work has appeared in leading journals as well as in popular magazines such as the *Harvard Business Review*. He is also co-author of numerous books, including *Negotiation in Social Contexts*, *The Psychology of the Social Self*, *Trust in Organizations*, *Power and Influence in Organizations*, *The Psychology of Leadership*, *Trust and Distrust Within Organizations*, *Organizational Trust* and, most recently, *Social Decision Making*. Professor Kramer has been a Visiting Scholar at numerous institutions, including the Bellagio Center, London Business School, Oxford University, Harvard University and the Hoover Institution.

Torsten M. Kühlmann is Professor in the Department of Law, Economics and Business Administration at the University of Bayreuth, and he teaches human resource management. His research interests include expatriate management, opportunism, trust and control in transnational business relationships, and knowledge transfers in multi-national companies.

Roy J. Lewicki is the Irving Abramowitz Professor of Business Ethics and Professor of Management and Human Resources at the Max M. Fisher College of Business, Ohio State University. Professor Lewicki maintains research and teaching interests in the fields of negotiation, conflict management and dispute resolution, trust development, managerial leadership, organizational justice and ethical decision-making. His work on trust is currently focused on calibrating trust and distrust dynamics, and measuring trust development and repair. He is the author/editor of numerous research articles and 35 books, including *Essentials of Negotiation*, (McGraw Hill/Irwin, 2010), the leading academic textbook on negotiation.

Edgar Meyer is Senior Lecturer at the School of Management at the University of Southampton. His research interests cover a range of topics with special interests in knowledge, training transfer, learning in organizations, teamwork and leadership.

Miriam Muethel is Assistant Professor and the Chair of Leadership and Human Resource Management at WHU – Otto Beisheim School of Management. She has published in the *Journal of International Business Studies* (2010), the *Journal of International Management* (2010), the *Journal of World Business* (in press), *Management International Reviews* (in press) and in the *Academy of Management Proceedings* in 2007 and 2009. In 2009 she was awarded finalist of the Academy of Management Best Paper Award (TIM Division). Before joining WHU, Dr Muethel worked for over two years as a business consultant at Volkswagen in the area of international project management.

Robert Münscher is Head of Advisory Services at the Centre for Social Investment, Heidelberg University. He received his doctorate in Business

Administration from Bayreuth University in 2010. His research interests include trust, relationship management and intercultural collaboration in the business and the nonprofit sector.

Bart Nooteboom is the author of ten books, including *A Cognitive Theory of the Firm* (Edward Elgar, 2009), *Inter-firm Collaboration, Learning and Networks: An Integrated Approach* (Routledge, 2004), *Trust: Forms, Foundations, Functions, Failures and Figures* (Emerald Group, 2002), *Learning and Innovation in Organizations and Economies* (Oxford University Press, 2000), *Inter-firm Alliances: Analysis and Design* (Routledge, 1999), and some 300 articles on entrepreneurship, innovation and diffusion, organizational learning, transaction cost theory, interfirm relations and trust. He was awarded the Kapp prize for his work on organizational learning and the Gunnar Myrdal prize for his work on trust. He is a member of the Royal Netherlands Academy of Arts and Sciences.

José M. Peiró is Professor of Work and Organizational Psychology at the University of Valencia. He is Director of the Research Institute of Human Resources Psychology, Organizational Development and Quality of Working life (IDOCAL) and senior researcher at the Valencian Research Institute of Economics (IVIE). He is President-elect of the International Association for Applied Psychology, past President of the European Association of Work and Organizational Psychology and a Fellow member of the Society for Industrial and Organizational Psychology and the European Academy for Occupational Health Psychology. He has been Associate Editor of the *European Journal of Work and Organizational Psychology*.

Alex 'Sandy' Pentland is a pioneer in organizational engineering, mobile information systems and computational social science. His focus is the development of human-centred technology and the creation of ventures that take this technology into the real world. He directs the Human Dynamics Lab, helping companies to become more productive and creative through organizational engineering, and the Media Lab Entrepreneurship Program, which helps translate cutting-edge technology into real-world impact around the world. He is among the most-cited computer scientists in the world.

Richard L. Priem is the Robert L. and Sally S. Manegold Professor of Management in the Lubar School of Business at the University of Wisconsin-Milwaukee. He is founding Director of the M&I Marshall and Ilsley Corporation Center for Business Ethics and is a regular Visiting Professor at LUISS Guido Carli University in Rome. His research interests include: corporate governance, illegal behaviour, strategy-making processes, demand-side strategies, group- and organization-level trust and organizational theory. He serves on the editorial boards of the *Academy of Management Journal*, *Academy of Management Review*, *Journal of Management* and *Journal of Management Studies*.

Werner Raub is Professor of Sociology in the Department of Sociology and the Interuniversity Center for Social Science Theory and Methodology (ICS) of Utrecht University. His research interests include the development, application and test of formal theoretical models in various fields of the social sciences such as markets, organizations and households as well as experimental tests of such models. He has carried out research on trust in each of these fields and has published widely on these issues in sociology as well as economics, psychology and philosophy.

Robert A. Roe is Emeritus Professor of Organizational Theory and Organizational Behaviour at Maastricht University. He studied psychology and obtained his doctorate at the University of Amsterdam. He was Professor of Work and Organizational Psychology in Delft, Tilburg and Nijmegen, Director of the Work and Organization Research Centre in Tilburg, Director of the Netherlands Aeromedical Institute, and founding President of the European Association of Work and Organizational Psychology. He is currently President of the European Federation of Psychology Associations. His publications cover a broad range of topics in work and organizational psychology.

Denise M. Rousseau is the H.J. Heinz II University Professor of Organizational Behavior and Public Policy at Carnegie Mellon University's Heinz College and Tepper School of Business; she gained her doctorate in Psychology at UC Berkeley. Professor Rousseau is two-time winner of the Academy of Management's Terry Award for best management book. Recognized for developing psychological contract theory, her work addresses the powerful reach of individual employee understandings of the employment relationship on work, firms and society. A past President of the Academy of Management, she is a founder of the Evidence-Based Management Collaborative, promoting the better uptake and use of organizational research in management education and practice.

Rosalind H. Searle is a Senior Lecturer in Occupational Psychology at the Open University. Her overarching research interest is organizational trust, especially in human resource management (HRM) contexts: recruitment and selection, and performance management. She has researched in the UK, Europe and South Asia. Recent work has focused on trust and controls in HRM, early trust formation for applicants and the impact of trust in UK voters' decisions. She has co-edited a book on trust and HRM, co-leads an ESRC seminar series and EGOS SWG in these areas. She sits on the editorial board of the *Journal of Trust Research*.

Malin Tillmar is Associate Professor at the Division of Business Administration, Department of Management and Engineering, and board member at the HELIX Centre for Working Life Research, at Linköping University. Her research has often been concerned with small businesses. Apart from cross-cultural research on trust in inter-organizational settings, Tillmar has studied entrepreneurship within and through public sector organizations. Currently, trust in the inter-sectoral interactions occurring on the constructed markets for care services has caught her interest.

Eric M. Uslaner is Professor of Government and Politics at the University of Maryland–College Park and Senior Research Fellow at the Center for American Law and Political Science, Southwest University of Political Science and Law, Chongqing. He the author of seven books, including *The Moral Foundations of Trust* (Cambridge University Press, 2002), *Corruption, Inequality, and the Rule of Law: The Bulging Pocket Makes the Easy Life* (Cambridge University Press, 2008) and *Segregation and Mistrust* (Cambridge University Press, forthcoming), and approximately 120 articles. In 2010 he held the US Fulbright Commission Distinguished Chair in American Political Science at the Australian National University.

Benjamin Waber is a doctoral candidate in the Human Dynamics Group at the MIT Media Lab and a graduate student affiliate at the Institute for Quantitative Social Science at Harvard University. Benjamin has been at the forefront of applying sensor and electronic data to management research, studying problems such as informal communication structure, office layout, team behaviour and employee training. His current research interests include dynamic organizational design, organizational behaviour, social networks, sensor networks, prediction mechanisms and information flow.

Antoinette A. Weibel is Professor of Management and Academic Director of the Undergraduate Studies Programme at the University of Liechtenstein and Fellow of Center of Research in Economics, Management, and the Arts at the University of Zurich. She is President of FINT and co-chair of the standard working group on trust in organizations at the European Group of Organizational Studies. Her research interests include: trust in organizations, trust and controls, inter-organizational trust and alliance governance, institutions and intrinsic motivation as well as wellbeing in the workplace.

Friederike Welter is Professor at Jönköping International Business School and Visiting Professor at the Small Business Research Centre at Kingston

University, UK. She was awarded the TeliaSonera Professorship of Entrepreneurship at Stockholm School of Economics in Riga, Latvia, for her research on entrepreneurship in a transition context. She has published widely, both nationally and internationally, on entrepreneurship-related topics; and she is Associate Editor of *Entrepreneurship Theory and Practice* as well as being on the review board of other international entrepreneurship and small business journals.

Michele Williams is Assistant Professor of Organizational Behaviour at Cornell University. Her research focuses on the development of co-operative, high-performance interpersonal relationships, especially on projects involving people from multiple organizations or groups within an organization. Her research concentrates on the influences of interpersonal processes, such as perspective-taking, on how interpersonal trust and co-operation evolve. Professor Williams has consulted on effective collaboration for public and private organizations such as Booz Allen and Hamilton and Massachusetts General Hospital. She is also co-author of the 4-CAP Leadership Assessment – a 360° assessment used by organizations to enhance the leadership potential of managers.

Acknowledgements

In compiling the *Handbook of Research Methods on Trust* we have been fortunate to have a large number of our friends and colleagues in the community of trust researchers who have helped us. While many of these are represented in this volume by their chapters, there are others to whom we are also extremely grateful. Invariably many of the methods discussed by our contributors have been discussed at conferences and seminars as well as in classes with students. We would therefore like to thank all those who have commented on and critiqued all the methods in this volume during their development. The development of methods used could not have been possible without research participants. These people, and in many instances the organization for which they work, give freely of their time and experiences thereby enabling us all, as trust researchers, to research this fascinating social phenomenon. On behalf of all trust researchers, we thank you.

Inevitably, as with any book, in addition to our contributors, there are a number of people whom we would like to thank personally. Tally Hatzakis (formerly of Brunel University) was involved in the early stages of this volume, in developing the overall structure and eliciting contributors and deserves a special mention. We thank Katinka Bijlsma-Frankema as former chair of the First International Network on Trust (FINT) who hosted the workshops in Amsterdam where our first specific discussions on trust and methods were started in a special track (2005) and a special plenary session (2007), giving rise to this handbook. We are also particularly grateful to Sue Engelbert of Middlesex University, UK, for her assistance in managing the editing process.

Ellen Dederichs has kindly given us permission to use her painting 'B.A. Urbano – Calle Comercial II' (2009) for the cover design. As editors, we think the blurred features of people and buildings represent very well the uncertainty encountered by trustors and trust researchers.

Last but not least we thank the people at Edward Elgar Publishing, especially Francine O'Sullivan as the original commissioning editor, who has been positive about the idea of this handbook ever since we mentioned it to her in November 2005, and also Jennifer Wilcox and Rebecca Hastie at the later stages for their admirable patience and support.

1 Introduction: the variety of methods for the multi-faceted phenomenon of trust

Fergus Lyon, Guido Möllering and Mark N.K. Saunders

A reader who picks up this handbook will, we imagine, share the excitement and frustration about trust that thinkers have experienced for millennia and that is still felt throughout the growing community of trust researchers nowadays: how trust is one of the most fascinating and fundamental social phenomena yet at the same time one of the most elusive and challenging concepts one could study. As scholars we have to reach past the undying topicality and apparent importance of trust as we apply our research methods to this challenge, only to realize their limitations when the object of study is trust. The chapters in this handbook show that we have a broad array of methods that help us rise to the challenge of capturing at least part of the multi-faceted phenomenon of trust.

To date, an overview of the many methods that can be used for studying trust has been missing. It is our aim to provide such an overview with this handbook, while recognizing that it cannot be fully exhaustive. Through this handbook we hope to encourage trust researchers to reflect on the methods they use, to acknowledge contributions from a variety of methodological positions and to improve methods and instruments according to the specific challenges posed by trust. Our optimism in this respect is based on the relative methodological openness and pluralism we have observed in the trust research community. Perhaps more than in other fields, our research topic prevents methodological hubris as it constantly reminds us how no method can provide the perfect understanding of a phenomenon.

In line with these considerations, the editors and contributors of this volume have explored trust from a variety of directions. As trust is a concept that cannot be easily observed or even defined, the trust research community has drawn on ideas across academia to gain a better understanding of it. This book reflects on the journeys of trust researchers and through the sharing of their experiences hopes to cast light on methods for those researching trust.

The origins of this book lie in conversations the editors have had with fellow researchers coming together at international events to share their work on trust over the past 10 years and more. In particular the growing number of publications on trust, the activities of FINT (First International Network on Trust), now in its tenth year, and the newly established *Journal of Trust Research* demonstrate a diversity of methods, disciplines, traditions and nations. Our common interest in trust coincides with wide-ranging ideas on how to study it.

As research on trust matures, the opportunity arises to consider the innovative developments by trust researchers in the methods they have used in order to examine this concept. In this book, a wide range of methods for researching trust are brought together for the first time. Our selected chapters are drawn from across a range of divides, with the aim to span boundaries whether they are between disciplines, between theoretical positions, methodological traditions or geographical regions. The chapter contributors demonstrate the true international nature of the interest in trust research, reflecting research in North America, Asia, Australasia, Africa and Europe. As trust research grows and more people aim to include an element of researching trust in their work, the chapters in this book can serve as a guide through a wide range of methodological approaches.

Research on trust can be traced back at least to work in the 1960s and 1970s with a range of influential exploratory pieces (such as Deutsch, 1973; Garfinkel, 1967; Rotter, 1967; Zand, 1972). In the 1980s and 1990s there was much research on conceptual aspects, followed by a wide range of empirical and experimental studies from the late 1990s to the present (see Bachmann and Zaheer, 2006; Möllering, 2006). The chapters in this handbook explore elements of this history and identify future directions, with particular emphasis on research process and methods.

Trust research traditions have given rise to a broad range of definitional debates which are well addressed by Rousseau et al. (1998), Möllering (2006) and Dietz and Den Hartog (2006), to name just a few. Seppanen et al. (2007) in their review found that there are over 70 definitions of the concept of trust (see also Castaldo, 2007). We have therefore taken a broad definition in giving guidance to the contributors, adopting Rousseau et al. (1998: 395): 'the psychological state comprising the intention to accept vulnerability based upon positive expectations of the intentions or behaviour of another'. However, debates on definitions in the English-language academic literature continue, paying little attention to the role of culture and language and the importance of understanding which word is used for trust, and its other interpretations (Saunders et al., 2010). In this book, we therefore recognize the diversity of trust concepts found in academic writing and readers will find variations between chapters.

This book does not aim to be a social science methods text; we accept that not all areas of research methods on trust have been included. We have tried to identify those areas that require additional attention to methods when looking at trust. We have also concentrated on the empirical elements of researching trust. We appreciate the value of theoretical and conceptual writings on trust (for example Baier, 1986; Hardin, 2002; Luhmann, 1979; Misztal, 1996; Nooteboom, 2002), but the remit we set ourselves and our fellow contributors was to look at practical concerns in empirical trust research.

The chapters are aimed at both new and established researchers. They will appeal to those new to trust who wish to explore possible methods as well as those who have been researching trust from a particular tradition interested in considering alternatives. The knowledge and understanding of research methods on trust is dissipated across the broad, multidisciplinary community of trust researchers, necessitating considerable detective work by those interested. This book seeks to draw together into one volume the wealth of research-method experience gained by trust researchers.

Each chapter summarizes the state of the art of an element of trust research as perceived by the authors. We have encouraged contributors to inspire others and give a flavour of this diversity of trust research rather than provide a full review. We believe that no one method – whether quantitative or qualitative, used on its own or in conjunction with others – is stronger or weaker than another. Rather, we ask our readers to consider each in its own context. For this reason, every contributor has presented their own experience of using a particular method. In each chapter, researchers examine different methodological issues and particular methods and share their experiences of what works, what does not work, their challenges and innovations. These reflections are central to the ethos of the book and distinguish it from other methods handbooks. We are not aiming to be definitive but sharing, because as researchers we learn by experimentation.

Part I of the book identifies conceptual issues and empirical approaches to researching them. The chapters by Roderick M. Kramer (Chapter 2) and Roy Lewicki and Chad Brinsfield (Chapter 3) consider how trust can be measured, raising points that are subsequently developed in chapters throughout the book, most notably in the chapter on quantitative measures by Nicole Gillespie (Chapter 17). The chapter by Bart Nooteboom (Chapter 4) introduces further measurement and conceptual challenges, particularly in cases when there is complex interaction between agents. He uses simulations to demonstrate the importance of trust and benevolence. The following two parts demonstrate qualitative and quantitative methods to researching trust at different scales: micro, meso and societal.

Part II of the book looks at qualitative methods and Part III examines quantitative methods, although many chapters demonstrate how qualitative and quantitative methods may be mixed in the same study. The final part draws conclusions for the future of trust research, the chapter by Katinka Bijlsma-Frankema and Denise Rousseau (Chapter 24) identifying future challenges for trust research.

CONCEPTUALIZING TRUST

As shown in later chapters, the current literature on the concept of trust can be divided in a number of ways. In each of these, trust research focuses on a particular element, often related to what is considered a suitable research subject within the disciplines of the researchers involved. These are not competing elements, rather they represent different ways in which to approach the exploration of trust. Six clusters can be identified and are examined in more detail below:

1.1   Antecedents

There has been much research on the preconditions for trust, building on the work of Mayer et al. (1995), who proposed that trust can be predicted by different factors of trustworthiness such as ability, benevolence and integrity. Drawing on organizational behaviour research and psychology, attention has been given to examining the differences between issues of trustworthiness, propensity to trust and trusting behaviour (Dietz et al., 2010). There is a wide range of survey measures, ranging from the consequences of trust, to trustworthiness and trusting attitudes. However, as Nicole Gillespie points out (in Chapter 17), there is a need to distinguish trust from perceived trustworthiness and a need to consider the willingness to be vulnerable.

1.2   Processes of Building Trust

Research on trust-building draws on a wide range of disciplines. Roy Lewicki and Chad Brinsfield (Chapter 3) provide an overview of the role of laboratory-based experimental strategies using simulation games to understand the underpinnings of trust judgements. Donald N. Ferrin, Michelle C. Bligh and Jeffrey C. Kohles (Chapter 18) also show the importance of seeing trust as interdependence, as explained by Rousseau et al. (1998). They note that much research has shied away from this, with methodologies assuming independent actors rather than examining dyadic relations where trust in one partner affects trust held by the other party. Field research on building trust has been an important element of the literature on trust and is explored in chapters by Friederike Welter and Nadezhda Alex (Chapter 5) and Malin Tillmar (Chapter 10) as well as others. Such approaches can focus on the personal relationships but may examine the institutional context as well, such as the political, legal and economic framework, and even the informal rules that make up culturally specific institutions.

1.3 The Context Shaping Trust-building

The chapters on trust-building demonstrate the importance of understanding culture and recognize the danger of assuming context away. Trust has been shown to be a process that is deeply embedded in social relations (Granovetter, 1985). Friederike Welter and Nadezhda Alex (Chapter 5) use a field study to examine how trust is part of entrepreneurial activity and how this is shaped by the cultural and regulatory context. Using a very different strategy – laboratory experiments – Davide Barrera, Vincent Buskens and Werner Raub (Chapter 19) examine how the concept of embeddedness can be brought into such controlled environments. Research on how context shapes trust is not without its challenges. Roderick M. Kramer (Chapter 2) describes the small and subtle context specific behaviours, both verbal and non-verbal cues, in trust-building.

1.4 Decision-making Processes in Trust

Linked to research on the antecedents of trust and the trust-building processes is a set of literature that debates the decision-making processes of trust. Distinctions can be drawn from those who examine trust as a rational choice or calculation (Williamson, 1993) in contrast to studies that take a wider view of trust that also includes the actions that are routinized, intuitive, habitual and often not explicitly stated (Kramer, 1996; Lyon, 2005; Möllering, 2006; Nooteboom, 1999). In this book, Richard L. Priem and Antoinette A. Weibel (Chapter 20) study the decision-making in trust, recognizing the importance of understanding when individuals face cognitive and emotional constraints. Similarly, Bart Nooteboom (Chapter 4), shows that, with incomplete contracts, calculative self-interest cannot explain everything and so there is a need to include other elements, such as benevolence.

1.5   Implications and Uses of Trust

There is a plethora of comparative studies that aim to compare organizations, individuals and the impact of different degrees of types of trust on performance or social outcomes. Research on consequences of trust in business and management has examined the effect on financial performance (Zaheer and Harris, 2005), alliances or innovation (Nooteboom, 2002), while there has been other research looking at the effect of trust on health outcomes and other aspects of human interaction (for example Brownlie et al., 2008).

These outcomes of trust can be examined at a range of scales, distinguishing between the micro, organizational/inter-organizational and societal levels (Bachmann and Zaheer, 2006; Nooteboom, 2002). In this book we present three conceptual chapters, each focusing on one of these scales. Friederike Welter and Nadezhda Alex (Chapter 5) look at the micro scale of interpersonal entrepreneurial relations. Boris F. Blumberg, Jose M. Pieró and Robert A. Roe (Chapter 6) look at a meso scale with networks of social capital, when researching inter-organizational relationships. There are also debates about the extent to which there is trust between organizations as entities themselves or between individuals within each organization (McEvily et al., 2003; Zaheer et al., 1998). At a societal scale, Eric M. Uslaner (Chapter 7) examines the applicability of surveys that ask about the degree of generalized or moralistic trust that people have in others who are not known to them.

1.6   Lack of Trust, Distrust, Mistrust and Repair

The final cluster of research focuses on distinctions made between lack of trust, distrust and mistrust. Research on the consequences of trust has also included the downside of trust when individuals put themselves at risk (McEvily et al., 2003) or over-trust (Goel and Karri, 2006) that can lead to trust violations (Lewicki and Bunker, 1996; Dirks et al., 2009). Boris F. Blumberg, Jose M. Pieró and Robert A. Roe (Chapter 6) show how trust can be eroded through lack of use or can suffer a radical loss if there is opportunism. Roy J. Lewicki and Chad Brinsfield (Chapter 3) discuss how trust is not always advantageous and can be misplaced. Furthermore, drawing on previous work (Lewicki et al., 1998), they point out that trust and distrust are independent constructs that can be held in the same relationship for different facets of that relationship. This leads to a further stream of research on relationship repair following violation, but the lack of longitudinal research has limited the insights in this area to date.

These categorizations may not do justice to the wide range of research, much of which aims to draw together the different elements outlined above. Some studies try to capture trust very broadly while others are only interested in a particular element of trust, because their main interest is in another concept. Hence, Möllering (2006) distinguishes between studies with trust as a central concern as opposed to those that examine it as a peripheral aspect. Moreover, some studies set out to study the concept from the start while others include trust as it emerges from a more inductive process or as an explanatory variable (see Möllering, 2006). It may be late in the research process when researchers stumble across the concept and decide to examine it in more detail (for example Sitkin and Stickel, 1996). When trust was not part of the original research design or was considered merely a control variable, perhaps one cannot expect as much methodological care and rigour as if it were at the core of the study. We hope that the overview given in this handbook, though, will also be useful to those for whom trust is peripheral, at least as they start out.

This section has examined the different approaches to conceptualizing the issues surrounding the concept of trust. These could be referred to as the ontological issues. It is not the purpose of this book to focus on ontology; rather, our aim is to shed light on the methodological issues behind research in each approach. In this way, this book is more about the epistemological challenges, although we recognize that this cannot be considered without clarity in ontology. The next section examines some of the methodological issues in more detail. In deciding on a structure, we have adopted the widely used division of qualitative and quantitative. Within this we acknowledge that trust research can and does mix both, either through drawing on different methods to examine different aspects sequentially, or by explicitly developing methods that use both qualitative and quantitative methods concurrently (Teddlie and Tashakkori, 2010). Examples of the latter include the card sort methods (Miriam Muethel, Chapter 12, and Mark N.K. Saunders, Chapter 11) or repertory grid methods (Reinhard Bachmann, Chapter 13, and Melanie J. Ashleigh and Edgar Meyer, Chapter 14).

QUALITATIVE METHODS

Traditions of qualitative research have been particularly important for shedding light on the processes of building trust and theory-building. Qualitative methods are found in both the inductive approaches of building theories, as in the chapters by Malin Tillmar on ethnography (Chapter 10) and by Reinhard Bachmann on the repertory grid technique (Chapter

13), and in deductive approaches that aim to test theories using qualitative data, such as in the chapter by Roderick M. Kramer (Chapter 2). In this section we explore some of the methods used in trust research, recognizing that there is much in common with issues in qualitative research more generally.

The inductive approach allows for more open and less structured data collection methods that might enable new concepts to emerge that were not previously found in the literature. Ethnographic methods have had a long tradition of such research but have only received limited use in trust research. Malin Tillmar (Chapter 10) shows how these methods may achieve insights and access to sensitive data that may involve learning the language in order to understand the facets of trust in different cultures. Through cross-case comparisons in two countries, she goes on to show how valuable insights can be made of one's own culture.

The use of qualitative methods also allows respondents to define what they mean by trust, and as Reinhard Bachmann (Chapter 13) shows, there is a need to question the assumptions of universality frequently found in many frameworks of trust. This is important in cross-cultural research that recognizes that people from different cultures and languages may develop and apply trust constructs in different ways. Melanie J. Ashleigh and Edgar Meyer, Robert Münscher and Torsten M. Kühlmann, and Calvin Burns and Stacey Conchie (Chapters 14, 16 and 22) examine how trust constructs differ according to culture.

With the depth of information required in qualitative research, access to subjects for an extended period of time becomes an issue. While qualitative research on trust can involve a large number of shorter interviews, many methods set out in the book require that the participants provide over an hour of their time. In some organizations, people can be instructed to take part, but in others there is the need to build up trust and relationships with the participant. The chapter by Fergus Lyon (Chapter 8) explores this in detail, showing how interviewees in his research made comparisons between the relationship with the researcher and their own practices of building trust in business. Access is a greater challenge when dealing with sensitive issues. Mark N.K. Saunders (Chapter 11) shows how methods, such as the use of card sorts, can be used to break the ice and build rapport prior to conducting in-depth interviews. Malin Tillmar (Chapter 10) found that if she was seen in the communities in which she was working and demonstrated that she was making an effort to integrate (such as by learning the language), respondents would tell her more.

Similarly, access becomes a crucial issue when dealing with what some refer to as 'hard-to-reach groups', often involved in more informal activities or even illegality. Friederike Welter and Nadezhda Alex (Chapter 5) examine entrepreneurs' cross-border trade that had elements of sensitivity relating to getting through customs, and Christine Goodall's chapter (Chapter 9) on trust between new arrivals and settled communities explores how she gained access to people who would otherwise be very suspicious of people asking about this topic.

While interviewing has dominated much qualitative research, there is a wide range of other methods as well. Malin Tillmar (Chapter 10) shows that observation is an element of ethnography that can yield important results as it shows what people are doing, rather than what they are claiming to be doing, or wanting the researcher to think they are doing. Robert Münscher and Torsten M. Kühlmann (Chapter 16) use the critical incident technique to focus on key moments in cross-cultural management within firms, using observations to gather data that complement interview-based data. Gerard Breeman (Chapter 15) uses the careful analysis of historical records and diaries, letters and other texts to understand trust, in what he refers to as the hermeneutic method.

There is also innovative work on researching non-linguistic approaches; pauses, silences and laughter, all of which are important indicators of how people respond to questions (Lyon, 2005). This is invariably lost in written responses to questions. There is also research on the role of emotions, shown through voiced utterances, emphasis, pitch and speaking speed. This presents challenges for coding and analysis although transcripts may capture it. Benjamin Waber and colleagues (Chapter 23) write on trust between medical staff when the subject has no time to stop, and they show how this can be coded, quantified and explored.

QUANTITATIVE METHODS

A wide range of quantitative trust scales and measures, highlighted earlier, have been explored using surveys of 'real-world situations' or through laboratory experiments. Whilst this diversity has allowed trust research to grow, the lack of convergence and replication is striking (see the review by McEvily and Tortoriello, 2011). Nicole Gillespie (Chapter 17) shows that a lack of common questions can limit the extent of replication in different contexts and cultures. She proposes a common set of psychometric measurements of trustworthiness and trusting behaviour that can be widely used for comparative purposes.

Questionnaire surveys have been used to explore all elements of trust research. Research on societal generalized trust has been common across a wide range of countries. Similar questions have been used, thereby allowing cultural comparisons to be made about trusting attitudes or moralistic trust (asking 'can people be trusted?'). Eric M. Uslaner (Chapter 7) examines the challenges of such questions, including how they might be interpreted in different cultures and how responses could be shaped by the ordering of questions in surveys. However, he also notes a consistency of responses, over time and between questions, suggesting that the established 'trust questions' are rigorous.

While much research has focused on the elements of trusting behaviour, other surveys focus on trust related to interaction with a specific person or actor, with valuable information collected on patterns of how trust can be built up. Rosalind H. Searle (Chapter 21) shows that a diary method can be used to collect data using structured questions to allow comparisons between people and changes over time. However, as for other research on trust, she is sensitive to the challenges of using the word 'trust' in surveys as it can change behaviour.

Other approaches look at measuring the frequency of trusting interactions and their nature. The methods of card sorting, ranking and repertory grid analysis (Chapters 11, 12, 13 and 14) show that there can also be a mixing of quantitative and qualitative methods and, consequently, an element of quantification of results. Using multiple quantitative methods can provide quantitative data such as recording the responses of individuals after they have read a vignette or a particular case study provided by the researcher (see Chapter 19 by Davide Barrera, Vincent Buskens and Werner Raub).

Laboratory experiments have been particularly important in trust research as a way to explore basic cognitive processes in a controlled setting. Roderick M. Kramer shows the power of such research in examining trust, particularly when it can be combined with other methods outside of the laboratory. Roy J. Lewicki and Chad Brinsfield (Chapter 3) review some of the interactive experiments or trust games that look at individual behaviour. Donald L. Ferrin and colleagues (Chapter 18) follow up on this work by looking at dyads, that is both sides of the relationship, recognizing that each side in a trust relationship is not working independently, whether they are co-workers, leaders/followers or partners in a joint venture.

Innovative approaches to laboratory experiments are also being developed in trust research. Calvin Burns and Stacey Conchie (Chapter 22) examine the more tacit side of trusting relationships that might not be evident from surveys or verbal responses. They measure the strength of associations related to trust concepts by calculating the time taken to respond to stimuli. Similarly, Roy J. Lewicki and Chad Brinsfield (Chapter 3) refer to the intuitive trust based on facial characteristics. There are also insights from neuro-economics, which has examined the roles of hormones such as oxytocin on trust (for example Kosfeld et al., 2005; Zak et al., 2004).

METHODOLOGICAL CHALLENGES

The methodological challenges of researching trust are illuminated throughout each chapter in this book, as authors reflect on their own work. Five key themes can be identified that present trust research with its specific challenges: the dynamic process of trust; researching tacit elements of trust; conceptualizing and describing trust in different cultures; the role of researchers in shaping the trust situation they are researching; and research ethics of trust. These challenges also point the way towards future research opportunities in the field.

As outlined earlier, trust is a dynamic process as it is built up, used, maintained, broken and repaired. The temporal element is rarely captured in trust research but longitudinal data collection methods can allow such processes to be captured. Nicole Gillespie (Chapter 17) shows how research on measures of trustworthiness can be related to trust behaviour, Rosalind H. Searle (Chapter 21) shows how diaries can be used to record processes over time (although as research progresses the dropout rate tends to increase) and Robert Münscher and Torsten M. Kühlmann (Chapter 16) show how high-quality interviewing skills used to examine critical incidents in relationships can capture the dynamism of changing trust relationships over time.

Methodologically, the less visible or tacit forms of trust are particularly hard to identify and collect data about as they may not be expressed explicitly by those involved. Research in this volume shows how trust can be captured by recording the non-verbal responses, with innovative approaches examining people's response to particular words (see Calvin Burns and Stacey Conchie, Chapter 22). However, research has to recognize that trust cannot be explained by rational choice alone as there are emotional constraints that can be intuitive or routinized.

The cultural dimension of trust is particularly important and increasingly recognized as central to trust research (Saunders et al., 2010). With cross-cultural research come methodological challenges of language translation and questions of whether the scales of trust commonly used can be transferred across cultures. This issue is discussed in detail by Katinka M. Bijlsma-Frankema and Denise M. Rousseau in their examination of the 'generality' of trust research results (Chapter 24). Friederike Welter and Nadezhda Alex (Chapter 5) show this is particularly difficult in comparative work between countries, and Christine Goodall (Chapter 9) shows the challenges of working on this topic with new arrivals in a UK community. Reinhard Bachmann (Chapter 13) cautions against assuming universality on any concept, although there are approaches which explore these differences. Miriam Muethel (Chapter 12) uses a board game to allow researchers to explore how people from different cultures use language related to trust. Malin Tillmar (Chapter 10) explores how ethnographic methods and a researcher's knowledge of the different languages can help. Replication of studies in different cultures along with careful analysis will allow for more insights into those conceptual elements that are more universal, although as both Nicole Gillespie (Chapter 17) and Roy J. Lewicki and Chad Brinsfield (Chapter 3) show, there has been little consistency in the questions being asked by different surveys.

The fourth methodological challenge identified here is the role of the researcher. Researching trust raises issues of reflexivity, including trust between researcher and the researched. Both Fergus Lyon (Chapter 8) and Malin Tillmar (Chapter 10) show that how the researcher is perceived shapes the information provided. These chapters and others show the significance of building up relationships of trust with interviewees and how important it is to pay careful attention to issues that might create mistrust (such as the use of interview recording in some situations). Research can also change relationships by talking about trust. Rosalind H. Searle (Chapter 21) refers to psychological reactance, Mark N.K. Saunders (Chapter 11) highlights that discussing trust can lead to stress or behaviour change, and Robert Münscher and Torsten M. Kühlman (Chapter 16) are sensitive to the distress that discussing critical incidents can have on respondents.

This leads to the final methodological challenge related to the ethics of research on trust. As mentioned earlier, trust research covers topics that are sensitive in nature, either within an organization or community, or between groups. Where these activities have an element of illegality or secrecy this becomes particularly challenging. Christine Goodall (Chapter 9) shows that there is a tendency for respondents to report trust in neighbours or authority as they wish to appear trusting; Calvin Burns and Stacey Conchie (Chapter 22) refer to the risk of people giving socially desirable answers in interviews. A further ethical dilemma arises when looking at different sides of a trust relationship when there are likely to be different views of the same situation and the potential for research to affect the relationship negatively.

LOOKING AHEAD

The more recent growth in trust research is evidenced by the large proliferation in publications on the subject. In this book we reflect on the different strategies for researching trust, the range of innovative methods that have been developed by trust researchers, and the methodological challenges that are particular to trust. As Roy J. Lewicki and Chad Brinsfield suggest (Chapter 3), trust research appears to be undergoing a process of divergence not convergence of paradigms. Parallel debates are taking place in the literature of different disciplines, whether they are management and organization studies, sociology, geography, anthropology, psychology, institutional economics, political science or emerging schools such as neuro-economics. There is a risk that each school of thought will develop a self-referential discourse and language, although we note that many trust researchers are trying to break across these boundaries.

Trust research is frequently going beyond disciplines and being carried out by interdisciplinary researchers or interdisciplinary teams. The methodological challenge of bringing different schools and different disciplinary methods together is touched on in a number of chapters. Friederike Welter and Nadezhda Alex (Chapter 5) show how the interaction in international interdisciplinary groups of scholars also requires an element of trust. However, such combinations of disciplines and professions provide their own challenges in terms of comparing findings or interpreting studies that test the same hypotheses using very different methods.

The future directions of trust research are therefore diverse, but a number of trends can be identified. There is an emerging focus on culture and a move beyond a focus on assuming universality of trust constructs developed in North America and Western Europe. The chapters in this volume illuminate methods and associated issues when researching how trust operates in different contexts and cultures. Such methods need to recognize cultural differences between countries, within countries, between professions and between sectors. Specific methods such as card sorts (Chapter 12 by Miriam Müthel) and ethnography (Chapter 10 by Malin Tillmar) offer alternative ways to explore the different underlying cultural interpretations.

Trust appears to be of growing interest following the breakdown of many institutions that were previously relied on, whether they were related to international financial systems or community-level engagement and relationships. These challenges to the status quo also throw up new forms of trust-building that are worthy of academic investigation. Examples include new forms of relationships arising from e-commerce and virtual networking, or new forms of organizing that rely on cooperation and collaboration. These may be at the bilateral level, at the community scale or at the macro scale in wider societal levels of trust in others and formal institutions. There are demands from different disciplines to explain changes in trust and new opportunities arising to challenge disciplinary conventions such as rational choice models in economics. These require clear thought regarding method.

As mentioned at the start of this chapter, this volume is an exercise of a community of researchers sharing their ideas and experiences of researching trust. It is not a definitive textbook, although it identifies a diversity of research methods that new researchers can explore in more detail elsewhere. It is part of the process of reflecting on methodology and demonstrating a stage in the maturity of trust research. As editors, we believe this handbook will contribute to the next stage of trust research as it cuts across boundaries, whether they are disciplinary, professional, sectoral or geographical.

REFERENCES

Bachmann, R. and A. Zaheer (2006), *Handbook of Trust Research*, Cheltenham, UK and Northampton, MA, USA: Edward Elgar.

Baier, A. (1986), 'Trust and antitrust', *Ethics*, **69** (2), 231–60.

Brownlie, J., A. Greene and A. Howson (2008), *Researching Trust and Health*, London: Routledge.

Castaldo, S. (2007), *Trust in Market Relationships*, Cheltenham, UK and Northampton, MA, USA: Edward Elgar.

Deutsch, M. (1973), *The Resolution of Conflict*, New Haven, CT: Yale University Press.

Dietz, G. and D.N. Den Hartog (2006), 'Measuring trust inside organisations', *Personnel Review*, **35** (5), 557–88.

Dietz, G., N. Gillespie and G.T. Chao (2010), 'Unravelling the complexities of trust and culture', in M.N.K. Saunders, D. Skinner, G. Dietz, N. Gillespie and R.J. Lewicki (eds), *Organizational Trust: A Cultural Perspective*, Cambridge: Cambridge University Press, pp. 3–41.

Dirks, K.T., R.J. Lewicki and A. Zaheer (2009), 'Repairing relationships within and between organizations: building a conceptual foundation', *Academy of Management Review*, **34** (1), 68–84.

Garfinkel, H. (1967), *Studies in Ethnomethodology*, Englewood Cliffs, NJ: Prentice Hall.

Goel, S. and R. Karri (2006), 'Entrepreneurs, effectual logic, and over-trust', *Entrepreneurship Theory and Practice*, **30** (5), 477–93.

Granovetter, M.S. (1985), 'Economic action and social structure: the problem of embeddedness', *American Journal of Sociology*, **91** (3), 481–510.

Hardin, R. (2002), *Trust and Trustworthiness*, New York: Russell Sage Foundation.

Kosfeld, M., M. Heinrichs, P.J. Zak, U. Fischbacher and E. Fehr (2005), 'Oxytocin increases trust in humans', *Nature*, **435** (7042), 673–6.

Kramer, R.M. (1996), 'Divergent realities and convergent disappointments in the hierarchic relation: trust and the intuitive auditor at work', in R.M. Kramer and T.R. Tyler (eds), *Trust in Organizations: Frontiers of Theory and Research*, Thousand Oaks, CA: Sage, pp. 216–45.

Lewicki, R.J. and B.B. Bunker (1996), 'Developing and maintaining trust in work relationships', in R. Kramer and T.R. Tyler (eds), *Trust in Organizations: Frontiers of Theory and Research*, Thousand Oaks, CA: Sage, pp. 114–39.

Lewicki, R.J., D.J. McAllister and R.J. Bies (1998), 'Trust and distrust: new relationships and realities', *Academy of Management Review*, **23** (3), 438–58.

Luhmann, N. (1979), *Trust and Power: Two Works by Niklas Luhmann*, Chichester: Wiley.

Lyon, F. (2005), 'Managing co-operation: trust and power in Ghanaian associations', *Organization Studies*, **27** (1), 31–52.

Mayer, R., J. Davis and F. Schoorman (1995), 'An integrative model of organisational trust', *Academy of Management Review*, **20** (3), 709–34.

McAllister, D.J. (1995), 'Affect- and cognition-based trust as foundations for interpersonal cooperation in organizations', *Academy of Management Journal*, **38** (1), 24–59.

McEvily, B. and M. Tortoriello (2011), 'Measuring trust in organisational research: review and recommendations', *Journal of Trust Research*, **1** (1), 23–63.

McEvily, B., V. Perrone and A. Zaheer (2003), 'Trust as an organizing principle', *Organization Science*, **14** (1), 91–103.

Misztal, B.A. (1996), *Trust in Modern Societies*, Cambridge: Polity Press.

Möllering, G. (2006), *Trust: Reason, Routine, Reflexivity*, Oxford: Elsevier.

Nooteboom, B. (1999), *Inter-firm Alliances: Analysis and Design*, London: Routledge.

Nooteboom, B. (2002), *Trust: Forms, Foundations Functions, Failures and Figures*, Cheltenham, UK and Northampton, MA, USA: Edgar Elgar.

Rotter, J.B. (1967), 'A new scale for the measurement of interpersonal trust', *Journal of Personality*, **35** (4), 651–65.

Rousseau, D.M., S.B. Sitkin, R.S. Burt and C. Camerer (1998), 'Not so different after all: a cross-discipline view of trust', *Academy of Management Review*, **23** (3), 393–404.

Saunders, M., P. Lewis and A. Thornhill, (2009), *Research Methods for Business Students*, 5th edition, Harlow: FT Prentice Hall.

Saunders M.N.K., D. Skinner, N. Gillespie, G. Dietz and R. Lewicki (eds) (2010), *Organisational Trust: A Cultural Perspective*, Cambridge: Cambridge University Press.

Seppanen, R., K. Blomqvist and S. Sundqvist (2007), 'Measuring inter-organisational trust: a critical review of the empirical research in 1990–2003', *Industrial Marketing Management*, **36** (2), 249–65.

Sitkin, S. and D. Stickel (1996) 'The road to hell: the dynamics of distrust in an era of quality', in R. Kramer and T. Tyler (eds), *Trust in Organizations: Frontiers of Theory and Research*, Thousand Oaks, CA: Sage, pp. 196–215.

Teddlie, C. and A. Tashakkori, (2010), 'Overview of contemporary issues in mixed methods research', in A. Tashakkori and C. Teddlie (eds), *Sage Handbook of Mixed Methods in Social and Behavioural Sciences*, 2nd edition, Thousand Oaks, CA: Sage, pp. 1–41.

Williamson, O.E. (1993), 'Calculativeness, trust, and economic organization', *Journal of Law and Economics*, **36** (2), 453–86.

Zaheer, A. and J. Harris (2005), 'Interorganizational trust', in O. Shenkar and J.J. Reuer (eds), *Handbook of Strategic Alliances*, Thousand Oaks, CA: Sage, pp. 169–97.

Zaheer, A., B. McEvily and V. Perrone (1998), 'Does trust matter? Exploring the effects of inter-organizational and interpersonal trust on performance', *Organization Science*, **9** (2), 141–59.

Zak, P.J., R. Kurzban and W.T. Matzner (2004), 'The neurobiology of trust', *Annals of the New York Academy of Science*, **1032**, 224–7.

Zand, D.E. (1972), 'Trust and managerial problem solving', *Administrative Science Quarterly*, **17** (2), 229–39.

PART I

CONCEPTUAL ISSUES

2 Moving between laboratory and field: a multi-method approach for studying trust judgments
Roderick M. Kramer

INTRODUCTION

Trust dilemmas arise whenever individuals perceive opportunities to benefit from engaging in trusting behaviour with others, yet recognize doing so entails the risk of exploitation. The research in this chapter examines the determinants of judgment and choice in such dilemmas by adopting a multi-method approach, including the use of both laboratory experiments and qualitative field research to investigate social psychological and organizational processes that influence trust judgments and decisions.

The benefits of trust have been amply established in many empirical studies, ranging from experimental investigations (Ostrom and Walker, 2003) to field studies in social and organizational settings (Sztompka, 1999). Obtaining the full range of benefits from trust, however, is often problematic in practice (Cook, Levi and Hardin, 2009; Hardin, 2002; Kramer and Cook, 2004). One problem is that the anticipated gains from trust materialize only when social actors happen to be dealing with others (that is, someone willing to reciprocate their own trusting behaviour). Misplaced trust – engaging in trusting behaviour with individuals who exploit that trust – can be enormously costly. Accordingly, it makes sense for individuals to trust, but only when that trust is likely to be reciprocated by others.

From a judgment and decision-making perspective, therefore, decision makers confront such fundamental questions as 'Whom can I trust?' 'How much can I trust them?' and 'Under what circumstances can I trust them?' Such questions constitute vexing judgmental challenges for decision makers. They direct our attention, moreover, to the thorny problem of discrimination – harvesting the benefits of trust clearly hinges, at least in part, on decision makers' ability to detect or assess trustworthiness accurately in others (Bacharach and Gambetta, 2001; Hardin, 2002). Mistakes cannot only be costly, they can be deadly (Fine and Holyfield, 1996; Gambetta and Hamill, 2005).

ılty of this judgmental task is amplified by the problem of ainty (Bacharach and Gambetta, 2001). We can never know ıe intentions or motives that animate another's actions or ınactions. Nor can we know, with certainty, what actions others are taking behind our backs. This uncertainty contributes directly to the trust dilemma. In a trust dilemma, decision makers hope to reap the perceived benefits from engaging in trusting behaviour with others. Pursuit of those opportunities, however, exposes them to the prospect that their trust might be exploited or betrayed. My research explores the antecedents of trust-related judgment and choice in such dilemmas. In particular, I explore the cognitive and social factors that influence judgment and choice in trust dilemma situations.

DESCRIPTION OF THE METHOD

My programme of research in this area adopts a multi-method approach. My initial research involved experimental studies of judgment and choice in trust dilemmas, using several well-known laboratory paradigms. These laboratory studies are useful when attempting to assess the causal importance of theorized social psychological processes. For example, in an early series of programmatic studies, Marilynn Brewer and I examined the effects of social categorization and decision framing on trust-related perceptions and choices in the context of an experimental simulation of an n-person trust dilemma (summarized in Kramer, Brewer, and Hanna, 1996). My colleagues and I then extended this work using a computer-based simulation of an iterative or repeated-play multi-actor trust dilemma (Bendor, Kramer, and Stout, 1991) in order to investigate the comparative efficacy of different decision rules for eliciting and sustaining mutual trust relations. I then turned to the use of qualitative techniques to study trust judgment in real-world trust dilemma situations (Cook et al., 2004; Kramer, 1996). Because my experimental work has been summarized at length elsewhere (Kramer, Brewer and Hanna, 1996), I focus in this brief chapter on my more recent qualitative work and its implications.

Before describing the individual methods and results of two representative studies, a few general remarks might be in order regarding the methodological assumptions and goals guiding my approach. A central value motivating my more recent research has been a commitment to exploring trust-related judgments as they occur in natural social and organizational contexts. Accordingly, my research is designed to probe people's judgments regarding trust in natural settings. By using methods that capture the real-world thought processes of real-world individuals in real-world contexts, my colleagues and I are able to explore the way people actually do (and don't) think about trust. The aim of such research is twofold. The first aim is to produce rich and faithful (that is, ecologically valid) accounts of trust judgments and choices. The second is to elucidate some of the psychological and social processes that drive those judgments and choices.

This ecological orientation towards trust judgments has other methodological implications. In particular, it suggests the utility of using methods that elicit 'on-line' or explicit cognitive processes that influence trust judgments in real-world domains. One advantage of these fairly direct, naturalistic approaches is that they enable us to learn something about how people confronting various real-world trust dilemmas actually think. In contrast with survey methods, where researchers determine in advance the universe of questions (and also how those questions are framed and anchored), researchers using more open-ended approaches allow their respondents to define for themselves the content and range of variables they consider valid, appropriate or diagnostic.

PERSONAL EXPERIENCE WITH THE MULTI-METHOD APPROACH

To illustrate these methods in action, I briefly describe two studies using different naturalistic methods of this sort and summarize some of the findings they yield. To place these studies in their proper context, let me preface the discussion by noting that both studies focus on trust judgments and choices that arise within the context of hierarchical relationships. Hierarchical relationships are characterized by asymmetries in power-dependence relations among the interdependent parties. As has long been appreciated by organizational theorists, hierarchical relationships are among the most important and prevalent form of social and organizational relation (Kanter, 1977). From the standpoint of trust, hierarchy creates interesting dilemmas for those involved in such relationships. First, for those individuals situated in positions of greater dependence and lower power, concerns regarding the motives, intentions and concealed actions of those decision makers who control their fate are likely to be consequential and chronic (Kanter, 1977). For individuals in the position of higher power and lower dependence, in contrast, monitoring the commitment, compliance, deference and trustworthiness of those below them is critical. As a consequence of these asymmetries in power-dependence, the specific content of trust-related concerns might be expected to vary as a function of one's location within the relationship. Additionally, one might expect that these specific concerns are driven also by contextual considerations.

For example, the concerns that govern trust-related expectations and choices in a relationship between faculty and graduate students at a research university might be expected to differ from those governing a relationship between physician and patient in a medical setting. These two presumptions motivate the studies described next.

Study 1: Using Autobiographical Narratives to Study the Role of Mental Accounting in Trust Judgments

Many experiment-based models of trust development emphasize the important role interpersonal interaction histories play in the trust-building process (Lindskold, 1978). As important as these experimental studies are in suggesting that history matters, they do not tell us much about what people really pay attention to in real-world trust dilemma situations (that is, what actually counts as history). For example, in the confines of the experimental laboratory, both expectations regarding others' reciprocity and feedback pertaining to the confirmation or violation of those expectations tend to be explicitly specified and therefore rendered completely unambiguous. This is a simple consequence of the fact that the parameters of such behaviour have been fully defined *ex ante* by the experimenter (for example, study participants can make either one of two choices in a binary-choice trust dilemma game). Similarly, the experimental participants learn with complete certainty how trustworthy the other has been (that is, the other either did or did not choose a cooperative response). In real-world trust dilemmas, of course, assessing reciprocity is apt to be a much messier and more complex judgmental process. The accuracy of interpretations regarding others' behaviour is likely to be impaired or clouded by incomplete information, social misperceptions, self-serving cognitive biases and imperfections in social memory.

It is important, therefore, to know more about what individuals in real-world trust dilemma situations actually pay attention to when trying to calibrate others' trustworthiness. One method that is appropriate and useful in this regard is the autobiographical narrative method (see Kramer, 1996 for a fuller description and justification of this method). Autobiographical narratives are generated by asking individuals to recall and describe significant events in their lives. These accounts can then be content analysed in terms of dimensions of theoretical interest to the researcher.

Using this approach, one of my studies investigated how university professors and their graduate students construe reciprocal trust and trustworthiness in their relationship (Kramer, 1996). Reciprocal trust is important in professor–student relationships for several reasons. First, from the professor's standpoint, trust is important because professors depend on students to collect research data and analyse that data in order to test their research hypotheses. Not only does the whole scientific enterprise depend on the integrity of that data collection and analysis process, but a professor's status and reputation depend on such integrity as well. Thus, professors must trust their students to execute the work in a competent and conscientious fashion. Although some oversight and monitoring is possible, it is difficult for professors in busy labs to supervise or oversee the collection of every data point. Thus, professors are dependent on their students' trustworthiness, and yet also to some degree always uncertain regarding their actual trustworthiness.

The graduate students in such relationships, in turn, depend on their professors to mentor them, to protect them and to help promote their professional well-being. This includes the willingness to invest the time and resources into helping them learn to do top-tier research, getting published, advancing their interests in the department and their field. In short, students are also dependent on the trustworthiness of their faculty advisors. In particular, they risk a great deal with this investment should their faculty members' generosity, priorities or loyalties shift.

To conceptualize how professors and students might monitor or 'audit' their trust-related transactions in this relationship, I drew on research on mental accounting. Mental accounting is an interesting cognitive phenomenon. There is considerable evidence that people tend to organize information about their economic and social transactions in terms of cognitive 'mental accounts', and that these mental accounts, in turn, can influence their subsequent judgments and preferences (Kahneman and Tversky, 1982; Kramer, Myerson and Davis, 1990). Based on this research, I assumed that individuals in relationships involving mutual trust would use mental accounts to encode and store trust-related information. In other words, they would pay considerable attention to the other's behaviour and code instances of trust-affirming versus trust-violating behaviour. This coded information, in turn, would be used to form impressions and render judgments regarding the other's trustworthiness. In particular, I hypothesized that both parties to the role would be vigilant about assessing the other's trustworthiness and that this vigilance would lead them to notice and remember trust-related actions. I further hypothesized that, because of their comparatively greater dependence and vulnerability, graduate students (who occupy the low power-status role in this dyad) would be comparatively more attentive to trust-related information. They would also tend to ruminate more about such information (that is, not only would they pay more attention to their professor's behaviours, but they would also ruminate about its significance or meaning for the relationship). These differences would be reflected, in turn, in the cognitive complexity or elaborateness of their mental accounting systems, with students possessing more differentiated 'fine-grained' mental accounting systems. Analysis of the autobiographical narratives I collected bore out this expectation.

Another interesting difference that emerged was in the content of their respective mental accounts. I had argued that, all else being equal, the faculty would tend to define student trustworthiness in terms of task-related considerations. After all, what professors really care about primarily is getting their research done (getting published, getting tenure, and so on). Therefore, the central issues of trust for them are construed largely in terms of their students' task-related behaviours, such as their competence and their reliability at executing data collection and analysis.

For graduate students, the picture is a bit more complicated. Obviously, students also care about a professor's technical competence and reliability (they also want to publish top-tier papers, graduate with distinction and obtain good jobs on completion of their degrees). However, they also care about relational considerations, such as their professor's good intentions towards them, interests in their long-term welfare. They care, for example, that their professors like them, are concerned about their professional progress and intend to support them. Thus, motives and intentions matter as well. Using this line of reasoning, I expected that relational considerations would tend to loom larger in how trustworthiness was construed by students. Consequently, such concerns would be reflected in the content of their mental accounts. Consistent with this theoretical expectation, I found that faculty recalled significantly more things their students had done and not done that affected the quality of their joint work (that is, instrumental or task-related concerns). The mental accounts of students, in contrast, revealed much more attentiveness to relational concerns, including how well students thought they were treated as persons.

Although this is only a partial summary of some of the findings from this study, I hope that it serves to illustrate how the autobiographical narrative method can be used to uncover the cognitive structures and content of trust judgments.

In a second study, described next, a different approach was taken to uncovering some of the cognitive structure and content of individuals' trust judgments in another important real-world context – the doctor–patient relationship.

Study 2: Exploring Trust Judgments in Patient–Physician Relationships

A large body of social cognitive theory and research indicates how readily people draw inferences regarding trust-related attributes such as others' cooperativeness, honesty, credibility, likability, fairness and intelligence from even very minimal social cues (see, for example, Bacharach and Gambetta, 2001). Drawing on this previous theory and research, my colleagues and I (Cook et al., 2004) explored the perceived determinants of trust and trustworthiness within the context of physician–patient relationships in a large, university-based research hospital.

Arguably, there are few relationships where concerns about trust loom larger than in the relationship between patients and their physicians (Barber, 1983). Patients' emotional and physical well-being, even their very lives, are often quite literally in the hands of their physicians. Although much less studied, physicians often care a great deal about the trustworthiness of their patients. Their professional standing and emotional well-being depends on the quality of their relationships with their patients. They depend on their patients, for example, to be honest when revealing information relevant to their successful treatment (for example, to report accurately their true level of compliance and not to withhold vital information). They also depend on their patients not to harm them through gossip or lawsuits should their care not turn out the way they expected. Despite recognition of the importance of this relationship, many fundamental questions regarding the antecedents and consequences of mutual trust in such relationships have remained unexplored and unanswered. Accordingly, my colleagues and I conducted a study in a major university-based medical centre, using semi-structured interviews to explore both patients' and physicians' trust judgments.

There are several findings that illustrate the kinds of social information patients and physicians attend to when forming judgments of each other's trustworthiness. Among the larger categories of cues that both patients and physicians emphasized, we found behavioural (verbal and nonverbal) cues construed as diagnostic of caring, concern and empathy. For example, one patient observed generally, 'I think it [trust] also depends on the doctor . . . on the way they [sic] treat you . . . are they looking at you when they examine you and how they treat you as a person, not only as a patient' (Patient 38, quoted in Cook et al., 2004, p. 71). Numerous patients cited the diagnostic importance of small and subtle behaviours and gestures, such as the amount of eye contact during an examination. One patient put it this way, 'I think eye contact is one of the most important things when you're talking to a doctor so that you don't feel like they are ignoring you' (Patient 38, in ibid., p. 71). Another elaborated, 'When she [my physician] is done, she puts her pen down, and she will make eye contact with me immediately after she's done writing. Her eye contact starts when she enters the room' (Patient 36, in ibid., p. 71).

There was also considerable evidence that cues construed by patients as diagnostic of physician competence were highly salient. As Brockner and

Siegel (1996) noted in this regard, judgments about trustworthiness reflect not only individuals' attributions regarding the benign intentions of others on whom they are dependent, but also attributions of competence at *being* trustworthy. Consistent with their argument, we found that patients attached considerable importance to the apparent knowledge and competence of their physicians. As one patient put it, 'He's pretty confident about his decisions. So that kind of helps. He seems to know what he's talking about. I'm not a doctor, so I couldn't tell you if what he's telling me is right, but it sounded pretty good' (Patient 37, quoted in Cook et al., 2004, p. 75).

Patients and physicians both drew attention to the deleterious impact of perceived unavailability or time-urgency on trust. One patient described her physician as 'Very sterile, very – no smile, no sense of humour, just quick, quick, let's get the job done' (Patient 21, quoted in Cook et al., 2004, p. 77). Related to this, the tendency for busy physicians to give incomplete or hurried explanations, and to make patients feel as if they are not respected was felt to undermine trust. One patient, for example, complained, 'I get very frustrated because so many doctors take an authoritative position . . . I'm going to tell you what to do, I don't have to explain it, I don't have to pay any attention to your knowledge or your awareness' (Patient 22, in ibid., p. 79).

To summarize, this second study added to our understanding of the cognitive complexity of social perceivers' judgments regarding trust and trustworthiness in their interpersonal relationships, especially as their relationships unfold in complex, real-world settings such as hospitals. This study also illustrates how stereotypes or beliefs regarding a context can colour such judgments independent of the actual behaviour of the individuals involved in the trust relationship. None of these subtle influences would emerge in experimental settings.

DISCUSSION

Contemporary theory and research on judgment and decision-making in trust dilemmas has relied almost exclusively on the use of simple, experimental games. Although such studies have proven enormously useful in helping researchers identify basic cognitive, affective underpinnings of trust judgment and choice, they obviously leave at the laboratory door many of the social and contextual variables that influence choice in real-world settings. As I hope the research discussed in this chapter illustrates, conceptualizing and studying individuals' trust-related judgments in terms of such ecologically sensitive, context-dependent factors thus allows us to develop richer, more domain-specific models of trust choice and behaviour.

REFERENCES

Bacharach, M. and D. Gambetta (2001), 'Trust in signs', in K.S. Cook (ed.), *Trust in Society*, New York: Russell Sage Foundation, pp. 148–84.

Barber, B. (1983), *The Logic and Limits of Trust*, New Brunswick, NJ: Rutgers University Press.

Bendor, J., R.M. Kramer and S. Stout (1991), 'When in doubt: cooperation in the noisy prisoner's dilemma', *Journal of Conflict Resolution*, **35**, 691–719.

Brockner, J. and P. Siegel (1996), 'Understanding the interaction between procedural justice and distributive justice: the role of trust', in R.M. Kramer and T. Tyler (eds), *Trust in Organizations: Frontiers of Theory and Research*, Thousand Oaks, CA: Sage, pp. 390–413.

Cook, K.S., M. Levi and R. Hardin (2009), *Whom Can We Trust? How Groups, Networks, and Institutions Make Trust Possible*, New York: Russell Sage Foundation.

Cook, K.S., R.M. Kramer, D.H. Thom, I. Stepanikova, S.B. Mollborn and R.M. Cooper (2004), 'Trust and distrust in patient–physician relationships: perceived determinants of high- and low-trust relationships in managed care settings', in R.M. Kramer and K.S. Cook (eds), *Trust and Distrust in Organizations: Dilemmas and Approaches*, New York: Russell Sage Foundation, pp. 65–98.

Fine, G. and L. Holyfield (1996), 'Secrecy, trust, and dangerous leisure: generating group cohesion in voluntary organizations', *Social Psychology Quarterly*, **59**, 22–38.

Gambetta, D. and H. Hamill (2005), *Streetwise: How Taxi Drivers Establish their Customers' Trustworthiness*, New York: Russell Sage Foundation.

Hardin, R. (2002), *Trust and Trustworthiness*, New York: Russell Sage Foundation.

Kahneman, D. and A. Tversky (1982), *Judgment Under Uncertainty: Heuristics and Biases*, Cambridge: Cambridge University Press.

Kanter, R. (1977), *Men and Women of the Corporation*, New York: Basic Books.

Kramer, R.M. (1996), 'Divergent realities and convergent disappointments in the hierarchic relation: the intuitive auditor at work', in R.M. Kramer and T.R. Tyler (eds), *Trust in Organizations: Frontiers of Theory and Research*, Thousand Oaks, CA: Sage, pp. 216–45.

Kramer, R.M. and K.S. Cook (2004), *Trust and Distrust in Organizations: Approaches and Dilemmas*, New York: Russell Sage Foundation.

Kramer, R.M., M.B. Brewer and B.A. Hanna (1996), 'Collective trust and collective action', in R.M. Kramer and T.R. Tyler (eds), *Trust in Organizations: Frontiers of Theory and Research*, Thousand Oaks, CA: Sage, pp. 357–89.

Kramer, R., D. Meyerson and G. Davis (1990), 'How much is enough? Psychological components of "guns versus butter" decisions in a security dilemma', *Journal of Personality and Social Psychology*, **58**, 984–93.

Lindskold, S. (1978), 'Trust development, the GRIT proposal, and the effects of conciliatory acts on conflict and cooperation', *Psychological Bulletin*, **85**, 772–93.

Messick, D.M. and R.M. Kramer (2001), 'Trust as a form of shallow morality', in K.S. Cook (ed.), *Trust in Society*, New York: Russell Sage Foundation, pp. 89–118.

Ostrom, E. and J. Walker (2003), *Trust and Reciprocity: Interdisciplinary Lessons*, New York: Russell Sage Foundation.

Sztompka, P. (1999), *Trust: A Sociological Theory*, Cambridge: Cambridge University Press.

Annotated Further Reading

Fine, G. and L. Holyfield (1996), 'Secrecy, trust, and dangerous leisure: generating group cohesion in voluntary organizations', *Social Psychology Quarterly*, **59**, 22–38. This beautiful study explores social and normative processes that regulate the emergence and maintenance of trust in a very interesting social setting: the world of amateur mushroom collectors. Fine and Holyfield demonstrate with rich examples how an organization can create a culture of mutual trust and, equally essential, mutual trustworthiness among members.

Gambetta, D. and H. Hamill (2005), *Streetwise: How Taxi Drivers Establish their Customers' Trustworthiness*, New York: Russell Sage Foundation. This imaginative field study investigates the personal, social and situational cues taxi drivers working in dangerous areas rely on when attempting to make swift assessments of potential customers' trustworthiness.

Sztompka, P. (1999), *Trust: A Sociological Theory*, Cambridge: Cambridge University Press. This well-written book provides a careful and thoughtful overview of contemporary trust theory and research. It then provides a rich and suggestive case study of the role trust plays in rapid social change in a real-world setting (change in Polish society in the 1990s).

3 Measuring trust beliefs and behaviours
Roy J. Lewicki and Chad Brinsfield

INTRODUCTION

In this chapter we discuss issues associated with operationalizing trust as a psychological state comprising one's willingness to accept vulnerability and the measurement of resultant trusting behaviours. We also discuss implications arising from conceptualizing trust and distrust as distinct constructs, as well as measurement challenges associated with trust development, decline and repair over time.

Trust has been conceptualized, defined, modelled, and operationalized in a wide variety of ways, and over a longer period of time than most contemporary trust researchers are aware of. Even decades ago, Stack (1978) and Wrightsman (1991) provided comprehensive reviews of then-existing trust measures in use in the field of social psychology. Trust has been viewed as an individual disposition (Rotter, 1967, 1971; Worchel, 1979), a psychological state (Lewicki et al., 1998; Rousseau et al., 1998), or a behaviour (Deutsch, 1962; Mayer et al., 1995). Different disciplines have emphasized different components; psychologists have emphasized the importance of individual differences, intentions and expectations over behaviours, while economists have minimized the psychological aspects over the behavioural 'evidence'. Some approaches to trust have described it as only from the perspective of the trustor (Rotter, 1967; Stack, 1978), while others have argued that a full understanding of trust must incorporate the qualities and behaviours of the trustee, or the person being trusted (for example, Mayer et al., 1995). Others have argued that trust is not a single, unidimensional construct; some have argued that trust and distrust are independent constructs (Lewicki et al., 1998) while others have argued that there are different types of trust (Lewicki and Bunker, 1996) and that distinctly different types of trust judgments occur when trust-relevant information is processed more 'rationally' or more 'intuitively' (Kramer, 1996). Finally, some authors explore how trust changes form and shape as it develops and builds, or as it is broken and declines (cf. Lewicki et al., 2006).

What has led to this proliferation of views, perspectives and representations? Several dynamics in the evolution of our understanding of trust can be identified. First, as a psychological state, trust itself cannot be seen or observed directly. Thus, understanding it requires that researchers come to some agreement as to the nature of the internal dynamics of trust – the makeup of beliefs, emotions, intentions and expectations that constitute trust. This consensus has taken a long time to emerge, and in the interim numerous definitions and measures have proliferated, no less arguments about which measures are more reliable or valid. Second, in viewing trust as behaviour, one is inferring trust from the observed behaviour compared to the other alternative behaviours, which were not chosen. A trusting behaviour or choice cannot be absolutely specified unless we know what other choices or alternatives are available. Thus, third, and relatedly, understanding a trust choice and/or behaviour is strongly shaped by context, and hence trust 'behaviours' might look quite different, depending on the context in which they occur (cf. Dietz et al., 2010, for one perspective on trust across cultures). Finally, trust has been of interest to multiple social science disciplines – predominantly psychologists, economists and sociologists – and therefore, not surprisingly, each discipline has tended to focus on aspects of the phenomenon that are most relevant to and consistent with its dominant theoretical paradigms. Thus, while we would hope to have a convergence of views on trust across disciplines, instead it continues to be difficult to have cross-paradigm convergence on how to conceptualize trust and thus how to measure its presence, strength and changes over time.

In the following pages, we will summarize what we believe to be the current state of measurement of trust beliefs and behaviours. Specifically, we look at current practices and make recommendations regarding the measurement of: (a) beliefs regarding another's intentions and willingness to accept vulnerability; (b) trusting behaviours; (c) conceptualizing and measuring trust and distrust as distinct constructs; and (d) trust development, decline and repair over time. We will point to areas where there is an emerging consensus, and to those areas where significant work remains to be done. Because measurement of the phenomenon is so closely tied to how it has been defined, we will include sample definitions and then discuss the state of the measures related to those definitions.

BELIEFS REGARDING ANOTHER'S INTENTIONS AND WILLINGNESS TO ACCEPT VULNERABILITY

Although important distinctions exist across the various conceptualizations and definitions of trust, beliefs and expectations about the intentions of another party and the willingness to accept vulnerability are common to the majority of these various perspectives. Frequently cited definitions of trust in this paradigm include:

- Trust is a psychological state comprising the intention to accept vulnerability based on positive expectations of the intentions or behaviour of another (Rousseau et al., 1998).
- Trust is a willingness to be vulnerable to another party based on both the trustor's propensity to trust others in general, and on the trustor's perception that the particular trustee is trustworthy (Mayer et al., 1995).
- Trust is a belief in, and willingness to act on the basis of, the words, actions and deeds of another (McAllister, 1995).

Moreover, notable survey measures of trust have sought to assess both the trustor's beliefs concerning the trustee's intentions (that is, trustworthiness), as well as the trustor's willingness to accept risk or vulnerability based on said intentions. For example, McAllister (1995) developed items to assess both cognition-based and affect-based dimensions of trust. Cognition-based items include, 'I can rely on this person not to make my job more difficult by careless work', and affect-based items include, 'If I shared my problems with this person, I know (s)he would respond constructively and caringly'. Similarly, Mayer and Davis (1999) developed items to assess trustworthiness for another party along the three dimensions of ability, benevolence and integrity. Items for these respective dimensions include, 'I feel very confident about top management's skills', 'Top management would not knowingly do anything to hurt me', and 'Top management tries hard to be fair in dealings with others'. In addition to items designed to assess trustworthiness (perceptions of a counterpart's intentions), Mayer and Davis also developed items to assess 'trust' in addition to 'trustworthiness'. Their trust items include, 'I would be willing to let top management have complete control over my future in this company' and 'I really wish I had a good way to keep an eye on top management (reverse coded)', which are essentially measures of a willingness to accept vulnerability.

More recently, scholars have suggested that perceptions of trustworthiness may also develop intuitively, in addition to traditional deliberative processes. One way that this has been tested is through assessing people's perceptions of trustworthiness based on their responses to the trustee's facial characteristics. For example, Todorov et al. (2008) built a computer-based model representing face trustworthiness and used these faces as stimuli in a functional magnetic resonance imaging study. They found that although participants did not engage in explicit evaluation of the faces, the amygdala response changed as a function of face trustworthiness.

TRUSTING BEHAVIOURS

Trust Games

Much of the recent scholarship on trust began half a century ago as social psychologists and game theorists explored trust dynamics through simple laboratory games. Perhaps the most common game was the Prisoner's Dilemma (for example, Deutsch, 1958, 1960; Loomis, 1959), in which each of two players made a simultaneous decision about whether to 'trust' or 'defect', leading to different combinations of payoffs for each player. A decade-long stream of research explored the impact of variations in economic payoffs, information, motivation, interparty communication, power and other variables on choices and payoff outcome (cf. Rubin and Brown, 1975, for one review).

The research stream was strongly criticized for its efforts to over-interpret the often complex and context-driven meanings of the two simple 'trusting' and 'defection' choices (for example, in any given multi-trial game, was a 'defection' choice an intent to exploit the other, a move to protect one's self from the other's possible defection, or a retribution for the other's earlier defections)? The research was very limited for a decade, but in recent years, organizational researchers and experimental economists have popularized a more sophisticated research tool called the Trust Game (Berg et al., 1995; Kreps, 1990) to examine trusting and trustworthy behaviour (for a review, see Camerer, 2003). In the simplest version of the Trust Game (Dasgupta, 1988; Kreps, 1990), each player is given $1. Player A must choose whether to send the dollar to player B, or keep it for themselves. If they decide to keep it, the game ends and each player gets $1. If player A sends the dollar to player B, the dollar is tripled by the experimenter and delivered to the player B, who now has $4. Player B must then decide whether to keep the $4 (leaving A with $0) or to split it, keeping $2 and returning $2 to A. Player A's decision to send the money to B thus satisfies the definition of trust as the willingness of a person to make themselves vulnerable to the actions of another, since A is potentially out $1 but stands to make $2 or even more based on B's decision (Rousseau et al., 1998).

Games such as the Prisoner's Dilemma and the Trust Game are typically instruments of laboratory research, and their feasibility for field research is limited. Although there is a variety of incarnations of trust games, they essentially place research subjects into interactions where risk-taking behaviours are assessed. The game appears to offer a clear measure of one player's willingness to trust another and a similarly clear measure of the extent to which this degree of trust is justified.

Cross-sectional Surveys

Survey measures have also been developed to assess the intention to perform trusting behaviours. McEvily and Tortoriello (2008) contend that most studies of trusting behaviour captured two aspects of behavioural trust identified by Zand (1972): reliance, 'representing trusting behavior in which an individual depends on another's skills, knowledge, judgments or actions, including delegating and giving autonomy', and disclosure, 'sharing work-related or personal information of a sensitive nature' (Gillespie, 2003: 10). Gillespie's 'behaviour trust inventory' was designed to capture intentions of managers to behave in each of these two domains across several different organizational settings. Moreover, Gillespie developed the behavioural trust inventory to provide a measure of trust that is generalizable across multiple organizational activities. According to Gillespie, an important feature of this instrument is its explicit focus on measuring one's willingness to engage in behaviours that would objectively subject the trustor to be harmed if trust was violated. Gillespie contends that few studies actually operationalize trust as the willingness to be vulnerable by engaging in trusting behaviours, but rather assess perceptions of trustworthiness that are more distal and less accurate indicators of trust. Items include, 'How willing are you to depend on your leader to handle an important issue on your behalf?' and 'How willing are you to share your personal feelings with your leader?' Finally, Currall and Judge (1995) designed an instrument to capture an individual's behavioural reliance on another person under a condition of risk, designed for boundary role situations. They identified four component dimensions which they believed to be critical to boundary role behaviour: communicating openly and honestly, relying on informal agreements (rather than formal contracts), coordinating interdependent tasks and managing surveillance to monitor for possible trust violations. The authors used multiple samples of data to test their instrument, collected data in real, on-going work contexts and performed rigorous statistical analyses on their data and is seen as one of the more valid and reliable measures of organizational trust.

TRUST AND DISTRUST AS SEPARATE CONSTRUCTS

Based on earlier work by Luhmann (1979) and others, Lewicki et al. (1998) argue that the typical approach to trust has been to view it as a unidimensional construct. There is no argument that 'high trust' exists at one end of the continuum, but it is not clear what is at the other end. Is it low trust? No trust? Or even distrust? It is not clear what it is, but it is not necessarily the 'opposite' of high trust. Second, the tendency has been to view 'trust' as positive and advantageous, but to see 'distrust' as negative and disadvantageous. But trust is not always advantageous – it may lead an actor to be naive or blind in their trust, offering trust too quickly and without appropriate verification (Rotter, 1980; Solomon and Flores, 2001). Gargiulo and Ertug (2006) point out that while trust is certainly critical for positive and productive relationships, it can also lead to complacency and to sacrificing high-quality outcomes in the name of not wanting to 'damage' trust by attempting to maximize gains. Third, not only is it not clear what exactly exists at the 'low' end, but Lewicki et al. also argue that this oversimplified view of trust derives from a very undifferentiated and unspecified view of individuals in relationships with others. Thus, in any complex interpersonal relationship, people trust others to do some things (for example be on time for an appointment) but may also not trust them to do others (for example remember to bring the driving directions on how to get to the appointment). Instead, the authors argue that trust and distrust in another party are separate judgments and that individuals in a complex relationship can hold both trusting and distrusting intentions and expectations towards another, based on different facets of their complex relationship. Trusting intentions and expectations are grounded in optimism, hope, confidence and positive expectations about the conduct of the other. Distrusting intentions and expectations are grounded in pessimism, fear, lack of confidence and negative expectations about the conduct of the other. Both can readily exist in a complex, multifaceted relationship. Across facets, individual relationships can then be characterized as low trust and low distrust (a benign or neutral relationship); high trust and low distrust (a positive, productive relationship); low trust and high distrust (a relationship of caution, suspicion and vigilance), and high trust and high distrust (a relationship characterized by many approach-avoidance conflicts and ambivalence).

Although the theory is more than 10 years old, efforts to measure trust and distrust as separate constructs has lagged. The measurement challenges lie in being able to find both attitudinal and behavioural measures that would clearly represent each of the four 'states', particularly the high–high and low–low states. With regard to measuring attitudes, Lewicki (2007) proposed a scale that separately measures trusting and distrusting orientations to another party, but it requires further refinement and validation. Other work has been under way to establish reliable descriptors of trustworthy and untrustworthy people. For example, Saunders and Thornhill (2004) developed an interview protocol that allowed participants to define parallel descriptors of trusting and distrusting attitudes.

Wildman et al. (2009) have also constructed a similar scale, distinguishing between perceptions of trust-based and distrust-based competence and intent. With regard to calibrating behaviours, our own laboratory work has been experimenting with variations of the Trust Game that will reliably distinguish trust-based behaviour from distrust-based passing behaviour. However, significant work remains to be done, and Schoorman et al. (2007) have questioned whether it is even fruitful to pursue this line of investigation.

TRUST DEVELOPMENT, DECLINE AND REPAIR OVER TIME

Trust is an evidentiary phenomenon: that is, it changes with evidence in favour of, or against, further trust. Thus, a crucial issue is, how do we measure the ways people update and recalibrate their trust judgments? For example, Mayer et al.'s (1995) model includes a feedback loop, illustrating that the favourability of the outcomes will cause the trustor to update earlier perceptions of trustworthiness. Moreover, theoretical work on trust has suggested that there are multiple forms of trust in professional relationships (Lewicki and Bunker, 1996; Mayer et al., 1995), and that these various forms of trust represent stages that are evolutionary, such that as relationships develop, deeper and more complex levels of trust are attained. For example, Lewicki and Bunker (1996) described a basic level of trust as calculus-based trust (CBT), which applies to arm's-length transactions in professional relationships. Accordingly, CBT represents a primarily cognitive assessment of one's trustworthiness that is transaction focused. Although CBT usually develops first in a relationship, it often leads to a second type of trust, based on identification with the other's desires and intentions, which Lewicki and Bunker termed identification-based trust (IBT). Similarly, Mayer et al.'s (1995) three-component model of trustworthiness proposes that judgments of ability and integrity would form relatively quickly in a relationship and that benevolence judgments would require more time to develop.

In addition, there has been considerable theorization about trust repair. Lewicki and Bunker (1996) articulate a process by which trust violations lead to consequences that must be addressed by both actor and victim. A number of empirical studies have examined the nature of trust repair and its key component elements (cf. Bottom et al., 2002; Ferrin et al., 2007; Shapiro, 1991; Tomlinson et al., 2004 as examples). These studies have examined the adequacy of explanation following trust violations; the nature, timeliness and sincerity of an apology and how the apology was phrased and framed; and whether it was more effective to apologize for a violation or deny one's guilt in order to repair violations of competency vs. integrity. Finally, several authors (for example, Gillespie and Dietz, 2009; Rhee and Valdez, 2009) have proposed broader frameworks for understanding trust repair and relationship repair in organizational settings.

Unfortunately, the cross sectional research and primitive measurement tools, which dominate the literature in this area, cannot adequately capture the evolutionary nature of trust development, decline and repair. Rather, more resource-intensive longitudinal research, in field settings where relationships have had time to develop, is required to assess how and why trust develops into its psychologically deeper manifestations, how and why it may decline and how it can be repaired. Moreover, as Dirks et al. (2009) point out in their critique of the relationship repair research, considerable work remains to be done at both the conceptual and measurement levels. First, at the theoretical level, researchers have approached trust repair from the attributional, social equilibrium and structural perspectives. From an attributional theory perspective, violations lead the victim to draw negative judgments about the actor, and repair strategies must address mechanisms for changing those attributions to positive ones. From a social equilibrium approach, a trust violation creates imbalance in favour of the actor, and subsequent actions must restore the victim's perceptions of the social equilibrium. Finally, in the structural approach, a trust violation suggests an inadequacy and/or breakdown in existing structural monitoring and control mechanisms, and repair strategies usually suggest remedies such as tightening control mechanisms, introducing new monitoring procedures, or legalistic remedies.

These authors also point out that the problems of trust measurement are compounded when one attempts time-series research on trust repair. First, to measure trust repair most effectively, one needs at least three data points: a measure of the level of trust before the transgression, a measure of the level of trust after the transgression and a third measure of trust after the 'repair' efforts. Most studies of trust repair do not attempt to secure these three data points, let alone attempt the challenges of measuring the cognitive, affective and behavioural components of more complex trust, or the 'collateral damage' that a trust violation may cause to other aspects of a relationship. These measures will also have to vary to avoid problems of overusing the same measurement tools and minimizing variance. Second, studies have been vague about what constitutes a criterion of 'repair'. Are trust repair efforts expected to restore trust to its full pre-transgression state? Is trust ever fully 'repaired' – that is, so that all visible traces of the violation are eliminated – or is 'repaired' trust different from 'never-broken' trust? For example, Lewicki et al. (1998) argue that previously broken and then repaired trust has introduced some level of distrust, such that the party may trust again but is also somewhat vigilant to possible future violations and takes appropriate cautionary action (the more frequent or serious the violation, the greater the likely distrust to be introduced). Dirks et al. (2009) use the metaphor of a pottery vase which was broken, reglued, sanded and reglazed so that the original cracks are not visible, as opposed to a vase which has been glued but the fractures are still clearly visible. Clearly, the area of trust repair has some significant conceptual and methodological challenges that must still be addressed.

DISCUSSION

As the vast body of literature suggests, trust is a multifaceted construct comprising cognitive, affective, behavioural, economic and ethical components. Trust is distinct from trustworthiness; it may be positive or negative, manifesting at the individual, group, organizational and societal levels. Moreover, in their review, McEvily and Tortoriello (2008) indicate that of the 96 studies they reviewed, there were 42 different instruments used to measure trust. Only 19 of the 96 endeavoured to replicate their results with the same instrument and one third of those did not provide enough information about the replication to enable an assessment of its accuracy. Almost 80 per cent of the measures treated trust as a unidimensional construct and hence it is most difficult to generalize about the construct, convergent and divergent validity of the measures across these studies. While McEvily and Tortoriello identify five measures which they consider to be the strongest and most noteworthy (Cummings and Bromiley, 1996; Currall and Judge, 1995; Gillespie, 2003; Mayer and Davis, 1999; McAllister, 1995), it is clear that significant refinement work, at both the construct and measurement levels, remains to be done.

REFERENCES

Berg, J., J. Dickhaut and K. McCabe (1995), 'Trust, reciprocity and social history', *Games and Economic Behavior*, **10**, 122–42.

Bottom, W.P., K. Gibson, S.E. Daniels and J.K. Murnighan (2002), 'When talk is not cheap: substantive penance and expressions of intent in rebuilding cooperation', *Organization Science*, **13**, 497–513.

Camerer, C.F. (2003), *Behavioral Game Theory: Experiments in Strategic Interaction*, Princeton, NJ: Princeton University Press.

Cummings, L.L. and P. Bromiley (1996), 'The organizational trust inventory (OTI)', in R.M. Kramer and T.R. Tyler (eds), *Trust in Organizations: Frontiers of Theory and Research*, Thousand Oaks, CA: Sage, pp. 302–30.

Currall, S.C. and T.A. Judge (1995), 'Measuring trust between organizational boundary role persons', *Organizational Behavior and Human Decision Processes*, **64**, 151–70.
Dasgupta, P. (1988), 'Trust as a commodity', in D. Gambetta (ed.), *Trust Making and Breaking Cooperative Relations*, Oxford: Basil Blackwell, pp. 49–72.
Deutsch, M. (1958), 'Trust and suspicion', *Journal of Conflict Resolution*, **2**, 265–79.
Deutsch, M. (1960), 'Trust, trustworthiness and the F scale', *Journal of Abnormal and Social Psychology*, **61**, 138–40.
Deutsch, M. (1962), 'Cooperation and trust: some theoretical notes', in M.R. Jones (ed.), *Nebraska Symposium on Motivation*, Lincoln, NB: University of Nebraska Press, pp. 275–319.
Dietz, G., N. Gillespie and G. Chao (2010), 'Unravelling the complexities of trust and culture', in M.N.K. Saunders, D. Skinner, N. Gillespie, G. Dietz and R.J. Lewicki (eds), *Trust: A Cultural Perspective*, Cambridge: Cambridge University Press, pp. 3–4.
Dirks, K.T., R.J. Lewicki and A. Zaheer (2009), 'Repairing relationships within and between organizations: building a conceptual foundation', *Academy of Management Review*, **34**, 68–84.
Ferrin, D.L., P.H. Kim, C.D. Cooper and K.T. Dirks (2007), 'Silence speaks volumes: the effectiveness of reticence in comparison to apology and denial for responding to integrity- and competence-based trust violations', *Journal of Applied Psychology*, **92**, 893–908.
Gargiulo, M. and G. Ertug (2006), 'The dark side of trust', in R. Bachmann and A. Zaheer (eds), *Handbook of Trust Research*, Cheltenham, UK and Northampton, MA, USA: Edward Elgar, pp. 165–86.
Gillespie, N. (2003), 'Measuring trust in working relationships: the behavioral trust inventory', paper presented at the Academy of Management Conference, Seattle, WA.
Gillespie, N. and G. Dietz (2009), 'Trust repair after an organization-level failure', *Academy of Management Review*, **34**, 127–45.
Kramer, R.M. (1996), 'Divergent realities and convergent disappointments in the hierarchic relation: trust and the intuitive auditor at work', in R.M. Kramer and T.R. Tyler (eds), *Trust in Organizations: Frontiers of Theory and Research*, Thousand Oaks, CA: Sage, pp. 216–45.
Kreps, D. (1990), *Game Theory and Economic Modelling*, Oxford: Oxford University Press.
Lewicki, R.J. (2007), 'The trust scale', in R.J. Lewicki, B. Barry and D. Saunders, *Negotiation: Readings, Exercises and Cases*, Burr Ridge, IL: McGraw Hill-Irwin, pp. 696–700.
Lewicki, R.J. and B.B. Bunker (1996), 'Developing and maintaining trust in work relationships', in R.M. Kramer and T.R. Tyler (eds), *Trust in Organizations: Frontiers of Theory and Research*, Thousand Oaks, CA: Sage, pp. 114–39.
Lewicki, R.J., D.J. McAllister and R.J. Bies (1998), 'Trust and distrust: new relationships and realities', *Academy of Management Review*, **23**, 438–58.
Lewicki, R.J., E.C. Tomlinson and N. Gillespie (2006), 'Models of interpersonal trust development: theoretical approaches, empirical evidence and future directions', *Journal of Management*, **32**, 991–1022.
Loomis, J.L. (1959), 'Communication, the development of trust and cooperative behavior', *Human Relations*, **12**, 305–15.
Luhmann, N. (1979), *Trust and Power*, New York: Wiley.
Mayer, R.C. and J.H. Davis (1999), 'The effect of the performance appraisal system on trust for management: a field quasi-experiment', *Journal of Applied Psychology*, **84**, 123–36.
Mayer, R.C., J.H. Davis and F.D. Schoorman (1995), 'An integrative model of organizational trust', *Academy of Management Review*, **20**, 709–34.
McAllister, D.J. (1995), 'Affect- and cognition-based trust as foundations for interpersonal cooperation in organizations', *Academy of Management Journal*, **38**, 24–59.
McEvily, B. and M. Tortoriello (2008), 'Measuring trust in organizational research: review and recommendations', unpublished manuscript, University of Toronto; updated version (2011) in *Journal of Trust Research*, **1** (1), 23–63.
Rhee, M. and M.E. Valdez (2009), 'Contextual factors surrounding reputation damage with potential implications for reputation repair', *Academy of Management Review*, **34**, 146–68.

Rotter, J.B. (1967), 'A new scale for the measurement of interpersonal trust', *Journal of Personality*, **35**, 651–65.

Rotter, J.B. (1971), 'Generalized expectancies for interpersonal trust', *American Psychologist*, **26**, 443–52.

Rotter, J.B. (1980), 'Interpersonal trust, trustworthiness and gullibility', *American Psychologist*, **26**, 1–7.

Rousseau, D.M., S.B. Sitkin, R.S. Burt and C. Camerer (1998), 'Not so different after all: a cross-discipline view of trust', *Academy of Management Review*, **23**, 393–404.

Rubin, J. and B. Brown (1975), 'Bargainers as individuals', in J.Z. Rubin and B.R. Brown (eds), *The Social Psychology of Bargaining and Negotiation*, New York: Academic Press, pp. 157–96.

Saunders, M.N.K. and A. Thornhill (2004), 'Trust and mistrust in organizations: an exploration using an organizational justice framework', *European Journal of Work and Organizational Psychology*, **13**, 493–515.

Schoorman, F.D., R.C. Mayer and J.H. Davis (2007), 'An integrative model of organizational trust: past, present and future', *Academy of Management Review*, **32**, 344–54.

Shapiro, D.L. (1991), 'The effects of explanations on negative reactions to deceit', *Administrative Science Quarterly*, **36**, 614–30.

Solomon, R.C. and F. Flores (2001), *Building Trust in Business, Politics, Relationships and Life*, New York: Oxford University Press.

Stack, L. (1978), 'Trust', in H. London and J. Exner (eds), *Dimensions of Personality*, New York: Wiley, pp. 214–327.

Todorov, A., S.G. Baron and N.N. Oosterhof (2008), 'Evaluating face trustworthiness: a model-based approach', *Social Cognitive and Affective Neuroscience*, **3**, 119–27.

Tomlinson, E.C., B.R. Dineen and R.J. Lewicki (2004), 'The road to reconciliation: antecedents of victim willingness to reconcile following a broken promise', *Journal of Management*, **30**, 165–87.

Wildman, J., S.M. Fiore and E. Salas (2009), 'Development of trust and distrust measures', White Paper, University of Central Florida: Institute for Simulation and Training.

Worchel, S. (1979), 'Cooperation and the reduction of intergroup conflict: some determining factors', in W. Austin and S. Worchel (eds), *The Social Psychology of Intergroup Relations*, Monterey, CA: Brooks/Cole, pp. 262–73.

Wrightsman, L.S. (1991), 'Interpersonal trust and attitudes toward human nature', in J.P. Robinson, P.R. Shaver and L.S. Wrightsman (eds), *Measures of Personality and Social Psychological Attitudes*, San Diego, CA: Academic Press, pp. 373–412.

Zand, D. (1972), 'Trust and managerial problem solving', *Administrative Science Quarterly*, **17**, 229–39.

Further Reading

Dirks, K.T., R.J. Lewicki and A. Zaheer (2009), 'Repairing relationships within and between organizations: building a conceptual foundation', *Academy of Management Review*, **34**, 68–84.

Lewicki, R.J., D.J. McAllister and R.J. Bies (1998), 'Trust and distrust: new relationships and realities', *Academy of Management Review*, **23**, 438–58.

Lewicki, R.J., E.C. Tomlinson and N. Gillespie (2006), 'Models of interpersonal trust development: theoretical approaches, empirical evidence and future directions', *Journal of Management*, **32**, 991–1022.

4 Agent-based simulation of trust
Bart Nooteboom

INTRODUCTION

Agent-based simulation is useful for exploring possible worlds, seeing what might happen under what conditions as a result of complex inter-action between agents, as in the building and breaking of trust. In this chapter, a survey of some attempts is given, and a specific case is summa-rized; shortcomings and problems are also indicated.

With a variety of associates I had done a number of statistical/econo-metric studies of trust (Noorderhaven et al., 1998; Nooteboom et al., 1997, 2000) but when you find statistical associations between antecedents and outcomes of trust, it does not tell you how trust processes work. So with other associates I turned to case studies (Klein Woolthuis et al., 2005), studying the development of trust over time, but this still does not trace how interactions produce the trust outcomes you find. Therefore with yet other associates I turned to agent-based simulation. Trust is an interactive phenomenon. People adjust their trust or distrust in others on the basis of observed actions and their interpretation. This becomes especially complex when there are multiple agents. In such complex interaction virtuous cycles of trust-building and vicious cycles of collapse may arise. A natural method for investigating this is that of agent-based simulation, in which interaction is explicitly modelled. With this method one can study emergent properties that would be hard or impossible to tackle analytically.

A SURVEY

Many attempts have been made at agent-based modelling of trust and related issues. The purpose of the models varies widely. Some study the effectiveness of sanctions and/or reputation mechanisms and agencies to support them – for example in information systems or supply chains (Diekmann and Przepiorka, 2005; Meijer and Verwaart, 2005; Zacharia et al., 1999), or in artificial societies (Younger, 2005). Some study self-organization, for example in the internalization of externalities in a common pool resource (Pahl-Wost and Ebenhöh, 2004), the emergence of leadership in open-source communities (Muller, 2003), or the emergence of cooperative social action (Brichoux and Johnson, 2002). Others investigate the working of decision heuristics (Pahl-Wost and Ebenhöh, 2004; Marsella et al., 2004).

The general set-up is that of multiple agents who can profit from each other but are uncertain about the quality or competence that is offered, sometimes allowing for multiple dimensions of quality, and dependencies between them (Maximilien and Singh, 2005). Other studies focus on the benevolence or intentions of agents: absence of cheating, in free-ridership, defection or expropriation of knowledge or other resources, and many look at both competence and intentions (Breban, 2002; Castelfranchi and Falcone, 1999; Gans et al., 2001; Muller, 2003; Pahl-Wost and Ebenhöh, 2004).

Mostly, agents are oriented only towards their self-interest, such as maximum profit, but some studies also allow for fairness and equity as objectives or dimensions of value (Marsella et al., 2004; Pahl-Wost and Ebenhöh, 2004). Generally, trust is measured as a number between zero and one, and, following Gambetta (1988), is often interpreted as a subjective probability that goals will be achieved or no harm will be done. On the whole, conduct is individual, but sometimes allowance is made for coalitions (Breban, 2002). Few studies of defection explicitly model both sides of the coin: the expectation of defection by others (trust) and one's own inclination to defect (trustworthiness).

Trust is generally updated on the basis of experience, sometimes only one's own experience in interaction, sometimes (also) on the basis of reputation mechanisms, sometimes with the services of some 'tracing agency' (Diekman and Przepiorka, 2005; Meijer and Verwaart, 2005; Zacharia et al., 1999). Few studies are based on an explicit inference of competence or intentions, and even fewer explicitly model the decision heuristics used. Exceptions to this are Pahl-Wost and Ebenhöh (2004) and, with great psychological sophistication, Marsella et al. (2004). A key question is whether agents have 'a theory of mind' on the basis of which they attribute competencies and intentions to others.

Most studies model trust as adaptive, in the sense that it develops as a function of private or public experience. However, there is very little research, as far as I know, of the adaptiveness of the importance attached to trust relative to profit, and of the adaptiveness of one's own trustworthiness or inclination to defect.

AN EXAMPLE

In the following I summarize a model of the emergence and adaptation of trust first published by Klos and Nooteboom (2001). We focused on intentional trust, in terms of loyalty or defection, based on private experience (no reputation effects). Trust is adapted on the basis of observed defection, but only with simple reinforcement, without a theory of mind and explicit decision heuristics. What is special is that next to trust it includes one's own trustworthiness, that is, inclination to defect. Both trustworthiness and the importance attached to trust are adaptive, as a function of experience.

The analysis is conducted in the context of transaction relations between multiple buyers and suppliers, which is the classical setting for the analysis of transaction costs. I summarize the aim of the model, its basic theoretical features, its basic logic and some results from simulation.

Is Trust Viable in Markets?

The exercise was inspired by a (largely virtual) debate with transaction cost economics (TCE) (and some personal debate with Oliver Williamson) that claimed that trust beyond self-interest cannot exist in markets. We thought that, under certain conditions, it might exist. The question then was: under what conditions? The purpose of the model was to develop a tool for assessing the viability of trust, in the sense of benevolence, between firms in markets. According to TCE, under competition in markets, firms are under pressure to utilize any opportunistic opportunity for profit (Williamson, 1993). However, under the uncertainty and volatility of innovation, reliance on the basis of control (fairly) complete contracts and reputation mechanisms are infeasible or unreliable. Therefore benevolence is needed as a basis for governance, as a substitute or complement for necessarily incomplete contracts (Nooteboom, 1999, 2004) and reputation mechanisms. Thus it is of some theoretical and practical importance to investigate whether, or when, benevolence may be viable. I propose that benevolence, going beyond calculative self-interest, can exist in markets but is nevertheless subject to contingencies, such as pressures of survival, depending on intensity of competition and the achievement of profit (Pettit, 1995) and experience. The purpose of the model is to explore these contingencies.

Elements of Theory

For a good test of TCE claims, not to thrash a straw man, we should set up a strong case of TCE, and the model we propose should incorporate essential elements of TCE logic. TCE proposes that people organize to reduce transaction costs, depending on conditions of uncertainty and specific investments, which yield switching costs and a resulting risk of 'hold-up'.

The model we propose employs TCE logic, but also deviates from TCE in two fundamental respects. First, while TCE assumes that optimal forms of organization will arise, yielding maximum efficiency, we suggest that this is problematic. The making and breaking of relationships between multiple agents with adaptive knowledge and preferences may yield complexities and path-dependencies or cycles of action and response that preclude the achievement of maximum efficiency. Even if all agents can in principle access all relevant partners, and have relevant knowledge about them, actual access depends on competition for access, and on unpredictable patterns of making and breaking relations among multiple agents. The methodology of agent-based modelling is well suited to modelling complexities of multiple interactions, and to seeing to what extent theoretical benchmarks of maximum efficiency can in reality be achieved.

Second, while TCE assumes that reliable knowledge about loyalty or trustworthiness is impossible (Williamson, 1975), so that opportunism must be assumed, we postulate here that to some extent trust may be based on inferences from observed behaviour. Here, trust is based on experience with agents defecting, that is, breaking relationships.

Basic Logic of the Model

In the model, buyers and suppliers are matched on the basis of preferences based on both potential profit and intrinsic value of trust, with different weights set as parameters at the beginning of a simulation and adapted on the basis of experience. In this matching, depending on their preferences, agents continue or break transaction relations according to their preferences. Trust is based on the observed loyalty of partners, on an absence of switching to a different partner. In line with industrial economics, profit is a function of product differentiation (which increases profit margin), economy of scale from specialization, and learning by cooperation in ongoing relations. Use is made of the notion (from TCE) of specific investments in relationships. Those have value only within the relationship, and thus would have to be made anew when switching to a different partner. Specific, dedicated investments yield more differentiated, specialized products, with a higher profit margin (since product differentiation reduces price competition). Economy of scale yields an incentive for buyers to switch to a supplier who supplies to multiple buyers, thus generating more sales volume. This yields a bias towards opportunism, in breaking relations with smaller suppliers. However, this can only be done for activities that are based on general-purpose assets, not relation-specific investments for speciality products.

The percentage of speciality products is assumed to be equal to the

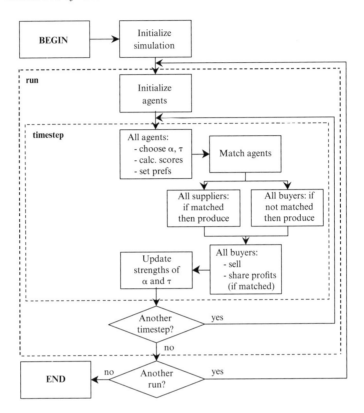

Source: Klos and Nooteboom (2001).

Figure 4.1   The simulation sequence

percentage of specific investments, as a parameter of the model that can be set. The speciality part, which is relation specific, yields higher profit and is subject to learning by cooperation, as a function of an ongoing relation. Thereby, it yields switching costs, since in switching partners one would lose that advantage, and thus yields a bias towards loyalty.

In sum, the model combines the essential features of TCE: opportunism by defection, specific investments, economy of scale for non-specific investments, and switching costs. However, the model adds the possibility of trust as a determinant of preference, next to potential profit.

In the model, agents are adaptive in three ways. In the preference function ('prefs' in Figure 4.1) the relative weights of potential profit and trust (parameter α in Figure 4.1) are adaptive, as a function of realized profit.

In this way, agents can learn to attach more or less weight to trust, relative to potential profit. Agents adapt their trust in a partner as a function of his loyalty, exhibited by his continuation of the relationship. As a relationship lasts, trust increases incrementally, but with decreasing returns, and it drops discontinuously when defection occurs. Agents also adapt their own trustworthiness, modelled as a threshold of exit from a relation (parameter τ in Figure 4.1), on the basis of realized profit. Agents only defect, in switching, when incremental preference exceeds the threshold. This models the idea that, while agents may be loyal, that has its limits. Thus, agents can learn to become more or less trustworthy in the sense of being loyal.

Note that adaptation of both the weight attached to trust and the threshold of defection occur on the basis of realized profit. This biases the model in favour of Williamson's (1993) claim that trust cannot survive in markets that demand maximum profit. As a result, in the model trust and trustworthiness can only emerge when they enhance realized profit. The model allows us to explore under what proportion of conditions, in terms of parameter settings, trust and loyalty increase, or are stable, that is, when they are conducive to profit, and hence viable in markets.

Starting values of agent-related parameters, such as initial trust, threshold of defection, and weight attached to trust, can be set for each agent separately. This allows us to model initially high or low trust societies, in setting parameters accordingly for all or most agents, or to model high-trust agents in low-trust societies, and vice versa, to study whether and when trust is viable, or is pushed out by opportunism. Other, not agent-related parameters such as the percentage of product differentiation and specific assets, strength of economy of scale, strength of learning by cooperation, speed with which trust increases with duration of a relation, number of buyers, number of suppliers and number of time steps in a run, are fixed per experiment.

For further technical details of the model, see Klos and Nooteboom (2001). The simulation logic is given in Figure 4.1.

Some Simulation Results

Initial expectations of outcomes were as follows:

- In interactions between multiple, adaptive agents, maximum efficiency is seldom achieved, due to unforeseeable complexities of interaction.
- In conformance with TCE, in the absence of trust outsourcing occurs only at low levels of asset specificity.

- High trust levels yield higher levels of outsourcing at all levels of asset specificity.
- Under a wide range of parameter settings, high trust levels are sustainable in markets (where performance is judged in terms of realized profit).
- The choice between an opportunistic switching strategy and loyalty depends on the relative strength of scale effects and learning by cooperation.

The first two expectations were borne out in Klos and Nooteboom (2001). The remaining three are borne out in simulation experiments by Gorobets and Nooteboom (2006).

The overall outcome is that both trust and opportunism can be profitable, but they opt for different strategies. This suggests that there may be different individual agents or communities, going for different strategies, of switching or of loyalty, which settle down in their own self-sustaining systems. If we compare across the different settings of high, medium and low initial trust, under different conditions concerning the strength of scale effect relative to learning by cooperation, and concerning initial weight attached to trust and initial thresholds of defection, profit declines more often than it increases, as we go from high to low trust. For further details see Gorobets and Nooteboom (2006).

INSIGHTS

Apart from the expected result that loyalty may survive and even help in markets, under some plausible conditions, the following insight emerges from the analysis. Potential profit from learning by cooperation is highest for the highest level of product differentiation, but precisely then, when trust is low, buyers prefer to make rather than buy, and thereby forgo the opportunities for learning by cooperation. When buyers focus on profitability rather than on trust, profit from economy of scale is instantaneous, while learning by cooperation is slow, and the potential for economy of scale is low at high levels of differentiation. Thus, under low trust and low weight attached to it, buyers lock themselves out of the advantages of collaboration. When they outsource, it is mostly at low levels of differentiation, when learning by cooperation yields only modest returns, but then they learn to appreciate its accumulation in lasting relationships. They end up outsourcing at high differentiation only 'by mistake', then learn to appreciate it, and once learning by doing gets under way, a focus on profit keeps them in the relationship. In time, as profit turns out to be consistent with loyalty and trust; they learn to attach more weight to those qualities.

This illustrates a principle noted before in the trust literature. As a default – that is, a stance taken until reasons for an alternative stance appear (Minsky, 1975) – trust is to be preferred to distrust. Excess trust can be corrected on the basis of experience with untrustworthy partners, while distrust prevents one from engaging in collaboration to learn that partners are in fact trustworthy, if that is the case, and that this is beneficial.

DISCUSSION

In the trust literature, interest in simulation studies has been limited, compared to the empirical studies. That is partly no doubt due to the technical nature of the models. Secondly, of course simulation is not equivalent to empirical testing. It looks at possible worlds, not the actual world; the test is virtual rather than real. It has only been shown that under certain parameter settings emergent properties of interaction satisfy theoretical expectations. The significance of this depends on how reasonable the assumptions in the model and the parameter settings are considered to be. An advantage of agent-based modelling compared to empirical study is that one can explore situations and conditions that cannot be observed. Extreme situations that do not actually occur can yield useful 'stress tests' of theoretical logic. An obvious problem with agent-based modelling is empirical validation: how realistic are underlying logics and assumptions? Another problem is calibration: what parameter settings are realistic? A particularly large problem with agent-based modelling is that even with few aspects of interaction, in a simple model structure, complexity of inter-action and the range of what can happen as a function of permutations of parameter values tends to explode, and it quickly becomes difficult to trace and understand what, precisely is going on. This yields a paradox: agent based modelling is useful to investigate complexity, but that soon yields a difficulty in understanding and assessing what is going on. Of course, that is also the case in reality.

So, agent-based modelling is only one method; it has its uses and limitations, and is best used in conjunction with empirical work to test its realism. Empirical work may be used to test and calibrate simulation models, and simulation models may yield hypotheses to test in empiri-cal work. They also help to decide theoretical debates on whether some outcome is possible or not, as in the example summarized here.

REFERENCES

Breban, S. (2002), 'A coalition formation mechanism based on inter-agent trust relationships', AAMAS conference, 15–19 July, Bologna.
Brichoux, D. and P.E. Johnson (2002), 'The power of commitment in cooperative social action', *Journal of Artificial Societies and Social Simulation*, **5** (3), http://jasss.soc.surrey.ac.uk/5/3/1.html.
Castelfranchi, C. and R. Falcone (1999), 'Social trust: a cognitive approach', CAiSE conference, Heidelberg.
Diekmann A. and W. Przepiorka (2005), 'The evolution of trust and reputation: results from simulation experiments', unpublished paper, Department of Humanities, Social and Political Sciences, Swiss Federal Institute of Technology, Zürich.
Gambetta, D. (1988), 'Can we trust trust?', in D. Gambetta (ed.), *Trust; Making and Breaking of Cooperative Relations*, Oxford: Blackwell, pp. 213–37.
Gans, G., M. Jarke, S. Kethers, G. Lakemeyer, L. Ellrich, C. Funken and M. Meister (2001), 'Towards (dis)trust-based simulations of agent networks', *Proceedings of the 4th Workshop on Deception, Fraud and Trust in Agent Societies*, May, Montreal, pp. 13–25.
Gorobets, A. and B. Nooteboom (2006), 'Adaptive build-up and breakdown of trust: an agent based computational approach', *Journal of Management and Governance*, **10** (3), 277–306.
Klein Woolthuis, R., B. Hillebrand and B. Nooteboom (2005), 'Trust, contract and relationship development', *Organization Studies*, **2** (6), 813–40.
Klos, T.B. and B. Nooteboom (2001), 'Agent-based computational transaction cost economics', *Journal of Economic Dynamics and Control*, **25**, 503–26.
Marsella, S.C., D.V. Pynadath and S.J. Read (2004), 'PsychSim: agent-based modelling of social interactions and influence', *Proceedings of International Conference on Cognitive Modelling*, Mahwah, Earlbaum, pp. 243–8.
Maximilien, E.M. and M.P. Singh (2005), 'Agent-based trust model involving multiple qualities', AAMAS conference, 25–29 July, Utrecht.
Meijer, S. and T. Verwaart (2005), 'Feasibility of multi-agent simulation for the trust and tracing game', in M. Ali and F. Esposito (eds), *Proceedings of IEA/AIE*, Heidelberg: Springer, pp. 145–54.
Minsky, M. (1975), 'A framework for representing knowledge', in P.H. Winston (ed.), *The Psychology of Computer Vision*, New York: McGraw-Hill, pp. 211–77.
Muller, P. (2003), 'On reputation, leadership and communities of practice', EAEPE conference, 7–9 November, Maastricht.
Noorderhaven, N.G., B. Nooteboom and H. Berger (1998), 'Determinants of perceived inter-firm dependence in industrial supplier relations', *Journal of Management and Governance*, **2**, 213–32.
Nooteboom, B. (1999), *Inter-firm Alliances: Analysis and Design*, London: Routledge.
Nooteboom, B. (2002), *Trust: Forms, Functions, Foundations, Failures and Figures*, Cheltenham, UK and Northampton, MA, USA: Edward Elgar.
Nooteboom, B. (2004), *Inter-firm Collaboration, Learning and Networks: An Integrated Approach*, London: Routledge.
Nooteboom, B., J. Berger and N.G. Noorderhaven (1997), 'Effects of trust and governance on relational risk', *Academy of Management Journal*, **40** (2), 308–38.
Nooteboom, B., G. de Jong, R.W. Vossen, S. Helper and M. Sako (2000), 'Network interactions and the role of mutual dependence: a test in the car industry', *Industry and Innovation*, **7** (1), 117–44.
Pahl-Wostl, C. and E. Ebenhöh (2004), 'Heuristics to characterise human behaviour in agent based models', in C. Pahl-Wostl, S. Schmidt, A.E. Rizzoli and A.J. Jakeman (eds), *Complexity and Integrated Resources Management,* proceedings of 2nd biennial conference IEMSS, 14–17 June, Osnabrück, pp. 177–84.
Pettit, P. (1995), 'The virtual reality of homo economicus', *The Monist*, **78** (3), 308–29.
Williamson, O.E. (1975), *Markets and Hierarchies*, New York: Free Press.

Williamson, O.E. (1993), 'Calculativeness, trust, and economic organization', *Journal of Law and Economics*, **36**, 453–86.

Younger, S. (2005), 'Reciprocity, sanctions, and the development of mutual obligation in egalitarian societies', *Journal of Artificial Societies and Social Simulation*, http://jasss.soc. surrey.ac.uk/8/2/9.html.

Zacharia, G., A. Moukas and P. Maes (1999), 'Collaborative reputation mechanisms in electronic marketplaces', *Proceedings of the 32nd Annual Hawaii International Conference on Systems Sciences*, HICSS-32. IEEE Comput. Soc., Los Alamitos, CA, p. 7.

Annotated Further Reading

J.F. Rennard (ed.) (2006), *Handbook of Research on Nature-inspired Computing for Economics and Management*, Idea Group reference: Hershey, PA, 2006. A recent volume on developments in agent-based modelling that aims to reflect human nature.

5 Researching trust in different cultures
Friederike Welter and Nadezhda Alex

INTRODUCTION

In this chapter, we want to explore approaches, pitfalls and possible lessons in researching trust in entrepreneurial activities. The chapter draws on experiences and empirical data from three research projects in which one or both of the authors have been involved. Key issues discussed concern the operationalization of different concepts of trust and the choice of adequate empirical methods.

In recent years there has been a growth of interest in the role of trust in business behaviour, because of its potential influence on reducing transaction costs (for example, Fukuyama, 1995; Höhmann and Welter, 2005; Welter and Smallbone, 2006; Williamson, 1993). However, trust is not an 'objective' phenomenon that can easily be measured and understood across cultures and countries. Trust, in particular its understanding and interpretation, is also a socially constructed and context-dependent phenomenon, which renders its measurement and empirical analysis difficult. Key issues concern the operationalization of different concepts of trust and the choice of adequate empirical methods. As trust has proved difficult to define conceptually, this also has consequences for researching it empirically, especially across countries and cultures. In addition, there is a danger that academics concerned with different aspects of human behaviour may sometimes be guilty of exaggerating the role of trust, which emphasizes the importance of developing robust methodologies to identify and assess it.

With this chapter, we want to explore approaches, pitfalls and possible lessons in researching trust across different cultures by looking at entrepreneurial activities. The chapter draws on experiences from three projects in which one or both of the authors have been involved. This includes (i) a project on trust in small businesses, both in internal and external business relations and in relations to the institutional environment, in a West–East context (2001–3, financed by the VW Foundation), where a large standardized survey in Estonia (100 small and medium sized enterprises – SMEs), Germany (200 SMEs) and Russia (400 SMEs) had been coupled with in-depth interviews with entrepreneurs and key informants (approximately 50) (cf. Höhmann and Welter, 2005); (ii) a project named 'Cross-border cooperation and EU enlargement: fostering entrepreneurship in Ukraine, Moldova and Belarus' (2005–7, financed by INTAS, 04-79-6991), in which the role of trust in cross-border partnerships was analysed empirically through in-depth interviews with institutions, entrepreneurs and petty traders (a total of 300 interviews in six regions) (cf. Welter and Smallbone, 2008); and (iii) a project on the same topic which involved two border regions each in countries such as Germany, Poland, Finland, Estonia, Bulgaria and Greece (2006–8, financed by the EU 6th Framework Programme) and where interviews with institutions, enterprises and individuals, all involved in cross-border co-operations, have been conducted (cf. Smallbone et al., 2007).

The experiences from the first project resulted in a shift towards qualitative methods to be applied in the subsequent projects, mainly in order to capture the process element of trust and trust building. Moreover, our empirical results also made us question the operationalization of our trust concepts. Nevertheless, both of the later projects faced additional challenges. For example, we included petty traders in a cross-border context in the sample, which required 'innovative' approaches for identifying potential respondents. In the last project, we started using a computer programme for analysing qualitative empirical data. The experiences made in all three studies are the basis for a review and analysis of what works and what does not work in researching trust in different cultures. This allows for conclusions to be drawn regarding future trust research in the entrepreneurship field, which are taken up in the final section.

GETTING STARTED: CONCEPTUALIZING TRUST AS AN EMBEDDED PHENOMENON

A first question in researching trust across cultures concerns its conceptualization. Trust research has identified two major concepts, namely personal and institutional trust. Personal trust signals trust at the individual level. High levels of personal trust mainly reflect repeated positive experiences made over time and longstanding relations, building on initial knowledge about the partner. Personal trust may depend on the characteristics of a group such as an ethnic or kinship group, but it also occurs in bilateral (business) relationships, often longstanding ones, where persons have come to know each other (Williamson, 1993). Institutional trust reflects the functioning of the overall political, legal or economic framework and its informal rules, with low levels of institutional trust generally taken as indicators for a deficient institutional framework. For example, laws reflect formal institutions, while their implementation might also reflect informal institutions in those cases where individuals need to know someone in the legal system in order to access it – and this consequently might result in low institutional trust, namely trust in the legal system. Institutional trust is essential for the efficient operation of a market economy, because in an economy characterized by a high level of institutional trust agents are able to enter into transactions with only limited information about their partner's specific attributes, with the scope of trust extending beyond the number of people that are known personally (Welter and Smallbone, 2006).

Trust is embedded in cultures. From an institutional perspective, trust plays a role as a sanctioning mechanism, thus acting as an informal institution. However, trust is more than an informal institution; rather it is embedded in informal institutions, with both the degree of trust and the ability to trust depending on the context for trust (Welter, 2005). Therefore, trust environments might be similar across countries, but may still differ within one country. One example refers to rural contexts across countries where spatial proximity might result in a higher level of trust, compared to metropolitan areas within the same country. Moreover, not only do the level and degree of trust differ across countries, but so does the nature of trust, as trust has culture-specific dimensions. Therefore, the context for trust plays an important role. Context can be interpreted as a function of factors which generally influence trust building, and of triggers for trust, which reflect situational influences. For example, trust building is facilitated between communities that have a common history, some common 'rules' or other shared experiences such as having lived in socialist societies. In this regard, Nuissl (2001) identified two alternative positions in the literature. Some authors support the hypothesis that 'real socialism' was incompatible with a cultural proclivity for trusting behaviour. As a consequence, in a post-socialist environment, there is a risk of being caught in a development trap stemming from a lack of interpersonal trust between strangers. Others claim that the necessity of relying on informal networks in everyday life under 'real socialism' results in a legacy of an ideology of solidarity, which supported the development of trust between actors.

Thus, while cultures with a common background (for example, ethnicities living on both sides of the border) might draw on their mutual history in building trust, trust building will mainly appear through repeated (business) exchanges where communities and cultures do not share a background or experiences. In this regard, on the one hand a joint regional identity of (neighbouring) countries might foster trust building, while on the other hand collective memories of a society could impede trust building when they hinder 'de-learning' because of previously negative

experiences. To sum up, trust is a context-bound phenor
by cultural traditions and settings.

CHOOSING A RESEARCH DESIGN: HO\
RESEARCH TRUST?

Many trust studies in the management and economics fields have applied
large-scale surveys and quantitative or experimental research designs,
albeit mainly relying on artificial laboratory experiments (for an overview see Kautonen et al., 2004). In our first research project on trust,
we designed the project using a cross-sectional method and combining
a survey, case studies and expert interviews to analyse entrepreneurial
behaviour and trust in West and East European environments. The
survey-based approach helped us in collecting quantitative data on occur-
rences of trust within business relations, within the firm and in relation to
the environment. It provided insights into the nature of trust-related contacts with entities such as banks, employees and business partners, into the
ways in which entrepreneurs regulated such contacts, for example through
contracts or oral agreements, and into the specificities of such regulations.

Some of our empirical results also started to cast doubt on the value
of a survey for this topic, especially in terms of analysing and measuring
different trust categories and trust levels across firms, sectors and regions.
For example, for Germany we started questioning the apparent role of the
written contract as a safeguard and of oral or no agreements as reflecting personal trust, because case studies revealed that written agreements
were often needed for bookkeeping and internal revenue. In retrospect, a
longitudinal case-study approach would have been more appropriate. The
survey researching the role of trust in entrepreneurial behaviour assisted
in reporting how frequent or common particular forms of (assumed) trust-
based behaviour were in different cultures, while a longitudinal case-study
approach would have allowed us to capture the process nature of trust in
different contexts. In this regard, Smallbone and Lyon (2002) argued that
quantitative data on trust is difficult to collect, especially with respect to
how trust-based relationships evolve, the intensity of trust and the value of
different types of trust-based business relations. Thus, we concluded that
quantitative and survey-based studies could be helpful in investigating the
nature and the extent of trust-based business links and relationships while
a qualitative approach can help to explore how trust is built up and lost
(Welter and Smallbone, 2006).

We switched to a qualitative approach in the following projects, which
studied cross-border entrepreneurship with, amongst other topics, a

particular emphasis on the role of trust in facilitating or hindering such co-operations. In general, investigating trust empirically is difficult because of its elusive and habitual nature, which can only be inadequately captured by survey studies. This takes on particular importance in a cross-border context and in investigating partly informal cross-border activities, as was the case in both research projects. In this context, qualitative research can help to provide an insight into individual attitudes, behaviours, value systems, motivations, aspirations, culture or lifestyles. Methodologically, the nature of the research questions under investigation, which included the motives, aspirations and experiences of those involved in cross-border activity – much of which was taking place outside the formal economy – made a qualitative approach essential. Interviews with petty traders and enterprises in both projects were conducted on a semi-structured basis, using a topic guide. Traders were identified by researchers at random, through observation of petty trading activities at markets on both border sides and/or railway stations at border crossing points; enterprises were also identified through assistance from institutions.

Of course, there are shortcomings to a qualitative approach in researching trust. Although the nature of the sampling methods used in the qualitative studies limits generalizations, there is no reason to believe that the profile of the cases studied across the various countries is not typical of those engaged in entrepreneurship and/or cross-border trading activities. But a cross-sectional empirical approach, as employed in all our research projects, clearly has its limitations. This mainly refers to a lack of dynamic orientation in researching trust processes, the changing nature of trust and the reasons for (not) trusting one another in business relations.

PREPARING FOR THE EMPIRICAL WORK: OPERATIONALIZING TRUST ACROSS CULTURES

All three projects adopted an indirect approach to operationalize trust, following Offe (2001), who rejects questions asking 'how much trust do you have in . . .' because of cross-cultural and intra-cultural semantic differences concerning the meaning of trust. Such questions would also imply that individuals are capable of identifying and evaluating the level of trust in their actions. Since trust is habitual and based on tacit knowledge, it might be difficult for entrepreneurs to identify 'what it is that may make his business partner appear to be trustworthy' (Bachmann, 2001: 357). However, an indirect approach to operationalizing trust has worked well in other projects studying entrepreneurship and small businesses. For example, Nuissl et al. (2002), in their study on inter-firm co-operation, reported that their interviewees were able to explain exactly why co-operation is sought, how it should be organized and which qualities should be primarily considered when assessing the potential partner.

Relevant questions in the survey and topic guidelines of the first trust project asked for the nature, extent and regulation of inter-firm relations with customers, suppliers and business partners, and intra-firm relations with employees as well as relations with the external environment, which refers to banks, links with the regulatory environment and sources of assistance. We also included questions on criteria used to select business partners, customers, suppliers, the governance mechanism and the sources of assistance.

The guidelines used in the interviews of the two cross-border entrepreneurship projects paid particular attention to the nature and extent of cross-border entrepreneurial activities; the motives of entrepreneurs and individuals for engaging in such activities; their entrepreneurial practices and the factors either inhibiting or favouring the development of their entrepreneurial activities; and the role of trust and learning in this regard as well as policies and support. In the case of interviews with individual traders, the role of different members of the household and families in the cross-border entrepreneurial activities was discussed. Since cross-border partnerships are part of a wider trading system, a key aspect of the investigation was the nature and extent of the 'co-operation' with trading partners for all groups.

In all projects, we also paid attention to the institutional embeddedness of trust, thus combining micro-level aspects of trust in individual behaviour with macro-level aspects that are required in order to explain differences in trust behaviour and levels of trust across countries. For example, institutional embeddedness was a key concept in our cross-cultural study of trust in Estonia, Germany, Italy, Russia and the UK. Related survey questions concerned linkages of the entrepreneurs with the regulatory environment as well as external sources of assistance in various stages of business development. In the cross-border projects, we also asked for attitudes towards neighbouring countries, in an attempt to identify macro factors influencing trust building.

In all research projects, the teams applied the same guidelines, which were jointly developed in English and then translated into the respective languages. This posed additional challenges in researching trust across cultures: differences in research cultures in the various countries might have an impact on how questions are phrased and how the concept of trust is interpreted. Team members might interpret questions differently because of their individual experiences and background. Training sessions were conducted in all projects to ensure that interviewers involved in the projects had a similar understanding of the research topic and the guidelines.

ASKING FOR TRUST: CHALLENGES ARISING DURING THE INTERVIEW PROCESS

In all projects, the in-depth interviews were conducted face to face based on topic guidelines. Some of the West and East European countries where the research projects took place are difficult environments for any empirically based entrepreneurship research because of the suspicion which entrepreneurs have of anyone approaching them and asking questions about their activities. This was made worse by the sensitive nature of the trust topic, especially as we also tried to capture mistrust towards the institutional framework, or, as in the case of the cross-border projects, the specific activities that were the focus of the interviews often happened outside the law. As a consequence, researchers had to work particularly hard to establish the trust-based relationships with potential interviewees necessary for conducting their interviews successfully.

In practice, a variety of approaches were used to overcome this problem. In all projects, researchers came from the respective countries themselves, which allowed them to draw on a common cultural understanding and which created an initial level of trust with their interviewees. They also sought assistance from contacts in administrations, local relatives and colleagues to help identify respondents whom they might approach, thus using recommendations to gain the trust of their respondents. In the case of cross-border traders, researchers approached potential interviewees personally. For example, in Belarus, which is one of the harshest environments for entrepreneurship and entrepreneurship-related research, researchers observed respondents on the Polish side of the border in local markets, railway stations and in cross-border trains. As soon as they had identified potential cross-border traders, they would offer to help with the transport of goods (Welter et al., 2006). This was considered helpful by potential interviewees as border regulations stipulate upper limits for goods imported by individuals. Many traders circumvent these regulations by drawing on an elaborate system of transport workers. Interviewers were thus winning the goodwill of their respondents and facilitating the way for a successful interview.

Another challenge concerned the documentation of the interview. In most cases, interviews could not be recorded because of the sensitive nature of the topic. Also, especially in the case of traders, interviewers were unable to take notes during the interview. Instead, the interviews were written up directly after the interview had taken place. Arguably, one might criticize this procedure for not accurately depicting the data; however, it takes into account both the sensitive nature of the research topic and the situations in which the data were collected.

ANALYSING TRUST DATA ACROSS CULTURES

Qualitative research into trust poses additional challenges after the data are collected – namely that of analysing the data. Again, keeping in mind that these projects had been conducted with teams originating from different cultures, inter-cultural differences play an important role. This refers both to translating the interview protocols and their interpretation. As interviews in all projects had been conducted in the respective country languages, they were translated into English, in order to allow for a joint analysis of the data. Naturally, the accuracy of the English protocols were influenced by the language skills of the respective national research teams and/or their translator, thus in the worst case 'distorting' our interpretation of trust-related issues. In this context, it helped that in all projects the majority of teams had longstanding experiences of working together.

Moreover, important information visible 'between the lines' in one's own language might disappear when interview protocols are translated into a foreign language. Therefore, in the last research project, we started using a computer programme for analysing qualitative data (N-Vivo), which not only allows for a structured and deep analysis, but also systematically keeps track of 'hidden' and situational information important for interpreting the results. Qualitative research software can help to manage, shape and make sense of unstructured information. It does not, though, take over the role of the researcher, who has to understand the 'meaning' of the interviews (Gibbs, 2004). Such software also helps in providing additional information. As trust is a context-bound phenomenon, we had to make sure that we had access to background information and any situational comments from interviewers. For example, when conducting case interviews, an experienced interviewer can often tell where entrepreneurs report 'half-truths', which is something that is important for the researcher interpreting the results to know.

In order to ensure consistent coding and interpretation of trust issues, interviews were coded by the authors as the research team responsible for the trust topic. We used a concept-driven approach to code the data, complemented by data-driven coding where interesting results came up during the coding process (Gibbs, 2004). Related to trust, the aim of the project was to identify and assess economic, social, cultural and institutional factors influencing the development and sustainability of different forms of cross-border partnerships between the various actors in the selected border regions. Therefore, our coding concentrated on factors facilitating or hindering trust building on a personal level, on the emergence of trust and on levels of trust on personal and institutional levels which we attempted to assess indirectly after having coded the interviews. Of course, we could have run the risk of over-interpreting trust-related data from a non-familiar country context. In order to prevent this, all the cross-cultural research projects included feedback rounds between research teams.

DISCUSSION: SOME FINAL REFLECTIONS ON THE ROLE OF CULTURE FOR TRUST (RESEARCH)

Instead of recapping the challenges in conducting empirical trust research in different cultures, we would like to finish this chapter by outlining some of our empirical results on the role of culture for building trust (we refrain from entering into a discussion on how to define culture, cf. Welter, 2005). This applies not only to trust in entrepreneurial behaviour and business relations, but also to international research teams studying trust across different cultures. Not surprisingly, trust building is facilitated in situations where individuals can draw on collective identities, as reflected in music, heroes, national symbols and common languages, as well as shared positive experiences. The latter enhance trust, especially where they go hand in hand with cultural proximity. In this context, trust is built through familiarity with one another's mentality and habits. Where communities and individuals do not share such a background, trust will be built through repeated (business) exchanges, which over time has facilitated all our research projects and mitigated cultural differences between the research teams. Individual personal experiences themselves might also foster cultural proximity.

On the other hand, negative experiences are often reinforced by cultural distance, and they also reinforce cultural distance. Prejudices, retentions and stereotypes can hinder the emergence of trust. Cultural stereotyping is often a result of disappointment and negative individual experiences. In the projects on cross-border entrepreneurship, interviewees often tended to classify the whole neighbouring nation as one deserving or not deserving trust, generalizing from their individual experiences. Such stereotyping, however, is important as it allows individuals to cope with situations and partners unfamiliar to them in drawing on something familiar and trusted, namely the stereotype. Symbols such as the stereotype help to reintroduce the unfamiliar into the familiar world (Luhmann, 2000; Möllering, 2006).

Culture also is visible in individual behaviour, which refers to partners acting in a business-like way, both at the level of our interviewees and at the level of participating research teams. Western 'identities', in the sense of familiar behaviour, facilitate the emergence of trust respectively; these are prerequisites if trust is to emerge. Partners have to earn trust through adhering to familiar behaviour which is visible in business relations – for example, paying creditors on time, or, in both business and research relations, in providing acceptable quality products and timely deliveries.

In summary, our results highlight the diversity of trust environments across and within countries, thus drawing attention to a culturally sensitive approach in researching trust which has implications for trust research beyond the European country results presented in this chapter. In this regard, there is a case to be made for more comparative studies across countries, preferably applying a mixed research design and incorporating longitudinal elements for the reasons discussed in previous sections. Researching trust across different cultures helps to understand the importance of institutions, in this case the cultural context, for the emergence and nature of trust because we are likely to 'see' this better in contexts we are not familiar with than in examples from our own cultural contexts, which we often take for granted.

REFERENCES

Bachmann, R. (2001), 'Trust, power and control in trans-organizational relations', *Organization Studies*, **22** (2), 337–65.

Fukuyama, F. (1995), *Trust: The Social Virtues and the Creation of Prosperity*, New York: Free Press.

Gibbs, G.R. (2004), *Qualitative Data Analysis: Explorations with NVivo*, Maidenhead and New York: McGraw Hill.

Höhmann, H.-H. and F. Welter (eds) (2005), *Trust and Entrepreneurship: A West–East Perspective*, Cheltenham, UK and Northampton, MA, USA: Edward Elgar.

Kautonen, T., A. Klymova and F. Welter (2004), 'Researching trust empirically: a note', in H.-H. Höhmann and F. Welter (eds), *Entrepreneurial Strategies and Trust: Structure and Evolution of Entrepreneurial Behavioural Patterns in 'Low Trust' and 'High Trust' Environments of East and West Europe. Part 1: A Review*, Forschungsstelle Osteuropa Arbeitspapiere und Materialien, 54, Bremen, pp. 26–34.

Luhmann, N. (2000), 'Familiarity, confidence, trust: problems and alternatives', in D. Gambetta (ed.), *Trust: Making and Breaking Cooperative Relations*, Oxford: Blackwell, pp. 94–107.

Möllering, G. (2006), *Trust: Reason, Routine, Reflexivity*, Oxford: Elsevier.

Nuissl, H. (2001), *Can 'Post-socialist' Entrepreneurs Trust Each Other? Empirical Findings on East German IT-Entrepreneurs' Cognitive Background of Trust*, Frankfurt/Oder: FIT.

Nuissl, H., A. Schwarz and M. Thomas (2002), *Vertrauen – Kooperation – Netzwerkbildung:*

Unternehmerische Handlungsressourcen in prekären regionalen Kontexten, Wiesbaden: Westdeutscher Verlag.

Offe, C. (2001), 'Wie können wir unseren Mitbürgern vertrauen?', in M. Hartmann and C. Offe (eds), *Vertrauen: Die Grundlage des sozialen Zusammenhalts*, Frankfurt/Main: Campus, pp. 241–94.

Smallbone, D. and F. Lyon (2002), 'A note on trust, networks, social capital and entrepreneurial behaviour', in H-H. Höhmann and F. Welter (eds), *Entrepreneurial Strategies and Trust: Structure and Evolution of Entrepreneurial Behavioural Patterns in East and West European Environments – Concept and Considerations*, Bremen: Forschungsstelle Osteuropa, pp. 19–24.

Smallbone, D., L. Labrianidis, U. Venesaar, F. Welter and P. Zashev (2007), *Challenges and Prospects of Cross Border Cooperation in the Context of EU Enlargement*, Deliverable 7: State of the Art Review of Literature, Kingston: Kingston University.

Welter, F. (2005), 'Culture versus branch? Looking at trust and entrepreneurial behaviour from a cultural and sectoral perspective', in H.-H. Höhmann and F. Welter (eds), *Trust and Entrepeneurship: A West–East Perspective.* Cheltenham, UK and Northampton, MA, USA: Edward Elgar, pp. 24–38.

Welter, F. and D. Smallbone (2006), 'Exploring the role of trust in entrepreneurial activity', *Entrepreneurship Theory and Practice*, **30** (4), 465–75.

Welter, F. and D. Smallbone (2008), 'Entrepreneurship in a cross border context: the example of transition countries', paper presented to the ICSB World Conference, June, Halifax.

Welter, F., D. Smallbone, A. Slonimski, O. Linchevskaya, A. Pobol and M. Slonimska (2006), 'Enterprising households in a cross-border context', paper to RENT XX, November, Brussels.

Williamson, O.E. (1993), 'Calculativeness, trust and economic organization', *Journal of Law and Economics*, **36** (2), 453–86.

Annotated Further Reading

Höhmann, H.-H. and F. Welter (eds) (2005), *Trust and Entrepreneurship: A West–East Perspective*, Cheltenham, UK and Northampton, MA, USA: Edward Elgar – an edited volume with several empirical chapters reflecting the diversity of trust environments in Europe.

Möllering, G. (2006), *Trust: Reason, Routine, Reflexivity*, Amsterdam: Elsevier – develops and discusses an interesting conceptual framework for trust research.

Williamson, O.E. (1993), 'Calculativeness, trust and economic organization', *Journal of Law and Economics*, **36** (2), 453–86 – a seminal article on trust which questions the concept of trust for business relations, instead suggesting that it is calculated risk.

6 Trust and social capital: challenges for studying their dynamic relationship[1]

Boris F. Blumberg, José M. Peiró[2] and Robert A. Roe

INTRODUCTION

In this chapter the dynamic nature of trust and social capital is explored. By showing how networks and social capital change over time, the challenges of measuring trust within these networks are set out and the implications for researching trust using longitudinal studies are identified.

The idea that trust is an important phenomenon in social networks has been acknowledged by many researchers. It is commonly assumed that a certain degree of trust among members is necessary for a social network to emerge and be maintained. A decline of trust can easily result in erosion or rupture of a social network. Several researchers have linked the notion of trust to social capital, suggesting that resource sharing by network members depends on their trust in one another. Trust has even been seen as an inherent part of social capital. In this chapter we present another view of the relation between trust and social capital. In contrast to earlier work in which trust was seen as part of social capital we consider trust as a factor in the dynamics of social networks that affects both the use of social capital and its effects. Taking a dynamic look at trust, we reflect on how declining and increasing trust will influence the magnitude of social capital as well as its depletion and its replenishment after having been used. Investigating this model empirically poses several challenges to researchers. At present dynamic research is seriously hampered by a general lack of methods for assessing changes in trust as well as changes in network characteristics and social capital. There is also a lack of methods to analyse co-variation and causality over time.

Social Capital

Social capital has been defined in a multitude of ways (see for example Bourdieu, 1986; Coleman, 1990); the core of the notion is the idea that members of a social network can share resources. By being part of a social network, members have access to resources beyond those that they own themselves. However, social capital is a socially mediated resource, one that cannot be fully and directly controlled by an individual member, as she/he relies on the willingness of another party to share its resources. Moreover, the resource must be asked for and hence is merely a potential resource. In this respect it differs from individual financial capital, which is under the immediate control of its owner. Social capital can only be used if it is claimed and if network members agree to make it available.

An individual's capacity to obtain resources is based on direct and indirect ties with other members in the network. Thus, social capital derives from the influence of the individual on other members' willingness to provide resources in an open exchange situation where the latter accept that they are vulnerable – this is where trust comes in – as reciprocity is not simultaneous. Those providing resources accept this vulnerability under the assumption that they will get something in return later on. This means that they expect to switch roles and use their own social capital by asking others to provide resources.

Trust

Trust is a dynamic phenomenon defined as 'a person's willingness to be vulnerable in order to obtain benefits from someone or something' (cf. Mayer et al., 1995). The willingness to be vulnerable clearly varies over time (see for example, McAllister, 1995). For instance, trust between two persons develops through shared experiences and mutual exchange of favours, starting with minor exchanges of little risk before they engage in major exchanges. Dyer and Chu (2000) find that the duration of the relationships and the continuity of the transactions in inter-organizational relationships have a positive influence on the development of trust, with conditional trust giving way to unconditional trust.

The actual dynamics of trust is not well studied, but the proverb 'it takes years to build up trust, and only seconds to destroy it' suggests that its development is characterized by gradual increase and great stability, unless there is ground for a sudden drop. It seems likely that the loss of trust involves two different mechanisms. One operates as a slow erosion that occurs if no interaction or exchange take place during extended periods of time. The other is the process of sudden and radical loss because one part perceives that the other behaves opportunistically, that is, takes advantage of his/her vulnerability (Bies and Tripp, 1996). While the sudden drop of trust, for example by the violation of a psychological contract, is well-documented, little is known about the way in which trusts builds up and gradually declines over time.

DESCRIPTION OF THE METHOD: A DYNAMIC MODEL FOR TRUST AND SOCIAL CAPITAL

Although rarely acknowledged in the literature, it is hard to conceive social capital without reference to the notion of time. Time is intrinsically linked to social capital as it implies an expectation that resources may be drawn upon at some future moment in time. If it were impossible ever to call upon another network member and ask them to make a resource available, one's social capital would be void. Having said that, another issue emerges: can social capital be assumed to retain its value over time? We propose that social capital is subject to change; it grows and shrinks as time passes. It is important to study this process and to clarify the role of trust. Figure 6.1 depicts the dynamic relations between the social network, the social capital of individual members and trust.

Social Networks

Social networks and the ties implied in them provide the setting in which social capital emerges. Since individual members' ties are crucial for their social capital one would expect changes in social capital to follow, at least partly, from changes in the network. This has been emphasized by authors who have described the structural dimension of social capital

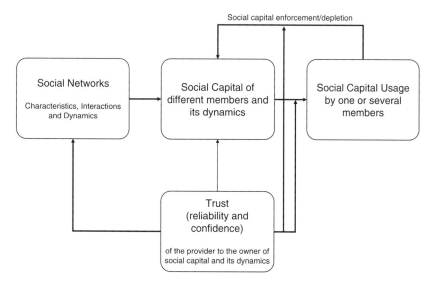

Figure 6.1   The role of social networks and trust in the development of social capital

(Burt, 1992; Coleman, 1990). When the network expands – that is, new members are acquired and new ties are formed – it is likely that the social capital will augment, simply because there are more members to rely on. The increase is not necessarily additive, however. An extensive literature suggests that adding network members that form a bridge to yet unrelated networks or circles will produce a greater increase in social capital than adding members that are already well-connected and are therefore redundant (Burt, 1992). Members filling structural holes in the social networks will contribute more to social capital creation than those whose relationships overlap with those of other members in the network. In an opposite direction, contraction of a social network can be expected to reduce social capital. If well-connected members leave for another network or die, the possibilities for remaining members to access their resources may diminish dramatically.

Changes of social capital may occur for various reasons. First of all, one would expect a gradual decay of social capital over time in response to general network erosion, that is, the weakening and breaking of ties associated with the ageing of networks (Burt, 2005). Secondly, there are changes due to members' agency. Following from individual members' actions in building new relations or giving up existing relations, structural changes in a network will result in direct growth or decline of social capital. In giving up existing relations or engaging in conflicting relations members may affect the social capital of others, namely by blocking their access to certain resources. And third, apart from these structural changes, there can also be changes in the nature of relations – for instance, when functional work ties are supplemented by friendship ties. Emerging friendship ties will increase the ties' overall strength and enhance social capital, while broken friendships will have the opposite effect. This refers to the relational dimension of social capital (Nahapiet and Ghoshal, 1998).

Changes in networks' perceived characteristics, that is, in the way they are regarded by their members, may also change social capital. For instance, over time norms may develop (or vanish) and values can become more (or less) shared. A larger consent on norms and values within a network, a larger value homophily, aligns the network identity with the members' identities and will increase social capital among the members (McPherson and Smith-Lovin, 2001). It should, however, be noted that a very strong alignment of norms might create in-group effects preventing members to build social capital beyond their core network. These processes refer to the cognitive dimension of social capital (Nahapiet and Ghoshal, 1998).

Social Capital Use

Following authors such as Coleman (1990: 302) and Knoke (1999: 18), who have emphasized that social capital is actionable, that is, can be utilized, we posit that social capital also changes due to an actual exchange of resources. Thus, individuals may augment their social capital – and that of other network members – by offering favours to resourceful parties which these parties should sooner or later reciprocate. Inversely, social capital might decrease by asking for access to other parties' resources and actually using them if the provider is not inclined to ask for reciprocal favours in the future. This effect can be explained by the temporal asymmetry of the exchange, where one request for access to a member's resource can precede the opposite request. By the same token, a decline in social capital will not occur when parties engage in a simultaneous exchange of resources or a serial exchange within a reasonable amount of time.

Not all changes in social capital can be attributed to individual agency. Changes produced by external sources, such as non-intended encounters, new opportunities to meet and communicate (for example due to infrastructure or technology) and natural events that sever the ties between people, such as the death of network members, will produce change in social capital as well.

The Role of Trust in the Development of Social Networks and Social Capital

Although several authors have suggested a link between trust and social capital (see for example Costa and Peiró, 2009; Martinez-Tur and Peiró, 2009), few have explored the conditions for its change in relation to trust. A truly dynamic view that considers the role of trust in the development of social capital has not yet been presented.

In order to investigate the role of trust in network changes within and across organizations there is a need to distinguish between trust people have in the members of their network and in outsiders. We posit that, other things being equal, members' trust in outsiders will facilitate the establishment of new contacts and expansion of the network, which will be accompanied by an increase of social capital (bridging social capital). Members' trust in insiders, that is, other members of their network, will help to develop stronger ties (bonding social capital). Inversely, lack of trust, in outsiders or insiders will restrain networks and make them vulnerable to ruptures, which may reduce social capital.

While these effects may surface in cross-sectional studies, they are more likely to emerge in longitudinal studies. Increasing trust (for example better than expected outcomes) will favour network expansion and cohesion, whereas decreasing trust (worse than expected outcomes) will promote network contraction and a weakening of ties among network members.

It must be acknowledged that trust is neither homogeneously distributed nor stable. Within any network there will be relations characterized by different levels of trust. Also, people will actively invest in some relations, which will raise trust over time, and hardly maintain other relations, accepting the erosion of the relation and the decrease of trust. For the network as a whole, these variations in trust matter, as the main sources for social capital will shift within the network depending on which trust relations are strongest. Where overlapping networks exist, or in cases of people moving from one network to another, the picture will be even more complex. One would expect that changes in networks and consequent changes in social capital will vary with changes in trust.

Trust and the Use of Social Capital

Several aspects of trust are relevant to the use of social capital. First, it is inherent in the notion of trust, as a person's willingness to expose herself/himself to the risk of the other party behaving opportunistically, that the person relies on the expectation that she/he will obtain and be able to use the resources made available through her/his contacts. In other words, the expectation that allows the person to bridge a time interval until the moment of gaining access to desired resources is rooted in trust. Trust can be seen as a general precondition for actually using social capital. Second, trust facilitates the utilization of social capital as it raises the likelihood that a member is granted access to other members' resources and that these resources can actually be used. We assume that two processes play a role in this: it is harder to refuse access to people one trusts and is trusted by, and trust supports the expectation of future reciprocation. If trust is high it makes people believe that at some point in time they may get something in return for granting a network member access to their resources. If trust is low, the opposite holds: access will more often be refused and little reciprocation will therefore occur.

Depletion of Social Capital?

An open question is what happens after a member of the network has asked for access to the resources of other members, that is, he/she has used social capital? Two different scenarios are possible. In the first scenario, the access to those resources is denied or fails. In this case, an existing network relation does not provide social capital. This may initiate a reassessment of the relation with regard to its potential benefits. It is possible that such a denial results in a depreciation of the trust in this relationship, which would in turn reduce the available social capital. In the second scenario the person activating social capital actually uses the resources of other members. What happens in this case seems to depend on the temporal symmetry of reciprocation that was mentioned above. After an episode of asymmetric use – one member using the other's resources but the other not yet reciprocating – the remaining social capital will be less; the chance that the person can successfully use more social capital decreases. However, the degree of decline will depend on the level of trust: if trust is high the non-reciprocation time lag is likely to be larger. Symmetric use of social capital will, on the contrary, restore or even enhance the social capital, as the reciprocity in the exchange of favours deepens the relationship and might also lead to a rise in trust.

While trust seems critical for the time lag until reciprocation, other factors that may influence the decline or growth of social capital, such as the perceived (im)balance in the resources exchanged, which may influence the perception of fairness and the status or power of each party. For instance, if an exchange is perceived to be unbalanced or unfair, or if it is disproportional to the status or power of the parties, social capital depletion is the most probable outcome. However, as has already been said, this outcome may only occur after a period of time, given that these types of exchanges do not usually happen concurrently.

RESEARCH VALIDITY AND CAVEATS

Investigating the Model

Above we have argued that the concept of trust can play an important role in understanding the phenomenon of social capital by combining it with notions from social network research. More particularly, trust can shed a new light on the use of social capital by network members and the issue of social capital accumulation or depletion. However, as earlier research on trust has largely been cross-sectional in nature, a rather drastic change in the research approach is needed to reveal its dynamic features and effects. We see a number of challenges that researchers should meet (see also Roe, 2009). The first is to move to a temporal way of conceptualizing phenomena, that is highlighting the fact that trust is continuously changing, even if it may have relatively stable episodes. Likewise, it must be acknowledged

that social networks are in constant flux, which produces temporal variations in size, density and so on, as well as in members' social capital. Our
model is meant to facilitate thinking in terms of temporal variation and
co-variation. Second, there is a need for temporal measurement. That
requires moving away from measuring instruments that are built for single
moment snapshots and developing new instruments that are suitable for
repeated measurement and sensitive enough to pick up change. Such
instruments, focused on trust on the one hand and network features on
the other, are needed to build time series that are long enough to analyse
temporal dependencies between the key phenomena. Third, there is a need
for adopting and developing alternative methods for analysing change, as
well as temporal and causal relations. The fourth and perhaps most difficult challenge is to manage the process of sampling and longitudinal data
acquisition. A variable pool of network members has to be assessed over
a time period of perhaps months or years. It seems almost unrealistic to
expect that researchers will be able to meet these challenges. On the other
hand, there are encouraging developments on the methodological side
and examples of long-term longitudinal studies from other disciplines that
provide hope that trust researchers can also move in this direction.

Modelling and Conceptual Issues

What we have proposed is not without caveats, of course. The dynamic
conceptualization of social capital and trust implies a broader range of
issues than addressed in this chapter. For instance, the role of trust in the
build-up and maintenance of social capital under conditions other than
utilization has not been addressed. Nor is the reverse relationship – the
influence of social capital on trust – being studied. Yet, it seems unlikely
that the use of social capital remains without influence on trust.

In trust research it has been common to distinguish between competence-
based and motive-based trust (McAllister, 1995). So far we have neglected
this important distinction. Both forms of trust will affect the usage of
social capital. Regarding the effects of attempts to use social capital on
trust, we expect, however, that failed attempts do not change competence-
based trust but lower motive-based trust, and that successful attempts
increase both forms of trust.

Another limitation is that we do not cover other mechanisms that may
affect the utilization of social capital. Obviously, control is a mechanism
that could substitute and/or complement trust (see for example Faulkner,
2000). Formal control is enforceable as it is based on a contract or institutional rules, while informal control is exercised through the mere observation of behaviour and the acknowledgement that it conforms with or

deviates from generally accepted social norms. Thus, in situations where control is present – which is typical for relations within organizations – missing trust might be substituted by control. Still, control mechanisms also have limits. Formal control suffers from the inherent incompleteness of contracts, while the efficacy of social control mechanisms, such as reputation concerns, are restrained by the dependency on other actors willing to enforce them (Williamson, 1996). Of course, control is also a dynamic phenomenon, and interesting questions arise when trust and control develop non-synchronously.

Measurement Issues

Our model clearly distinguishes between trust, social capital and social networks. While fine-grained measures for trust have been developed, such fine-grained measures are very demanding in network studies as it would be required to measure a respondent's trust with each tie over time.

Despite recent developments in social network and social capital research, these theoretical considerations are not taken up at a methodological level. Although the distinction between social networks and social capital is clear, researchers often use properties of social networks, such as density, centrality and so on, as indicators for social capital. Such structural measures neglect, however, the heterogeneity of members (providers) in terms of resource possessions.

DISCUSSION AND IMPLICATIONS FOR FURTHER RESEARCH

Our view of social capital as dynamic and actionable and of trust as a factor that, being dynamic itself, can influence both the development and use of social capital has a number of implications for future research.

First, in line with the temporal approach to organizational research proposed by Roe (2009), we would suggest that researchers first examine the dynamic properties of social networks, social capital and trust in isolation, and next their interrelationships. That is, research should first investigate these phenomena in their full lifecycle, from the beginning until the end, including processes of emergence, development and decline. Once their dynamic properties are known, research should be devoted to analysing how changes in social networks relate to changes in social capital. Here it would be worth focusing on the three layers or dimensions of networks (structure, type of relations and shared perceptions) that have been linked to social capital in earlier research (Nahapiet and Ghoshal, 1998).

Similarly, one would like to see research into the dynamic links between trust and social capital. A separate topic for investigation is the depletion and restoration of social capital upon use and its outcomes for both parties involved, and the effect that this might have on trust among them.

Obviously, one would need longitudinal research designs to study such dynamic patterns and relationships between them. Earlier research on inter-organizational networks shows that relations between colleagues are rather unstable; many relations do not survive the first year (Burt, 2005). This suggests that the dynamics of social capital and trust can be unravelled in designs spanning somewhat limited time periods as long as one measures at a sufficient number of time points.

NOTES

1. We thank participants of the BBVA international symposium on social capital and trust in organization hosted 2006 in Madrid and the 4th EIASM Workshop on Trust Within and Between Organizations 2007 in Amsterdam for fruitful comments on earlier versions of this chapter.
2. The author wants to thank the METEOR Institute for sponsoring a visit during September 2007. The contribution to this chapter was also supported by the Spanish National Foundation project CONSOLIDER 2006-14086/SIC. He also acknowledges the support of the Valencian Research Institute of Economics (IVIE), project numbers SEJ (200614086) and ENE 2005-08619/CON.

REFERENCES

Bies, Robert J. and Thomas M. Tripp (1996), 'Beyond distrust: "getting even" and the need for revenge', in Roderick M. Kramer and Tom R. Tyler (eds), *Trust in Organizations*, Thousand Oaks, CA: Sage, pp. 246–60.
Bourdieu, Pierre (1986), 'The forms of capital', in John G. Richardson (ed.), *The Handbook of Theory: Research for the Sociology of Education*, New York: Greenwood Press, pp. 241–58.
Burt, Ronald S. (1992), *Structural Holes. The Social Structure of Competition*, Cambridge, MA: Harvard University Press.
Burt, Ronald S. (2005), *Brokerage and Closure*, Oxford: Oxford University Press.
Coleman, James S. (1990), *Foundations of Social Theory*, Cambridge, MA: Harvard University Press.
Costa, Ana C. and José M. Peiró (2009), 'Trust and social capital in teams and organizations: antecedents, dynamics, benefits and limitations. An introduction', *Social Science Information*, **48**, 131–43.
Dyer, Jeffrey H. and Wujin Chu (2000), 'The determinants of trust in supplier–automaker relationships in the U.S., Japan, and Korea', *Journal of International Business Studies*, **31**, 259–85.
Faulkner, David O. (2000), 'Trust and control. Opposing or complementary functions', in David O. Faulkner and Marc de Rond (eds), *Cooperative Strategies: Economic, Business and Organizational Issues*, Oxford: Oxford University Press, pp. 341–61.
Knoke, David (1999), 'Organizational networks and corporate social capital', in Shaul M.

Gabbay and Roger Leenders (eds), *Corporate Social Capital and Liability*, Dordrecht: Kluwer, pp. 17–42.

Martínez-Tur, Vicente and José M. Peiró (2009), 'The trust episode in organizations: implications for private and public social capital', *Social Science Information*, **48**, 143–75.

Mayer, Roger C., James H. Davis and F. David Schoorman (1995), 'An integrative model of organizational trust', *Academy of Management Review*, **20**, 709–34.

McAllister, Daniel J. (1995), 'Affect and cognition based trust as foundations for interpersonal cooperation in organizations', *Academy of Management Journal*, **38**, 24–59.

McPherson, Miller and Lynn Smith-Lovin (2001), 'Birds of a feather: homophily in social networks', *Annual Review Sociology*, **27**, 415–44.

Nahapiet, Janine and Sumantra Ghoshal (1998), 'Social capital, intellectual capital and the organizational advantage', *Academy of Management Review*, **23**, 242–66.

Roe, Robert A. (2009), 'Perspectives on time and the chronometric study of what happens in organizations', in Robert A. Roe, Mary Waller and Stewart Clegg (eds), *Time in Organizational Research*, Oxford: Routledge, pp. 291–313.

Williamson, Oliver E. (1996), *The Mechanisms of Governance*, New York: Oxford University Press.

7 Measuring generalized trust: in defense of the 'standard' question[1]
Eric M. Uslaner

INTRODUCTION

This chapter reviews several key issues in the measurement of generalized trust: whether to include a single measure or multiple items, whether to measure trust as a dichotomy or on a scale with more values, what trust means in different cultures and languages, and whether trust means the same thing at the aggregate and individual levels.

The measurement of interpersonal trust has been as controversial as the debate over what trust means and what shapes faith in others. I review some of the controversies about the measurement of trust and offer evidence in defense of the 'standard' question in research on generalized trust: 'Generally speaking, do you believe that most people can be trusted or can't you be too careful in dealing with people?'

The standard question was first formulated by Elisabeth Noelle-Neumann in Germany in 1948. Morris Rosenberg expanded the measure of college students in the United States in 1956 by creating a misanthropy scale that includes trust and the perceptions that people are fair and helpful (Zmerli and Newton, 2008). It has now become common for researchers to use the misanthropy scale as a measure of 'trust.' Is 'misanthropy' the same as trust? Beyond the issue of whether the deity of 'trust' is one or three, there are controversies over what the standard question means, whether the traditional dichotomy (trust versus being careful) captures the range of variation in people's faith in others, and how best to measure trust. I consider each of these issues in this chapter.

DESCRIPTION OF THE METHOD

Any question on measurement must first begin with some notion of what we are measuring. When we consider whether 'most people can be trusted,' what do we mean? The most common notion of trust is based upon experience: Hardin (2002: 10) argues: '. . . my trust of you must be grounded in expectations that are particular to you, not merely in generalized expectations.' In contrast, my notion of moralistic trust is faith in people whom we don't know and who are likely to be different from ourselves. We can't base trust in strangers on their trustworthiness, because we don't know them. We must presume that others share our fundamental moral values. We learn trust early in life from our parents and it is largely consistent throughout our lives, resistant to many experiences both good and bad (Uslaner, 2002: 15, 26). Moralistic trust should be distinguished from knowledge-based 'strategic trust.' Moralistic trust does not refer to trust in specific persons, but rather trust in strangers more generally.

What does trust mean? Yamagishi and Yamagishi (1994) distinguish between generalized and particularized trust. Generalized trust is faith in people unlike yourself, while particularized trust is the notion that we should only have faith in people like ourselves. This is similar to, but not identical to, Woolcock's (1998) concepts of 'bonding' and 'bridging' social capital – but particularized trust is more narrow than bonding social capital since it reflects trust only in people like oneself. Empirically, this means that trust is multidimensional.

I found support for this view in a factor analysis of data from the 1996 survey of metropolitan Philadelphia conducted by the Pew Center for the People and the Press. This survey asked a wide range of trust questions. The factor analysis produces three distinct dimensions: trust in strangers, trust in friends and family, and trust in government. The generalized trust question is part of the same dimension as trust in people you meet on the street, people who work where you shop, and neighbors on the trust in strangers factor. It is distinct from the trust in friends and family factor, which is dominated by people at work, people at church, people at your club, your family, your boss, and neighbors (Uslaner, 2002: 53–5). There is a clear differentiation between trust in people you know (experience-based trust) and faith in strangers (moralistic trust). Indeed, there is no direct linkage between particularized and generalized trust either in this survey or the *New York Times* Millennium Survey of 2000 (Uslaner, 2002: 145–8). Trust is not a one-dimensional phenomenon based exclusively upon experience.

The multidimensional nature of trust challenges some alternative measurements of trust. Following Hardin's argument that trust is really trustworthiness, Putnam (2000: 135–6) argues that the question 'Most people are honest' used in the DDB Needham Lifestyle Surveys is a reasonable proxy for trust. Yet generalized trust is not the same thing as trustworthiness. While trust and honesty are related, they are hardly the same thing: The 1972 American National Election Study (ANES) asked people if they agreed that 'most people are basically honest': 86.4 percent agreed, compared to just 46.7 percent who said that 'most people can be trusted.'

The two measures are correlated, but the relationship is moderate (tau-c = .345). Almost all people who believe most people are dishonest say that 'you can't be too careful in dealing with people.' Yet barely more than half of people who say that most people are honest are ready to trust strangers. Even the aggregate correlation between the share of the public who say that 'most people are honest' and 'most people can be trusted' across 20 surveys – the General Social Survey (GSS) for trust and the DDB Needham surveys for honesty – from 1975 to 1998 is just .453.

Economists seem wedded to experience-based trust. While many economists define trust as cooperative behavior in an experimental game (Bohnet, 2008), others are more nuanced and see trust as a potential factor that would lead to more cooperative behavior in experiments on public goods production. Glaeser et al. (2000) employ both behavioral and attitudinal measures of trust in their experiments. The behavioral measures were previous 'trusting' responses in public goods games, while the attitudinal measures centered on the standard trust question. They also included other attitudinal measures such as fairness (whether most people are fair or would take advantage of you) and helpfulness (whether people would be helpful or are just looking out for themselves).

They find that neither the generalized trust question, an index of trust, fairness, and helpfulness, nor most other measures of trust from previous research have statistically significant effects on cooperating in public goods games. Past cooperative behavior – as well as social status, friendship networks, and altruistic behavior – was strongly related to behavior in current games. Numerous experimental games show similar results, although there are now results that show positive effects for the standard trust question on cooperation in 'trust games' (Capra et al., 2008).

What remains an open question is whether we should expect generalized trust – which does not refer to faith in specific persons – to be associated with cooperation in a repeated game. It is hardly surprising that previous behavior would have strong effects on cooperation in a trust game, but ought we to expect a measure of generalized trust to predict such strategic cooperation? And might it be far too strong for Glaeser et al. (2000: 841) to claim that 'standard survey questions about trust do not appear to measure trust'?

RESEARCH VALIDITY CAVEATS

Is the standard question measure reliable and valid? Three key issues stand out. First, Smith (1997) has argued that the standard question is subject to question order effects. In most years the GSS survey has at least two forms. In one version the trust question follows some queries on whether life is exciting, work values, how one gets ahead in life, and two sexual morality items. In the second version, trust follows items on political ideology, reducing gaps in income between the rich and the poor, divorce laws, legalization of marijuana some of the time and attitudes on crime in other years. Not surprisingly, the second trust series shows less trust than the first. Smith reports a 7.7 percent overestimate of trust in the first series compared to the second. He argues that the trust question calls 'for global assessments of people in general based presumably on one's entire life experience. Making judgments based on such massive, cognitive retrievals are difficult and open to variability' (Smith, 1997: 174). Smith's point is well taken and the estimates of trust in the ANES seem particularly prone to question order effects. However, over time, the bias in the GSS series seems to have fallen rapidly and the GSS estimates are generally quite close to those of other surveys (Uslaner, 2002: 68–9).

Second, Miller and Mitamura (2003) argue that the two parts of the standard question – trusting most people and being cautious – represent two distinct attitudes rather than parts of the same concept. They found that Americans are more likely than Japanese to say that 'most people can be trusted' and that 'you can't be too careful in dealing with people.' Being trusting and careful are not part of the same concept, they argue.

The best defense of the standard question lies in the extant research about trust. Perhaps the two strongest pieces of evidence supporting the standard question are: (1) 'think aloud' questions indicating that people do seem to understand the standard question; and (2) the strong stability of the question over time in panel studies. The ANES conducted a 'think aloud' experiment in its 2000 Pilot Study. Respondents were asked what the three misanthropy measures – trust, fairness, helpfulness – meant to them. If the trust question was more difficult to understand because it included carefulness as well, we might expect that more people would give answers that were difficult to code (into general versus specific responses) than for fairness or helpfulness. Yet, fewer people gave unclear responses to the generalized trust question: 20 percent for trust compared to 22 percent for fairness and 26 percent for helpfulness.

Trust is also very stable over time. Across the 1972, 1974 and 1976 ANES panel, about three quarters of people gave consistent responses to the trust question over time, making trust the fourth most stable question of 17 issues repeated over the three waves of the panel. Across the 1965, 1973 and 1982 panel study of high-school students and their parents conducted by Richard Niemi and M. Kent Jennings, 72 percent of parents and 64 percent of students gave consistent responses over the 17 years – so trust ranked as tied for fourth in stability among 17 questions (Uslaner, 2002: 60–65). In the 2006 ANES Pilot Survey, 75 percent of respondents gave the same response as they did two years earlier (Uslaner, forthcoming). Even with the 'you can't be too careful' option in the standard question, people have little difficulty understanding the question – and in giving consistent answers over time. Moreover, when the trust question is asked without the 'can't be too careful' anchor, responses tend to cluster in the center of the scale and to have only weak relationships with the standard question. The ANES experimented with a five-point scale on how often people trust others in 2006. Only five of 315 respondents said 'always' and only five said 'never,' so the two extreme values comprised only 3 percent of the sample (Uslaner, forthcoming).

Third, most researchers on trust do not rely on just the standard question. The argument for a scale rather than a single measure is straightforward: single-item measures have more measurement error and are less reliable. The trust measures originated in social psychology where virtually all measurement employs scales. After Rosenberg devised the misanthropy scale, Rotter (1967) created an 'interpersonal trust' scale that included disparate indicators, including trust, honesty, institutional bias, fear of social disgrace, and whether '[t]he United Nations will [ever] be an effective force in keeping world peace.' Chun and Campbell (1974) found that these diverse measures did not form a single dimension of trust, but rather reflected four distinct factors. The Rotter scale has not lasted in research on trust. The three-item misanthropy scale, which Zmerli and Newton (2008) call 'generalised social trust,' dominates most research (Brehm and Rahn, 1997). While the three measures scale well, the individual-level correlations among them are not always strong – and in the United States, where we have a considerable time series from 1960 to 2006, neither trust nor fairness correlates even moderately with helpfulness over time. There is general consensus that trust has fallen sharply over time in the United States ($r = -.857$, $N = 31$). However, neither helpfulness nor fairness show such a drop, and there has been a sharp increase in fairness over time ($r = .745$ after 1971).

The 2000 ANES 'think aloud' experiment leads to further skepticism of an underlying scale. Seventy-two percent of respondents who gave a codeable response to the trust question interpreted trust generally, without mention of specific experiences. Fifty-six percent of respondents gave general responses to the fairness question, but only 39 percent to the helpfulness question (Uslaner, 2002: 72–4).

While we can create reliable scales by adding the fairness and helpfulness measures to the standard trust question, what we gain is not so clear. Are we reducing measurement error by increasing the number of indicators? Or are we increasing measurement error by forming a scale from indicators that don't all seem to tap the same underlying concept?

Trust can be stronger or weaker. But the standard question is a dichotomy: In the late 1990s, the Swiss Household Panel and the Citizenship, Involvement, Democracy (CID) cross-national surveys in Europe shifted to an 11-point scale using the same questions as for the dichotomies. Shortly thereafter the new European Social Survey (ESS) adopted the 11-point scale as well. Scherpenzeel (n.d.: 1) argued: 'Scales with relatively few response alternatives force respondents to categorize their reaction towards an attitude object instead of directly mapping it onto the response continuum, thus causing information loss . . . respondents differentiate more between objects when offered response scales with greater numbers of categories . . .' Zmerli and Newton (2008) and Hooghe and Reeskens (2007) argue that the 11-point scale marks a great improvement over the dichotomous measure of generalized trust. They both find that the 11-point measure has more robust correlations with measures of trust in government than the dichotomy and argue that this helps us round out the theory of social capital.

I won't engage in a debate over whether we ought to expect a stronger relationship between these two types of trust. I do want to highlight a problem with the 11-point scale: the social psychological version of 'regression to the mean,' or what I call 'clumping' (Uslaner, 2009). Clumping is the tendency of people to respond to questions with multiple alternatives by 'clumping' their answers around the mean – at values of 4, 5, or 6 on the 11-point scale. The first two waves of the ESS and the CID surveys in Romania and the United States all use 11-point scales for both trust in people and confidence in government.

Clumping is a non-trivial problem. In the ESS, the share of respondents choosing the three middle values ranged from about 35 percent for trust in the police to almost 50 percent for trust in the European Parliament. In the United States CID, clumping ranged from about 25 percent for trusting neighbors to about 50 percent for confidence in Congress and political parties. People who clumped on one question of institutional confidence were likely to give central values on other indicators – though the link with generalized trust was modest.

Perhaps this just shows us that people trust their institutions and their fellow citizens about eight feet – a bit but not too much. People are expressing a healthy skepticism. However, across all institutions in the ESS, respondents don't discriminate well in the scores they assign. For clumpers, the average correlation for confidence in different institutions is about .17. The average correlation across trust in people and confidence in institutions for clumpers is .07 (Uslaner, 2009). The scores 4, 5, and 6 don't represent distinct values, so trusting your sister eight feet doesn't seem that different from trusting her 12 feet. For non-clumpers, the average correlations range from .410 for trust in people to .670 for trust in parliament.

The patterns of clumping across countries and institutions are not random among respondents. Clumping represents a 'social desirability' heuristic: People give higher scores on the 11-point scale to show that they are less mistrusting of other people but lower scores to indicate that they are not quite so positive about their leaders and institutions. Where there is a lot of mistrust of others, people are more likely to give scores of 4, 5, or 6 to the 11-point generalized trust question. The 4, 5, or 6 responses seem to represent the lower limit for popular institutions in countries where people are more generally confident in their institutions.

The Romanian CID asked respondents both the 11-point scale and the traditional dichotomy. The relationship between the two measures is modest ($r^2 = .164$). Seventy-six percent of Romanians scoring 4 on the 11-point measure are mistrusters on the dichotomous measure, as are 69 percent directly in the middle at 5, and even 58 percent who scored a 6 on the expanded measure. Only 6.8 percent of respondents gave responses of either 9 or 10 – and almost one third (32 percent) of them said that they were mistrusters in the dichotomy.

Clumping, together with the low correlations among clumpers, suggests that the 11-point scales may be problematic for many respondents. Miller (1956) argued many years ago that a seven-point scale is the most that people can handle in a survey question. Beyond seven options, people lose the ability to discriminate among alternatives. Yet even seven points can be problematic: in the 2004 American National Election Study there is substantial clumping on the seven-point scales. Clumping is especially prevalent on the ethnic and racial stereotyping measures (whether African Americans, Hispanics, Asians, and whites are intelligent, hard-working, or trustworthy). All of the other stereotype measures except for the intelligence of whites (65 percent) clump at between 65 and 82 percent. Fifty-two percent of all respondents clumped on 8 or more of the twelve stereotype measures, 60 percent on seven or more.

Survey respondents, especially in a low-trust country such as Romania, may not give 'accurate' answers to 11-point scales and even seven-point scales (for the 2004 ANES) or five-point scales (for trust in the 2006 ANES Pilot) seem to encourage a regression to the middle.

PERSONAL EXPERIENCE WITH THE TRUST QUESTION

I became a supporter of the 'standard' question – the dichotomy – when I first began my research agenda on trust. Unlike some others, I found the wording of the question to be compelling: Can we put our faith in strangers or need we be careful? Since my worldview on trust downplays the role of experience (Uslaner, 2002), being careful seems to be an appropriate response for people we don't know, unless we have a predilection to put our faith in others. Second, some of my initial research on trust showed that this standard question really was a measure of our trust in people we don't know, who may be different from ourselves. Trust (as measured) does not lead to greater participation in politics or in social groups where we are likely to interact with people like ourselves and who share our views and interests. It does lead us to volunteer for secular organizations and to give to secular charities where we help people who are likely to be very different from ourselves. And it does predict high levels of tolerance in minority groups. Third, when the ANES released the texts of the 2006 'think aloud' experiments to me, I had to ensure that my coding of respondents' interpretations was not colored by my own preconceptions. When I finished coding and analysed the data, my faith in the standard question was reinforced.

I admit that I had some concerns about responses in some national surveys, most notably in China, where survey after survey showed high levels of trust, but my own experience and the views of scholars in China suggested a low level of trust of people from different backgrounds. In my book, I simply dismissed the Chinese case as an anomaly (Uslaner, 2002). I was also initially intrigued – but a bit sceptical – when I discovered that the CID project was shifting to an 11-point scale. As part of the Romanian CID team, I was able to examine both issues: which measurement worked best and whether language or culture might suggest different interpretations for trust across nations. In the Romanian CID we asked both the standard question and the 11-point scale.

Alas, neither led clearly to the sorts of results found in the West, but two other questions I added to the Romanian CID survey on trust in people of different ethnic groups and of different religions showed stronger connections to volunteering and levels of education. Nevertheless, the strong connection of the standard question (in Romania and across nations) to inequality has led me to view the standard question more favourably than any alternative. In 2006, when the ANES was planning on shifting to a five-point scale, I convinced the survey's board of overseers to include both the new scale and the standard question in its pilot study.

The standard question performed at least as well as the new scale in the pilot, so that in 2008, the ANES included both questions. My work on the 2006 ANES pilot led me to re-examine the Romanian CID and the ESS to see if the clumping I found in the former survey was a general phenomenon. When I saw that it is, my faith in the standard question became firm.

There are no hard and fast criteria for proclaiming any measurement best. But any measurement strategy must have some underlying rationale. Glaeser et al. (2000) and others argue that the trust question does not predict cooperation in laboratory games. But there is little reason to expect that generalized trust or a moral trust in people we don't know will lead to cooperation among players who learn about each other through interactions. And then comes Beugelsdijk (2006), who both criticizes the measurement of trust and then claims that aggregated measures of trust are nothing more than proxy indicators of well-functioning institutions. This led to an exchange between us focusing at least as much on what trust means as on how to measure it. Beugelsdijk does not recognize anything like moralistic trust – trust is trust, he says, except when it isn't and then trust is just good institutions. He gathers data on 18 variables (some of which seem measured more than once) for 41 countries and reduces them by factor analysis to five dimensions. When nothing of substance emerges, he performs another factor analysis and then reports results (Beugelsdijk, 2006: 379) indicating that mistrust is part of a more general syndrome of corruption and poor contract enforcement without considering whether there might be some causal chain from one to the other (Uslaner, 2008, 292–4).

DISCUSSION

There have been many criticisms of the standard question, all quite reasonable. Yet this question has led to important findings and controversies. As for other questions that have been criticized (such as questions on party identification in the US), it is easier to spot the problems with any indicator than to propose new measures that clearly outperform the old one. The standard question has one key advantage: it permits longitudinal comparisons as far back as 1948 for Germany and 1960 for the United States, the United Kingdom, Italy, and Mexico. New strategies have emerged and it is always healthy to have a debate over the best way to measure trust. Any alternative must show real advantages and none has done so – at least to my satisfaction. The traditional dichotomy, by itself and not as part of a scale, may still be the best way to measure trust.

NOTE

1. I am grateful for the support of the General Research Board of the University of Maryland–College Park and for helpful discussions with Geoff Layman, Mike Hanmer, Marc Hooghe, Kerem Ozan Kalkan, Ken Newton, and Tim Reeskens. I am also grateful to my colleagues on the Romanian CID team, Gabriel Badescu and Paul Sum and to the Starr Foundation through the Institutional Researches and Exchanges Board of the United States Department of State for a grant under the IREX Capsian and Black Sea Collaborative Program (2001) to collect the data. I am also indebted to Marc Morje Howard of Georgetown University for the opportunity to work with the United States CID data.

REFERENCES

Beugelsdijk, S. (2006), 'A note on the theory and measurement of trust in explaining differences in economic growth', *Cambridge Journal of Economics*, **30**, 371–87.
Bohnet, I. (2008), 'Trust in experiment', in Steven Durlauf and Lawrence Blume (eds), *The New Palgrave Dictionary of Economics*, New York: Palgrave Macmillan.
Brehm, J. and W. Rahn (1997), 'Individual level evidence for the causes and consequences of social capital', *American Journal of Political Science*, **41**, 888–1023.
Capra, C.M., K. Lanier, and S. Neer (2008), 'Attitudinal and behavioral measures of trust: a new comparison', unpublished paper, Emory University Department of Economics.
Chun, K. and J. Campbell (1974), 'Dimensionality of the Rotter interpersonal trust scale', *Psychological Reports*, **35**, 1059–70.
Glaeser, E., D. Laibson, J. Scheinkman and C. Soutter (2000), 'Measuring trust', *Quarterly Journal of Economics*, **115**, 811–46.
Hardin, R. (2002), *Trust and Trustworthiness*, New York: Russell Sage Foundation.
Hooghe, M. and T. Reeskens (2007), 'To trust or not to trust: that's the question', presented at the 2nd Conference of the European Survey Research Association, June, Prague.
Miller, A. and T. Mitamura (2003), 'Are surveys on trust trustworthy?', *Social Psychology Quarterly*, **66**, 62–70.
Miller, G. (1956), 'The magic number 7, plus or minus two: some limits on our capacity for processing information', *Psychological Reports*, **63**, 81–97, www.well.com/user/smalin/miller.html.
Putnam, R. (2000), *Bowling Alone*, New York: Simon and Schuster.
Rotter, J. (1967), 'A new scale for the measurement of interpersonal trust', *Journal of Personality*, **35**, 651–65.
Scherpenzeel, Annette (n.d.), 'Why use 11-point scales?', at www.swisspanel.ch/file/doc/faq/11pointscales.pdf.
Smith, T. (1997), 'Factors relating to misanthropy in contemporary American society,' *Social Science Research*, **26**, 70–96.
Uslaner, E. (2002), *The Moral Foundations of Trust*, New York: Cambridge University Press.
Uslaner, E. (2008), 'The foundations of trust: macro and micro', *Cambridge Journal of Economics*, **32**, 289–94.
Uslaner, E. (2009), 'Is eleven really a lucky number? Measuring trust and the problem of clumping', unpublished manuscript, University of Maryland–College Park.
Uslaner, E. (forthcoming), 'The generalized trust questions in the 2006 ANES pilot study', in J. Aldrich and K. McGraw (eds), *Improving Public Opinion Surveys: Interdisciplinary Innovation and the American National Election Studies*, Princeton: Princeton University Press, also at www.electionstudies.org/resources/papers/Pilot2006/nes011889.pdf.
Van Deth, J., J. Montero and A. Westholm (2008), *Citizenship and Involvement in European Democracies: A Comparative Analysis*, London: Routledge.

Woolcock, M. (1998), 'Social capital and economic development: toward a theoretical synthesis and policy framework', *Theory and Society*, **27** (2), 151–208.
Yamagishi, T. and M. Yamagishi (1994), 'Trust and commitment in the United States and Japan', *Motivation and Emotion*, **18** (2), 129–66.
Zmerli, S. and K. Newton (2008), 'Social trust and attitudes towards democracy', *Public Opinion Quarterly*, **72**, 702–24.

Annotated Further Reading

Beugelsdijk, S. (2006), 'A note on the theory and measurement of trust in explaining differences in economic growth', *Cambridge Journal of Economics*, **30**, 371–87. A critique of the measurement of social trust, arguing that trust measured at the aggregate level is a different concept than trust measured at the individual level.
Smith, T. (1997), 'Factors relating to misanthropy in contemporary American society,' *Social Science Research*, **26**, 70–96. A history and review of measures of trust, fairness, and helpfulness and a critical examination of problems in the measurement of these problems.
Uslaner, E. (2008), 'The foundations of trust: macro and micro', *Cambridge Journal of Economics*, **32**, 289–94. A response to Beugelsdijk arguing that measures of trust must be the same at both the individual and aggregate level and that trust may lead to less corruption, but that it is not a surrogate measure of good government.

PART II

QUALITATIVE RESEARCH

8   Access and non-probability sampling in qualitative research on trust
Fergus Lyon

INTRODUCTION

Qualitative research on trust is frequently of a sensitive nature. The ability to access informants and build close relationships while ensuring validity therefore becomes a crucial factor. This chapter shows how accessing participants in trust research requires that researchers understand how trust is built and maintained in their own work.

Qualitative approaches present particular challenges both in terms of the actual practicalities of collecting research material and gaining access to informants or respondents who are willing to participate in the research. Sampling and access varies with different approaches used by researchers depending on the types of data being collected. This chapter shows the close interrelationship between issues of access and sampling in much in-depth trust research. There are also context-specific issues raised depending on the sector of research (such as health services, manufacturing or other services), types of trust relationships being investigated (inter-organisational, intra-organisational), and whether the research is looking at specific trust relationships between individuals or more generalised trust in institutions or professions. This chapter will only be looking at access and non-probability sampling issues in research on trust relationships between individuals, because other types of trust research are addressed elsewhere in the book.

My experience as a trust researcher shows the importance of building trust with research participants in order to obtain access, whether it is related to research on inter-organisational business relationships in Africa (Lyon and Porter, 2008), on conflict (Porter and Lyon, 2010), on refugees in the UK (Lyon et al., 2007), on relationships within cooperatives and social enterprises (Lyon, 2006) or business science relationships (Harris et al., 2009). Trust with the research participant is even more important when carrying out qualitative research on sensitive topics or with groups that might be harder to reach by other methods. Similarly Emmel et al. (2007) found that research with socially excluded groups in the UK required the building of trust and they provide a detailed analysis of the relationships involved.

If a definition of trust is used that includes an element of expectation and risk related to a leap into the unknown (Möllering, 2006), then the research methods used to understand this may be more likely to face difficulty in accessing participants, or ensuring that those being interviewed are willing to 'open up' and discuss sensitive issues. The following sections will briefly outline the key issues related to qualitative sampling when researching trust, while recognising that more general issues on sampling are well covered in other books of research methodology. There is a short section on the caveats and risk of bias in different forms of sampling. I then provide a short example of access and sampling issues related to a personal project researching trading relationships in Ghana, West Africa; this is a context where the lack of formal institutional forms means that personalised trust-based relationships are very important for the survival of the traders.

DESCRIPTION OF THE METHOD

While much attention is given to probability sampling in quantitative research, qualitative research often uses smaller non-probability samples with longer more detailed interviews. The number of interviews is therefore often shaped by resource constraints and issues of access rather than statistical requirements.

Within types of non-probability sampling a distinction can be made between sampling that is theory driven and sampling that is carried out progressively as the research unfolds (an approach necessary in grounded theory and more inductive research). The former is more common in deductive research looking to test hypotheses or theories. Theory-driven sampling is often carried out purposefully to ensure there is maximum variation (Guba and Lincoln, 1989) with existing knowledge of the types of participants used to stratify in this sampling method. Within this practical considerations shape the sampling approach and researchers have to rely on convenience and connections they have or are able to build up. Curran and Blackburn (2001: 67) show how building a sample of small enterprises can be very time consuming and the process of collecting this data from these businesses may actually damage the relationship with the firms.

Yin (1984) describes the different approaches for selecting case studies. These may be stand-alone cases or selected for comparative reasons, and therefore require similar elements. Saunders et al (2009) divide purposive sampling into four categories: extreme case or deviant sampling; heterogeneous or maximum variation; homogenous or subgroup; critical cases; and typical or illustrative profile using a representative case. Examples of each of these approaches can be found in the trust literature. Research on trust-based relationships has also used purposive sampling to examine a relationship from both trustor and trustee perspectives, raising ethical concerns about how much the researcher shares with the other party. Möllering (2006) also reports on the challenges of researching both sides of dyadic relationships where there is an element of distrust.

A distinction can also be made between sampling of organisations and sampling of employees within an organisation. Within organisations there is an issue of sampling of individuals or employees and the need to negotiate access through managers who may act as 'gatekeepers' diverting the researcher away from employees who may be more critical. Alternatively, permission can be granted by management but there are challenges to establishing credibility with the intended participants in the organisation and the extent to which the researcher is trusted with sensitive information (Saunders et al., 2009). There is also a need to consider the selection of activities within an organisation that should be examined in more detail and what Miles and Huberman (1994: 27) refer to as nested settings within settings. Similarly there can be sampling of 'critical incidents' that are explored in more depth, with selection based on the objectives of the research.

Where access is challenging due to the sensitive nature of trust research, many studies rely on personal connections where there is already trust between researcher and the research and a greater understanding of how the data may be used. Building on existing relationships, 'snowballing methods' can be used to access participants, where one participant will recommend another. In this way the first participant will act as a guarantor, intermediary or bridge-builder (Williams, 2002), between the researcher and the researched. This gives the person making the introduction more control over the research process and affects the balance of power between the two parties (Emmel et al., 2007).

Qualitative in-depth trust research requiring a closer relationship between the researcher and researched may also lead to the breaking down of the traditional models of a researcher gathering data from an informant, with alternatives such as collaborative action research to study or resolve a problem, or narrative inquiry where researcher and participant are both telling their stories (Miles and Huberman, 1994: 47). In longitudinal research the need to retain and strengthen the relationship requires reciprocity, and some researchers have become involved in the organisations they have studied as a way of ensuring the research continues; they are trusted by the informants, and they can collect data through participant observation.

The ethnographic approach (see Tillmar in this volume) is flexible and less intrusive, and, as an ethnographer, one has to be sensitive to the setting in which the interaction takes place; as shown in the research experiences described below, it is important to build up relationships and trust with the research subjects. A key challenge for this style of research is gaining access to positions where observations can be made. Where participant observation is used there are ethical challenges in terms of deciding how much those being observed know about the research (Curran and Blackburn, 2001: 82).

So far we have mainly examined sampling for individual participants, although there is a need to consider sampling issues when sampling for group interviews and focus groups. The advantages of group work are not only the overlapping range of knowledge, and 'observable mutual cross checking' (Chambers, 1997: 148) but also 'a means to set up a negotiation of meanings through intra- and inter-personal debates' (Cook and Crang, 1995: 56) that may 'bring forth material that would not come out in either the participant's own casual conversations or in response to the researcher's preconceived questions' (Morgan, 1988: 21). Morgan (1988: 11) found that the use of focus groups was useful for 'orienting oneself to a new field, generating hypotheses based on informants' insights, evaluating research sites, developing interview schedules and questionnaires and obtaining participants' interpretations of results from earlier studies'. In this way Morgan sees focus groups as a compromise between the strengths and weakness of participant observation and individual interviews. However, recruiting people to join focus groups is challenging, frequently leading to bias. Once in a focus group, there can be certain individuals whose voices become more dominant, making it harder to access the views of some members, particularly when discussing sensitive issues. The impact that this has on the overall efficacy of the group is dependent upon the skills of the focus group moderator.

RESEARCH VALIDITY CAVEATS

Purposive sampling will have a risk of bias, as certain groups may be excluded from the research either through being unknown to the researcher, through being hidden by the gatekeepers (for example employers directing the research away from certain employees), or through potential participants hiding themselves away due to suspicion and mistrust. There will always be an element of self-selection in qualitative research sampling as some people are more likely to put themselves forward to agree to participate than others. There may also be bias as certain potential participants may be more suspicious, perceive the researcher's involvement to be of greater risk and have less time available. This can create bias in the types of organisations included, and also the types of people interviewed within an organisation.

The snowball sampling approaches in which previous participants provide connections to a range of other participants also presents difficulties for the researcher as there is a higher likelihood of bias based on the networks of those involved earlier in the chains. This can be overcome by having several starting points for these chains and attention given to having a diverse range of participants based on the researcher's knowledge of the population being studied. For example, in the example given later in the chapter, attention had to be given to including marginalised groups of traders and farmers in Ghana. Certain groups, such as the poorer women, were less visible and so care had to be taken to include them in the sample.

PERSONAL EXPERIENCE OF ACCESS FOR TRUST-BASED RESEARCH

The food trading system of Ghana offers a rich insight into some informal entrepreneurship processes and the challenges of researching them. The study was based on field work carried out over two years conducted in a number of towns, cities and villages in Southern Ghana (Lyon, 2006). A key aim of the study was a detailed examination of how these (usually) women traders carried on their trade in what was a highly risky and difficult situation. The traders studied were mainly itinerant traders (*nkwainsofo*) who bought in rural areas and sold in different types of markets in urban areas. It presented a fascinating case of how rural-based entrepreneurs with very few resources or support find innovative ways of sustaining their enterprises and meet urban food demand in the absence of any formal regulations, finance or legal representation.

The research questions necessitated a qualitative in-depth approach with non-probability sampling. The major challenge faced during the research was gaining access to the traders and encouraging them to talk openly to me. This was particularly hard in Ghana (as it is in much of West Africa) as traders are suspicious of those observing them after many decades of government rhetoric and policy that appear to be predicated on an assumption that the traders exploit both rural producers and urban consumers. It was also necessary to make a formal introduction to the leader of the traders' associations in each market. These associations are discussed later. Once known to the traders, it was possible for me to stay for long periods in the market, observing the trading, disputes, the ways in which the latter were settled, and interviewing people after incidents in order to understand reasons behind each party's action.

Building up these relationships took much of the research time and involved me trying to change the way I was perceived as a way of 'enrolling' people into the project and building up cooperation (Latour, 1986). For example, when spending time with traders, I had to distance myself from any farmers, despite the fact that I had spent some months living in rural areas, researching the food trade from the farmers' perspective. The example above raises a number of ethical issues and I did not try to examine both sides of the trading relationship as this would have limited my access.

Cooperation from the entrepreneurs, and the outcome of the interview, was based on their trust in me. The similarity between the research process and the subject of the research (trust in entrepreneurial relationships) was often referred to both by the farmers as well as the traders: 'I got 1.5 million Cedis [approximately $650] from a customer trader . . . I work with traders; it depends on trust (*gyedei*) . . . Like I came to you because I have trust in you. This is because I got a message from my mother who knows you.'

My ability to gain access and the information that they shared with me was also shaped by how I was perceived, and who I was seen to be aligned to. It is very hard to know how anyone perceives an outsider although, in my case, several issues about my identity were referred to at various times, such as being white and British in an ex-British colony; being younger than them; and being from a comparatively wealthy country and conducting research in a country with considerable poverty.

My extreme outsider status sometimes played to my advantage as I was not perceived to be a threat to their businesses. That made it easier to tackle certain issues – such as the respondents' trust-based relationships and economic activities – that my Ghanaian colleagues found difficult to broach. Being male restricted some topics of conversation with women traders, particularly concerning their home life. Gender relations shaped how the research relationship was built up with people who were visited regularly. With men, I could draw on common gendered roles and customs, whilst with women I could distance myself from Ghanaian men because of my ethnicity and be jocular about my interest as a man coming to see them. The beginning of many interviews consisted of relaxed and informal conversation and joking, often centred on questions of my marital status, whether I was looking for a wife and whether I would take them (or their daughters) back to the UK.

My position was complicated further by working closely with Ghanaian research assistants and 'interpreters' whose image with the researched affected how I was perceived. A number of participants appeared to regard the background of the research assistants with as much importance, if not more, as my own background (cf. Twyman et al., 1999). This suggests that the issue of gender, race and class of the research assistant can shape the research outcome.

I used both formal and informal groups to explore certain issues. Informal group interviews and discussions were not planned but took place when there were a number of people together and willing to be involved. This may have been in peoples' houses or in public spaces such as bus stops, drinking bars, or the traders' association huts. Formal groups were planned in advance and were found to be particularly useful for certain activities such as wealth-ranking exercises, getting community-level information and discussing the meaning of key Twi words. Attention was paid to the composition and the role of the research assistants as moderators (Cook and Crang, 1995: 57) as this affected the behaviour and hence the information given (Herod, 1993: 308). I felt that group work marginalised some groups, especially the poor and women farmers, who did not appear to be so well organised or could not afford the time (Farrington and Bebbington, 1993). The power relations in the group meetings were problematic at times and this affected who was invited, who spoke and who was excluded, although some information on social relations within a group could be gained by observing the interaction in groups. We faced problems with domineering individuals and elites who put forward opinions that limited discussions (Cook and Crang, 1995: 61). However, this could be avoided if such individuals were taken on one side and interviewed alone by myself or one of the research assistants while the group discussions continued.

DISCUSSION

This chapter has identified some of the issues related to access and non-probability sampling in trust research. While much has been written on access for qualitative research, research on trust may face specific issues related to the sensitive nature of the subject matter. For example, in the case discussed above, trust-based relationships involved considerable sums of money being lent between traders.

There is a need to consider how sampling is carried out in in-depth qualitative research which explores these issues. The approach to sampling will vary according to the research question, although in most cases the issues of access will be closely linked to how sampling is carried out. Furthermore, the subject matter of trust is related to the research experience of building trust-based relationships between researcher and participant (see also Möllering, 2006). Within these relationships there is a need to understand how trust is built up and how the power dynamics between parties evolves. As trust research has shown elsewhere, concepts of power and trust are intertwined, with relationships of trust having an element of power underpinning them and shaping the sanctions that each party has on the other (Lyon, 2006). There is also power exerted through the influence of gatekeepers of the research process (Emmel et al., 2007), and power exerted by the researcher less explicitly or even subconsciously. This may come about where the participants in research perceive the researcher as able to bring them some direct benefit, or where there is deference to those who are perceived to be 'more educated'.

Access is also shaped by both the personal trust relationships between the researcher and the researched, and the 'generalised' trust in the researcher because of a shared understanding of how research is carried out and used. This is an example of institutionalised trust, where the institution of scholarship is trusted by many based on their understanding of what researchers do. However, this varies between contexts, between cultures and over time. Ensuring that academic research retains the highest degree of research ethics is therefore central to build on the current acceptance of researchers, continuing our ability to research trust and collect data on sensitive topics.

REFERENCES

Chambers, R. (1997), *Whose Reality Counts? Putting the First Last*, London: Intermediate Technology Publications.

Cook, I. and M. Crang (1995), *Doing Ethnographies*, Concepts and Techniques in Modern Geography (CATMOG) No 58, Norwich: GeoBooks.

Curran, J. and R. Blackburn (2001), *Researching the Small Enterprise*, London: Sage.

Emmel, N.D., K. Hughes, J. Greenhalgh, and A. Sales (2007), 'Accessing socially excluded people-trust and the gatekeeper in the researcher-participant relationship', *Sociological Research Online*, **12** (2), www.socresonline.org.uk/12/2/emmel.html.

Farrington, J.A. and A. Bebbington (1993), *Reluctant Partners? Non-Governmental Organisation, the State and Sustainable Agricultural Development*, London: Routledge.

Guba, E.G. and Y.S. Lincoln (1989), *Fourth Generation Evaluation*, Newbury Park, CA: Sage.

Harris, F., F. Lyon and S. Clarke (2009), 'Doing interdisciplinarity: motivation and collaboration in research for sustainable agriculture in the UK', *Area*, **41** (4), 378–84.

Herod, A. (1993), 'Gender issues in the use of interviewing as a research method', *Professional Geographer*, **45** (3), 305–17.

Hollier, G.P. (1986), 'The marketing of gari in North-West Province, Cameroon', *Geographiska Annaler*, **68B** (1), 59–68.

Latour, B. (1986), 'Powers of association', in J. Law (ed.), *Power, Action and Belief*, London: Routledge and Kegan Paul, pp. 246–80.

Lyon, F. (2006), 'Managing co-operation – trust and power in Ghanaian associations', *Organization Studies*, **27** (1), 31–52.

Lyon, F. and G. Porter (2008), 'Market institutions, trust and norms: exploring moral econo-
mies in Nigerian food systems', *Cambridge Journal of Economics*, **33** (5), 903–20.
Lyon, F., L. Sepulveda and S. Syrett (2007), 'Enterprising refugees: contributions and chal-
lenges in deprived urban areas', *Local Economy* **22** (4), 363–76.
Miles, M.B. and A.M. Huberman (1994), *Qualitative Data Analysis*, 2nd edition, Thousand
Oaks, CA: Sage.
Möllering, G. (2006), *Trust: Reason, Routine, Reflexivity*, Oxford: Elsevier.
Morgan, D. (1988), *Focus Groups as Qualitative Research*, Qualitative Research Methods 16,
London: Sage.
Porter, G. and F. Lyon (2010), 'Conflict and cooperation in market spaces: learning from
the operation of local networks of civic engagement in African market trade', *Human
Organisation*, **69** (1), 31–42.
Saunders, M., P. Lewis and A. Thornhill (2009), *Research Methods for Business Students*, 5th
edition, Harlow: FT Prentice Hall.
Twyman, C., J. Morrison and D. Sporton (1999), 'The final fifth: autobiography, reflexivity
and interpretation in cross-cultural research', *Area*, **341** (4), 313–25.
Williams, P. (2002), 'The competent boundary spanner', *Public Administration*, **80** (1),
103–24.
Yin, R. (1984), *Case Study Research: Design and Methods*, Sage: London.

Annotated Further Reading

Emmel, N.D., K. Hughes, J. Greenhalgh and A. Sales (2007), 'Accessing socially excluded
people: trust and the gatekeeper in the researcher–participant relationship', *Sociological
Research Online* **12** (2) – a detailed study of the relationships of trust between the
researcher and others involved in the research process, drawn from research on social
exclusion that required trust to be built up with gatekeepers.
Saunders, M., P. Lewis and A. Thornhill (2009), *Research Methods for Business Students*,
fifth edition, Harlow: FT Prentice Hall – textbook with detailed chapters on sampling and
access with case studies and discussions of ethical issues.

9 Working with difficult to reach groups: a 'building blocks' approach to researching trust in communities
Christine Goodall

INTRODUCTION

This chapter looks at conducting qualitative trust research within communities. It highlights some of the problems this type of research can throw up for the researcher, and proposes a 'building blocks' approach which is designed to examine the factors likely to promote or hinder the building of trust as individual components.

This chapter is based on my experience conducting qualitative trust research in a community setting in Stoke on Trent, UK, between 2004 and 2006. The purpose of the research was to propose a model for improved and more trusting relations between the settled host community in the city and new arrivals, primarily asylum seekers, and to use the findings to draw lessons for building trust across different cultures more generally.

Qualitative community research on trust is rare. Most research on trust is conducted through surveys, or through the analysis of large-scale surveys that incorporate trust questions, or those that can act as proxies, within them. Trust is also investigated through socio-psychological experiments, but during my research I did not come across any study where qualitative research was used in communities to investigate the components or causalities of trust. The only real qualitative example I found was the inclusion of the opportunity for respondents to 'think aloud' which was added to the Economic Incentive, Values and Subjective Well-Being Pilot Survey conducted in Detroit and Baltimore and reported in Uslaner (2002: ch. 4). This lack of qualitative community research on trust mirrors to an extent the situation regarding the concept of social capital; most research on social capital has been based on surveys and scales, and the qualitative in-depth study by Stewart-Weeks and Richardson (1998) was remarkable for its unique approach.

Additionally, qualitative research on discrimination, intolerance and attitudes to difference in communities to which asylum seekers have been dispersed is also rare (Castles et al., 2002). Castles et al. point out that broader social and economic problems in communities, and attitudes to change, need to be explored in order to understand the drivers of poor relations between settled communities and new arrivals (Castles et al., 2002: 86).

This chapter then will discuss my approach to conducting qualitative trust research in a community setting, the challenges I faced and how they were overcome. The 'difficult to reach' groups referred to in the title of this chapter are twofold but nested: first there are the more obvious difficulties of researching trust with a sample that includes refugees and asylum seekers, and less obviously – but of equal importance in my view – the difficulties of researching trust with members of the general public in a community with particular issues related to insularity, parochialism and distrust of difference (see for example Gadd et al., 2005).

The chapter briefly introduces the research and the context in which it was carried out. It then introduces the approach to researching trust developed for the study in terms of a conceptual framework, and how this framework was constructed.

THE RESEARCH CONTEXT

The aim of the study was to conduct community-based research and analysis, primarily with settled communities, in order to gain a greater understanding of intolerance, fear of difference and perceived threats to individual and collective identities, and to use the findings to propose a model of successful relations between local settled communities and new arrivals. More broadly the research aimed to explore attitudes to difference, and the environmental societal factors that can promote or inhibit openness, tolerance and a positive attitude to change.

The research was conducted in the city of Stoke on Trent. The city was chosen as it is one of the dispersal locations under the government's asylum dispersal policy, has not had a significant previous history of migration, has a largely white settled population, has experienced a sharp rise in voting for extreme right-wing candidates, and experiences many social and economic problems.

THE RESEARCH PROBLEM

The problem was to conduct qualitative research on trust in a community whose members were insular, wary of difference and change, and where there were already manifestations of distrust between groups, and those perceived to be 'insiders' and 'outsiders'. Most interviewees were to be members of the general public, of all ages ranging from teenagers to the very elderly, and including refugees and asylum seekers. Interviewees would also include local politicians and some key actors in the voluntary and statutory sectors. This posed a number of issues/problems to be overcome.

First, definitions of trust are not readily accessible to members of the general public, particularly those for whom English is not a first language. For example, a classic definition of trust often cited in the literature is that found in Rousseau et al. (1998: 395): 'a psychological state comprising the intention to accept vulnerability based upon positive expectations of the intentions or behavior of another'. Given that such definitions are not readily accessible, are the definitions of respondents themselves then the best to use? Members of the public are likely to have their own conceptions of what trust means for them and their community, and these could differ widely from person to person. While assessing different perceptions of the meaning of the term 'trust' might be interesting, this approach could not help me in understanding the apparent absence of generalized trust to be found in the community. Additionally, culture and language can have a substantial effect on discussions of a concept such as trust, sometimes rendering meanings unclear and hampering communication.

Secondly, overtly labelling the research as 'trust research' and asking specific questions about trust is likely (in the type of community discussed) to create defensiveness, and militate against a robust collection of data, and a frank and open discussion between interviewer and respondent. People do not generally like to admit to distrusting their neighbours and may also be wary of an admission of distrust of those in authority, when disclosed to someone that they might perceive to be in a position of power (such as the interviewer).

Additionally, due to the nature of the asylum process in the UK, and of the immigration debate more widely, those going through this system, or those who have gone through the system, or who have otherwise recently come to the UK, or who come from a minority background are likely to be naturally suspicious of being interviewed about trust in others. This group of respondents is generally wary of discussing personal experiences with anyone perceived to be in a position of power or authority, and presents particular challenges for the trust researcher.

THE RESEARCH METHOD AND THEORETICAL FRAMEWORK

The answer to the question 'how were these problems overcome?' lies in the nature of the model of trust selected to form the theoretical framework for this research, namely that of Uslaner (2002). In this example, the research method and the theoretical framework adopted are in essence one and the same.

The basis of the model proposed by Uslaner as a result of his analysis is that generalized trust of strangers has the property of a moral value (see also Chapter 7, this volume). Like a moral value it is relatively stable over time and not based on individual experience. Moralistic trusters see the best in people and rationalize away negative experiences, continuing to place trust in others even though they might experience disappointment. They are not blind to the likelihood of being let down, but go on putting faith in people anyway (see also Jones and George, 1998). Uslaner argues that this form of trust enables people to be open and tolerant to minority groups and to those whose life experience or culture are very unlike their own. This form of trust requires the 'leap of faith' discussed by Möllering (2006: ch. 5) and Eldred (2004), and is devoid of self-interested calculation.

So if direct personal experience is not relevant for this form of trust, what environmental or social factors can help to generate it, and what can assist people to form positive assessments of those they do not know, and take the 'leap of faith'? Uslaner argues that this form of trust is built on personal autonomy and a sense of control over one's own life, optimism and an environment of equality. His theory is that, in order to reach out to others unlike ourselves, we need to believe both that the future will be better and that we have the power to make it so. Therefore we require personal autonomy and some control over our own lives, and an optimistic view of life. Moralistic trusters, argues Uslaner, are not fatalistic, or believers in luck or chance to a great degree; things do not happen to them, rather they make things happen. This gives them the assurance to reach out to others and to withstand disappointment.

In addition to optimism and control, Uslaner argues for equality as another primary component for building a trusting society: equality promotes the idea of a shared fate and also promotes optimism by making a better future appear more possible. In other words it builds bridges between people and also makes optimism and an upbeat worldview rational. In addition, a sense of unfairness or injustice can be allied to perceptions of inequality.

Following this model, I was able to construct a framework where personal autonomy, optimism, perceptions of equality and fairness (or an absence of these) might be seen as the 'building blocks' of generalized trust. It was therefore possible for me to conceptualize research that would uncover whether these building blocks for trust were present within the community. With such an approach, it was more important to ask about these 'building blocks' than about trust itself, thereby solving the research problems outlined above. Semi-structured interview frameworks were constructed for individual respondents and groups that encouraged people to think about issues of personal autonomy and control; about hope and optimism (or lack of these); and about equality and fairness.

Two further elements were added to make a more robust framework through which to examine trust in communities, built upon the moralistic trust model; these were the role of leadership, and the importance of resilience. Cvetkovich and Earle (1995) consider leadership crucial for building cosmopolitan social trust, and it is also logical to see leadership as important for the creation of positive identities, optimism and a fair society. Resilience was added as a crucial element for building the form of trust where the 'leap of faith' is required. In order to have the resilience to go on trusting in the face of disappointments requires a certain amount of resources. Such resources might take a number of forms, from the economic to social support, but without resources it is much harder to discard calculation and keep on trusting as a 'leap of faith'. This point is made by Wildavsky (1993) in his study of risk, and also features in Uslaner's early development of his ideas on moralistic trust: 'When you have resources you can absorb occasional losses by people who exploit you; when things look bleak you look at people you don't know as rivals for what little you have' (Uslaner, 1999: 21). This quotation is particularly relevant to discussions of the perceived unfair distribution of resources such as housing, health services and education between settled communities and immigrants.

Hence the building blocks for trust could be investigated through initiating conversations about what it was like to live in the respondents' local community, how they perceived their environment, how they thought others perceived it, what concerned them, what they enjoyed about living in their community, how they felt about the future and so on. In this way, the presence or absence of factors likely to generate or inhibit the formation of generalized social trust, and thus foster openness, tolerance and positive attitudes to diversity and difference, could be investigated while avoiding overt discussions of trust.

DISCUSSION

How did this approach work in practice? The respondents were generally very ready to discuss their attitudes to living in Stoke on Trent and their local communities within the framework outlined above. Often discussions of practical matters such as poor local public transport developed in such a manner as to shed light on ties within communities, the role of extended family, attitudes to those perceived as 'outsiders', insularity, and so on. Sometimes respondents' general reaction to discussion questions told a story in themselves. For example a group of teenagers found genuine difficulty in considering the question of their plans for the future. It became clear that many considered 'the future' as something that 'happened' to them, rather than anything that they themselves could shape. People wanted to retain some control by clinging to the familiar and being quite resistant to change. The same group of teenagers claimed that a virtue of living in Stoke on Trent was that it almost never appeared on the news, because very little of note occurred. They knew most people around them and they knew what to expect of them. However, change and newcomers were seen as threatening and likely to make life uncomfortable and confusing.

The two groups of asylum seekers interviewed were accessed through a local college which they attended for English classes. I was therefore introduced to them by trusted intermediaries – their tutors. They were a little reticent at first, not knowing quite what to expect of me or the discussion, but once the conversation about their experiences of living in the city began to flow, they gained in confidence and began to provide extremely rich and relevant data concerning the 'building blocks' under investigation. I believe that interviewing them in groups was preferable to speaking with individuals, as the balance of power was shifted, and members of the group seemed encouraged to talk about their more negative experiences when others had done the same. They were also aware that others in the room had shared similar experiences and feelings.

CAVEATS AND VALIDITY

Overall, a wealth of relevant data concerning the 'building blocks' of generalised trust outlined above was collected, and people were happy to speak openly to me both in groups and as individuals. However, there was one topic – one that was very relevant to my investigations – on which people remained reticent and cautious. I did not ask people overtly about their attitudes to new arrivals or to people from ethnic minority backgrounds more broadly, but of course in an investigation on generalized trust with a specific aim of understanding the relationship between the settled community and new arrivals, and the seeming intolerance and significant rise in voting for the British National Party, such attitudes were of great interest.

There was a common tendency among respondents to describe anyone who was not of a white British background as a 'foreigner', whether or not they were new arrivals or people from ethnic minority backgrounds within the settled community. Respondents appeared nervous about expressing negative attitudes. Sometimes in group settings, if someone expressed some negative feeling about the 'foreigners' another member of the group would tell them to 'be careful what you say'. On another occasion a woman being interviewed as an individual, when talking about how she felt about living in the city, only expressed her negative feelings towards 'foreigners' once the tape had been turned off, with the comment that she knew that she 'was not supposed to talk about that'.

It was clear that the open discussion of how people felt about living in the city did not necessarily capture all the data on attitudes to difference that existed, but I feel that it captured more of people's genuine feelings than if an overt discussion of trust and attitudes to difference had taken place. I consider that this was also the case with the other topics discussed, and that examining the components thought to be required for the generation of social trust was a much more effective research method than asking people to talk about trust.

REFERENCES

Castles, S., M. Korac, E. Vaster and S. Verdivek (2002), *Integration; Mapping the Field*, Home Office Report 55-02, London: Home Office.
Cvetkovich, G. and T. Earle (1995), *Social Trust: Toward a Cosmopolitan Society*, Westport, CT: Praeger.
Eldred, M. (2004), *Heidegger's Restricted Interpretation of the Greek Conception of the Political*, Cologne: Artefact, October, www.webcom.com/artefact.
Gadd, D., W. Dixon and T. Jefferson (2005), 'Why do they do it? Racial harassment in North Staffordshire', Centre for Criminological Research, Keele University.
Jones, G. and J. George (1998), 'The experience and evolution of trust; the implications for cooperation and teamwork', *Academy of Management Review*, **23** (3), 531–46.
Möllering, G. (2006), *Trust: Reason, Routine, Reflexivity*, Oxford: Elsevier.
Rousseau, D., S. Sitkin, R. Burt and C. Camerer (1998), 'Not so different after all; a cross discipline view of trust', *Academy of Management*, **23** (3), 393–404.
Stewart-Weeks, M. and C. Richardson (1998), *Social Capital Stories: How Twelve Australian Households Live their Lives*, Sydney: Centre for Independent Studies.
Uslaner, E. (1999), 'Trust and consequences', paper presented at the Communitarian Summit, University of Maryland, February, www.bsos.umd.edu/gvpt/uslaner/working.htm.
Uslaner, E. (2002), *The Moral Foundations of Trust*, Cambridge: Cambridge University Press.
Wildavsky, A. (1993), 'The riskless society', in D. Henderson (ed.), *Fortune Encyclopedia of Economics*, New York: Warner Books, at www.econlib.org.library/Enc1/RisklessSociety.html.

Annotated Further Reading

Uslaner, E. (2002), *The Moral Foundations of Trust*, Cambridge: Cambridge University Press. This book will provide a full and accessible explanation of the model of trust used as a conceptual framework for this research, and therefore an explanation of how the 'building blocks' referred to were identified.

10 Cross-cultural comparative case studies: a means of uncovering dimensions of trust
Malin Tillmar

INTRODUCTION

The aim of this chapter is to highlight the value of cross-cultural case study design, as a means of maintaining reflexivity in uncovering dimensions of trust. This will be done through sharing experiences from my studies that were undertaken between 1997 and 2002 and led to my PhD thesis 'Swedish tribalism and Tanzanian Agency: preconditions for trust and cooperation in a small business context' (Tillmar, 2002). The research strategy was to carry out qualitative case studies in rural areas in my home country – Sweden – and in a different cultural and institutional context – Tanzania. My ambition in this chapter is to engage in an exercise of reflexivity that interprets my own interpretations (Alvesson and Sköldberg, 2000).

One ambition in the thesis was to acknowledge the context dependency of cooperation and trust by studying and comparing small business cooperation in two different settings. Another aim was to suggest a more general and coherent conceptual framework that would make it possible to distinguish the various facets of trust. The choice of conducting qualitative case studies was not too difficult for several reasons. Trust is a social phenomenon that is hard to measure adequately. At the time it was not as well explored and defined as it is today and I took special interest in contextual preconditions (Bryman and Bell, 2003). Since the studies were deductive in the sense that I started with a literature review on trust, the interview guide covered issues such as who the business owners chose to cooperate with and why, what enabled and constrained cooperation and so on. However, to understand the informants' situation fully, I sensed a need to interact on a more frequent and informal basis. Both case studies therefore combined semi-structured interviews and ethnographically inspired methods (Garsten, 1994, 2003). The latter implied participant observations in work settings and social events, as well as repeated informal conversations with key informants. I perceived that, to grasp the social situation in Tanzania, there was a greater need for an elaborated ethnographic component in that study. I lived there for one year and learned the language. The Tanzanian study also required a larger number of interviews (around 50), before the so-called sense of 'saturation' in empirical findings was achieved. In both studies, the interviewing was continued until such saturation was attained, when previous findings are being reinforced and nothing new is learnt (Merriam, 1994, 2009). In the Swedish study, this happened after around 20 interviews. During that study, I lived in my home town and stayed in the area studied for only a few days. In both studies four key informants – two male and two female – were selected. The informants were selected from among those who were active in cooperative ventures. These key informants were visited and interviewed on several occasions during the research period in order to grasp the longitudinal development of the cooperation studied.

DESCRIPTION OF THE STUDY

The overall research process can be divided into three phases: (1) conducting the studies; (2) interpreting the individual studies; and finally (3) comparative analysis. Here, I will attempt to highlight the considerations behind each phase as well as results obtained from the decisions made.

Phase 1: Conducting the Studies – Attempting to Blend in

For obvious reasons this was a challenge, especially in Tanzania. In other words, the 'observer effect' – as well as 'interviewer effect' on people's behaviour was one of my major concerns. Learning and always trying to speak the language – Kiswahili – as well as socializing with local people rather than merely with the few other *mzungos* (white people) became an important way to access rich information. Believing that a *mzungo* could ever 'blend into' a small Tanzanian town would of course have been naive; in retrospect, I believe I had a touch of that naivety, which was actually helpful. I remember wishing that I could change the colour of my skin, and I worked hard on my Kiswahili. The key informants and I had a lot of fun over my mistakes. What was said behind my back I will never know, and I did not think much about it at the time. Still, I was strengthened by their friendliness and patient assistance and was therefore able to master the language before starting to conduct interviews. Without doubt, the language was the key to the understanding that I attained – often over a beer in one of the local pubs (from male informants) or while playing with the informants' babies (in the case of female informants).

As the reader of this book is aware, trust – and how it is built and given or not given to people – may be a sensitive issue. To me, this became especially obvious in the Tanzanian context. In the lives of both the men and the women there, who to trust and how to enable that trust was a core issue in building their lives and livelihoods. At times, the spouse was involved in the business and for both men and women trusting the spouse in all aspects was by no means a matter of course. As an example, a businessman who involved his wife in the business once sent her out of the office to buy me a soft drink and as soon as she left he told me that she was very trustworthy concerning money – which was not very common (according to him). With one of my female friends and informants on cultural issues I often had long conversations regarding long-term strategies for trusting men with money and financial cooperation. The discussions I had with both men and women could thus become highly personal while also concerning deeply rooted cultural issues. Tribal affiliation, tribal organizations and the views held about the different tribes, not least concerning the trustworthiness of their members, were among the cultural issues which were explained to me in detail in various informal settings.

In the small Swedish town, the challenge was to recognize that the rules of the game there were different from in the larger city where I live and work. In rural Sweden, too, I was an outsider from academia in a metropolitan area. Keeping a very low profile, listening to a variety of actor groups and observing the social interaction facilitated the uncovering of the local rules of the game and the beliefs rooted among the actor groups. These included prejudices held by different people about locals as well as newcomers to the area. There was also reference to 'Jante's law'. The Jante law is a well-known norm in the Scandinavian context; essentially it implies that 'you should never think that you are something or that you are better than us [the others]'. It is so-called from its depiction in a 1933 novel by the Danish-Norwegian author Aksel Sandemose.

Phase 2: Interpreting the Individual Studies – Avoiding Ethnocentric Interpretations

This was a challenge not only in the Tanzanian study, but also in the Swedish study. At first, I was astonished by the resistance to cooperation shown between locals and newcomers from the larger cities. It all seemed so foolish. Then, I realized that we all trust people depending on the category to which we allocate them. In Tanzania, trust was based on tribal affiliation and gender. In rural Sweden, trust was based on whether people were locals or newcomers to the area. In our academic world, trust may be ascribed to people from faculties or even users of different methods.

In Tanzania, the importance of tribal affiliation when deciding who to trust did not surprise me that much, after all, I realized that it actually resembled the Swedish situation. The striking similarities interested me and inspired me to delve more deeply into the phenomenon of categorization and tribal issues. The experience is an example of an earlier observation by Brislin (1980; Brislin et al., 1973) that cross-cultural research may stimulate the researcher's learning and make him/her more sensitive to variations in human behaviour.

Phase 3: Uncovering Swedish Tribalism and Tanzanian Entrepreneurship

Studies of people with similar professions in different countries have been used to highlight both cultural differences (Hofstede, 1980, 1991) and similarities (Garsten, 1994; Salzer, 1994). In my study, differences and similarities also served as tools that facilitated the understanding of preconditions for trust and cooperation. As expressed by Ragin, case study oriented comparisons 'provide a powerful basis not only for identifying causes but also for differentiating among important types and subtypes of social phenomena' (1989: 43–4).

In this phase, closeness to the fields and the emic (context-specific) understandings were balanced by distance and etic (general) aspects of the phenomena (Molander, 1993; Triandis, 1994). This is where the cross-cultural comparison became an important means of accomplishing the aim, which was to suggest a more general and coherent conceptual framework that would make it possible to distinguish the various facets of trust. It was through the comparison that I could – at least to some extent – avoid ethnocentric interpretations and also recognize the Swedish prejudices as a kind of tribalism. Perhaps even more important, it was through comparing the actions, or agency, of the business owners in the two contexts that I could uncover how the Tanzanians struggled to create mechanisms imaginatively and entrepreneurially that enabled trust against all odds (see further Tillmar and Lindkvist, 2007). In the Swedish context I observed that the preconditions for cooperation were far better, but the business owners refrained from cooperation rather than striving to create trust.

VALIDITY AND CAVEATS

Cross-cultural comparisons of cases allow the researcher to achieve a combination of closeness and distance (Molander, 1993) that enables the uncovering of dynamics that would not otherwise be apparent. How the Tanzanian study would have been interpreted without an alternative pattern to provide a contrast is, of course, a hypothetical question, yet, I believe that there is a risk that the focus would have been more on the difficulties and cultural obstacles than on the imaginative creation of reasons for trust. Neither would I have drawn the conclusion that trust based on the possibilities of sanction and/or hostage-type situations was so important in situations of low general trust. Another point which could be made was that much of our early trust research had presupposed a well-functioning legal and formal institutional framework. Without the comparative design I am not sure if I would have reached that conclusion (at least not in 2002). So, what were the major mistakes made during the study?

In the Swedish study, I used a tape recorder to support my memory and avoid misunderstandings, as recommended in the majority of the literature on interview methodology (see for example Bryman and Bell, 2003). In Tanzania, I tried to do the same, but I did not manage to learn much. As I passed an informant – just to say hello – on my way to the fruit market a few days after an interview, he was much more eager to talk. I perceived a trade-off between supporting my memory with a tape recorder and receiving rich information, and chose the latter. To compensate for the risk of forgetting and misunderstanding, I took notes and transcribed each interview immediately after it had taken place. To double check, I returned to the key informants to check my information and early inter-pretations. When I later asked a local friend about the reluctance to talk in front of a tape recorder, she connected it to the former authoritarian government and the general suspicion of officials.

Before carrying out the study in Tanzania, I had been expecting to meet some difficulties due to the fact that I was white, female and relatively young. As mentioned, the first fact was a problem when it came to blend-ing in. I was suddenly regarded as an authoritarian figure and at times also as a potential source of funds or credit. Much effort thus had to be put into explaining that I was not going to distribute any funds or credit. At some stage I feared that such beliefs would affect the information I was given. It was some time before I felt confident that the majority of the business community in Singida realized that my questions would by no means be linked to any funding and I had to select my key informants from among those that I perceived had fully understood and accepted this fact.

The two latter facts – that I was young and female – proved to be much more positive than negative. It is my contention that they put me on a more equal basis with some Tanzanian men and that I was perceived to be more 'harmless' than an older male would be. My efforts (and at times failure) to speak the language may have contributed to this effect. The only obstacle related to my female sex that I encountered during my research was that I could not always stay late at the pub, chatting to the businessmen. That was not culturally acceptable unless I was accompanied by my husband (which I sometimes was since the local pubs showed African football on TV). Getting access was thus not an entirely easy process. I also needed to adjust my way of dressing and wore long skirts and sleeved tops. Although I thought I had understood the dress code and had adjusted at an early stage, I was approached by a small delegation of annoyed women who told me they suspected I didn't wear a proper underskirt. However, they were helpful enough to tell me where I could buy such a thing . . . and I went shopping.

In the Swedish study, I instead met scepticism towards academia. What was the point of research? Could I find out something that they did not already know? Apart from answering their questions as honestly and clearly as I could, socializing and talking about everyday issues at social gatherings connected to the studied project became my way of gaining access in this case, too. It should be noted that the actors in this context were not free from expectations of my research either. Some wondered if I, and my work, could help to market the region as a tourist area, and some wondered if I could influence the decisions connected to obtaining rural development support from the European Union. Here, too, I thus had to put effort into explaining that I could not influence the flow of funds. These expectations can be found in other empirical studies whether in Sweden, Tanzania or elsewhere. The difference is that the ethnographic approach encourages awareness and conscious handling of such biases. I cannot recall reflecting much on my clothing when conducting the Swedish study; the atmosphere was informal during meetings and interviews, and I believe I was also informally dressed. However, my awareness of this was not on the same level in the Swedish study as in the Tanzanian. The same applies to my awareness of trust between spouses. Perhaps this was also an issue also in the Swedish region, but I did not look for it.

DISCUSSION

Two of the main conclusions that I drew from the studies described here were: first, where few legal institutions safeguard against breaches of trust, people tend to invent 'reasons' to trust; secondly, 'category-based trust' is very significant and has not been given due attention in the literature. A more extensive discussion about these findings is outside the scope of this chapter, and reported elsewhere (Tillmar, 2006; Tillmar and Lindkvist, 2007). Here, we conclude that I would not have been able to reach those conclusions without the cross-cultural and comparative design.

I hope that my reflections on the cross-cultural research experience will stimulate others to undertake such an endeavour. I have attempted to show that an undertaking of this kind is far from trouble free, but it is very rewarding. To me, it was not only an inspiring and developing journey but also something fruitful for theoretical development. I believe that trust research (and social science research in general) would benefit from more qualitative cross-cultural comparative studies.

REFERENCES

Alvesson, Mats and Kaj Sköldberg (2000), *Reflexive Methodology,* London: Sage.
Bachmann, Reinhard (2001), 'Trust, power and control in trans-organizational relations', *Organization Studies*, **22** (2), 337–65.
Brislin, Richard W. (1980), 'Introduction to social psychology', in H.C. Triandis and R.W. Brislin (eds), *Handbook of Cross-Cultural Psychology, Volume 5*, Boston: Allyn and Bacon, pp. 389–444.
Brislin, Richard W., Walter J. Lonner and Robert M. Thorndike (1973), *Cross-Cultural Research Methods*, New York: Jon Wiley and Sons.
Bryman, Alan and Emma Bell (2003), *Business Research Methods*, Oxford: Oxford University Press.
Garsten, Christina (1994), 'The apple world: core and periphery in a transnational organizational culture', doctoral dissertation, Stockholm Studies in Social Anthropology 33, Stockholm: Department of Social Anthropology, Stockholm University.
Garsten, Christina (2003), 'Etnografi', in Bengt Gustavsson (ed.), *Kunskapande Metoder inom Samhällsvetenskapen*. Lund: Studentlitteratur, pp. 145–66.
Hofstede, Geert (1980), 'Motivation, leadership, and organization: do American theories apply abroad?', *Organizational Dynamics*, **1** (Summer), 42–63.
Hofstede, Geert (1991), *Organisationer och Kulturer: Om Interkulturell Förståelse*, Lund: Studentlitteratur.
Merriam, Sharan B. (1994), *Fallstudien som forskningsmetod*, Lund: Studentlitteratur.
Merriam, Sharan B. (2009), *Qualitative Research: A Guide to Design and Implementation*, San Francisco: Jossey-Bass.
Molander, Bengt (1993), *Kunskap i Handling,* Gothenburg: Daidalos.
Ragin, Charles C. (1989), *The Comparative Method: Moving Beyond Qualitative and Quantitative Strategies*, Los Angeles: University of California Press.
Salzer, Miriam (1994), 'Identity across borders: a study in the "IKEA-World"', dissertation, Linköping Studies in Management and Economics 27, Linköping: Linköping University.
Sandemose, Aksel (1933 [1977]), *En Flykting Korsar Sitt Spår*, Uddevalla: Forum.
Tillmar, Malin (2002), 'Swedish tribalism and Tanzanian agency: preconditions for trust and cooperation in a small-business context', dissertation, Linköping Studies in Management and Economics 58, Linköping: Linköping University.
Tillmar, Malin (2006), 'Swedish tribalism and Tanzanian entrepreneurship: preconditions for trust formation', *Entrepreneurship and Regional Development*, **18**, 91–107.
Tillmar, Malin and Lars Lindkvist (2007), 'Cooperation against all odds: finding reasons for trust where formal institutions fail', *International Sociology*, **22** (3), 343–66.
Triandis, Harry C. (1994), *Culture and Social Behaviour*, New York: McGraw-Hill Inc.

Annotated Further Reading

Alvesson, Mats and Kaj Sköldberg (2000), *Reflexive Methodology*, London: Sage. A thorough discussion of qualitative methods, on the bases of the philosophy of science.
Tillmar, Malin (2006), 'Swedish tribalism and Tanzanian entrepreneurship: preconditions for trust formation', *Entrepreneurship and Regional Development*, **18**, 91–107. Details of the empirical results from using the cross-cultural approach.

11 Combining card sorts and in-depth interviews

Mark N.K. Saunders

INTRODUCTION

Trust research invariably asks questions about sensitive issues, highlighting the need to build rapport and trust between the researcher and participant. It may also be necessary to ensure participants are not sensitized to the research focus on trust. This chapter outlines the use of a card sort, concurrent with an in-depth interview to help overcome these issues.

The problem of obtaining valid and reliable information when asking questions about sensitive issues is not unique to trust research. Notwithstanding the problems associated with gaining access, or increased non-participation due to individuals expecting negative consequences, participants' subsequent evasive answers or socially desirable responses can reduce the utility of data collected (Crowne and Marlowe, 1964). Participants' concepts of what is sensitive are socially constructed and so what matters is whether a participant finds the research sensitive for whatever reason (Arksey and Knight, 1999). Where this occurs, participants may use their answers to protect themselves from potential harm or embarrassment, to present themselves in a positive light, or to please the researcher. This, in turn, may threaten the accuracy or interpretation of data collected (Dalton et al., 1997). Not surprisingly, this issue is recognized widely; most research methods texts emphasize the need to minimize such problems by ensuring the research topic is salient to the participant, explaining the benefits to her or him and emphasizing privacy and anonymity (for example Kvale and Brinkmann, 2009; Saunders et al., 2009b).

Building on this and similar advice, research methods texts expound subsequently how, when conducted by a skilled interviewer, face-to-face interviews can elicit honest responses about sensitive topics, revealing much insightful information and, of equal importance, not causing upset or distress. Whilst the amount of advice on how to ask questions on sensitive topics such as trust varies enormously between texts, that in Lee's (1993) seminal text *Doing Research on Sensitive Topics* is extensive. Even though assurances of anonymity are normally given, it is clear that, especially in the early stages of an interview, posing a direct question on a topic perceived as sensitive is likely to give poor results (Van Der Heijden et al., 2000). This is due, at least in part, to disclosure of sensitive information being only likely to be possible once trust has been established between the researcher and participant. Consequently it is crucial in the early stages of an interview to introduce questions and collect data in such a way as to allow participants' cooperation and trust to be gained so that they will respond candidly without fear that this will be compromised (Dalton et al., 1997).

My experiences as a trust researcher have shown repeatedly the importance of building rapport with participants before asking questions about potentially sensitive issues such as reasons for their feelings of trust and distrust in relation to work colleagues. Asking such questions early on in the interview process is likely to result in either a noncommittal answer or, alternatively, a refusal to respond. At the same time it has highlighted the need to beware of sensitizing participants to the importance of trust in the research. If precise research foci are explained in detail at the outset of an interview, it is likely to raise their importance in participants' consciousness and, as a consequence, may introduce some form of bias in their responses; thereby compromising the research or limiting the scope to develop new understandings (Lee, 1993). As it is each participant's ethical right to have the reasons for the research explained, this raises a potential dilemma. If participants are provided with insufficient information regarding the purpose of the research, they will be unable to make an informed decision regarding whether or not to take part. Consequently, considerable care must be taken in how the purpose of the research is explained to allow informed consent without sensitizing.

In this chapter, I consider the use of a popular data-gathering technique, the card sort (Whaley and Longoria, 2009). Although not commonly used by trust researchers, when combined with an in-depth interview, this offers a method for researching the relative importance of a range of employees' feelings, including both trust and distrust, in response to organizational situations. Following an overview of sorting techniques and a discussion of the card sort method, I outline a concurrent mixed method approach in which a card sort is followed immediately by an in-depth interview that draws directly upon the card sort data. This is illustrated from my personal experiences of using this approach to explore the occurrence of trust in relation to other feelings in response to organizational change. By not sensitizing participants specifically to trust the concurrent card sort and interview allow the testing of: first, the strength of trust relative to other feelings; secondly whether trust and other judgments such as distrust are symmetrical, occurrence of one precluding the other; and, thirdly, whether trust and distrust judgments entail conceptually different expectations and anticipated independent outcomes and the reasons for these.

AN OVERVIEW OF SORTING

Sorting techniques, whereby participants sort items or stimuli such as physical objects, pictures or cards containing words into different groups, are useful in that they provide a way of eliciting agreement and disagreement regarding item categorization (Whaley and Longoria, 2009). The categories into which items are sorted may be chosen by the participant, the interviewer or a mixture of both (Rugg and McGeorge, 2005). As an elicitation technique, sorting – and in particular the card sort – has a number of distinct advantages, not least simplicity of administration for the researcher, ease of understanding for the participant and relative speed of the process (Fincher and Tenenberg, 2005). Combining it with other techniques, such as the in-depth interview, allows the reasons behind participants' categorizations to be explored and understood, making sense of the data collected.

Sorting techniques have their origin in Personal Construct Theory (Kelly, 1955). This is based on the belief that, although different people categorize items differently, there is sufficient commonality to enable understandings alongside sufficient differences to support individuality. Individuals reflect their own feelings by placing items into categories on the basis of one or more criteria. Consequently an individual may classify an item such as 'trusting' into one of a number of categories, reflecting the extent she or he feels it, based on criteria relating to how their employing organization has managed a particular process.

A card sort offers the simplest form of sorting technique, each item to be sorted being a card with a picture, drawing, word or phrase printed on it. Participants are asked to place (sort) these cards into their own categories or categories supplied by the researcher (such as 'felt strongly', 'felt to some extent', and 'not felt'), the latter being referred to as a constrained card sort (Rugg and McGeorge, 2005). Such researcher-supplied categories aid comparison of responses across participants, although it is important to ensure that those provided are both realistic and understandable. It is this form of card sort, where categories are supplied by the researcher, which is the focus of this chapter.

Within the research methods literature limited advice exists on the use of card sorts, a notable exception being Rugg and McGeorge (2005). In their 'tutorial' article on sorting techniques they begin to address this, highlighting how, compared to related techniques such as repertory grids (see Chapters 13 and 14 in this volume), sorting techniques have received little formal attention. Commencing with advice regarding choice and number of items to be sorted, they suggest these can be derived either through preliminary research or from the literature, stressing that items should be from within the same horizontal level in a hierarchy; for example employees' emotional responses to organizational change. They state there should be no fewer than eight items and a maximum of between 20 or 30 items for single criterion repeated sorts. However, they also add that a greater number of items can be used in some circumstances, as illustrated later in this chapter.

Once items have been chosen they need to be prepared for physical sorting by participants. Rugg and McGeorge (2005) advise that when preparing cards, all should be the same size, words or phrases on every card being printed using the same font and font size. Each card should be given a code number to aid the recording process, printed preferably on the back so as not to interfere with the sorting process. Where a constrained sort is used, they advise the researcher to provide clear labels for each category into which the cards will be sorted. Instructions to the participants regarding sorting criteria should be clear and the process explained precisely by the interviewer. Despite such careful preparation, where cards are sorted more than once, the first sort is likely to cause the most problems, participants being unfamiliar with the process and not always understanding precisely what is required.

For practical reasons I have found it helpful to have a clear table on which the cards can be spread and physically moved during the sorting process. Where participants develop their own categories, it is important that the researcher clarifies precisely the definition the participant is using for each. Advice from Rugg and McGeorge (2005) emphasizes that clarification is best done once the cards have been sorted into categories, as participants often change their minds during this process. Results of a card sort session are usually recorded on paper, noting the details of the sort, the categories used and the code numbers of each item sorted into each category. Using code numbers on the back of cards saves considerable time as only the number rather than the precise word or phrase needs to be recorded. These data are subsequently analysed, often quantitatively on their own, providing information on which feelings are felt most frequently and the relative strength of these feelings. However, as noted earlier it can be advantageous to use the card sort as a precursor to an in-depth interview, to explore the criteria and reasoning for the categorization. Such interviews can allow participants to explain seemingly contradictory strong feelings, for example 'trusting' and 'under pressure', in relation to their own particular context: in this example the need to perform to a high level following promotion (Saunders and Thornhill, 2003).

COMBINING CARD SORTS WITH IN-DEPTH INTERVIEWS

In recent years there has been an increased use of mixed method designs using a combination of data collection techniques (Bryman, 2006; Tashakkori and Teddlie, 2010). In concurrent mixed method designs, such as the card sort and subsequent in-depth interview, data are collected and analysed in parallel (Creswell et al., 2008). The findings are then integrated for the purposes of either triangulation or complementarity. While triangulation aims only at corroborating data and obtaining convergent validity (Scandura and Williams, 2000), complementarity emphasizes enhancement and clarification through the identification of additional rather than competing interpretations to explain more fully the phenomenon being researched (Hammersley, 2008). Consequently, an in-depth interview offers a way of understanding the reasons for the categorizations uncovered by the card sort. For topics where the researcher does not wish to sensitize the participant to the precise focus of the research, the card sort offers a way of establishing a rank categorization of the items of particular interest such as trust and distrust relative to each other and to other feelings, the in-depth interview allowing the underlying reasons to be explored.

Inevitably, the combining of a card sort with in-depth interviews means quantitative (rank) data are used in conjunction with quantitative (interview) data. This has been the subject of considerable epistemological debate since the early 1970s (Bryman, 2006), with some researchers arguing that the two methods are incompatible. However, in recent years there has been an increased use of mixed method designs. Such hybrid methods (Edmondson and McManus, 2007; see also Chapter 12 on the board game method in this volume) add value by providing additional complementary data and thereby increasing interpretive power.

Use of a concurrent card sort and in-depth interview (discussed next) integrates a quantitative constrained card sort of a variety of possible feelings in relation to an organizational situation or event with a qualitative subsequent in-depth individual interview to explore and understand each participant's reasons for their categorization represented by the sorted cards. It therefore collects data that establish the relative strength of different feelings, including trust, alongside the reasons for these within a specified context. During the card sort participants are asked to sort a randomly presented set of between 40 and 50 cards according to how strongly each is felt. Each card reports a different feeling that might be experienced in relation to an organizational situation. The words and phrases on the cards reflect the range of possible emotions and moods in response to similar situations as highlighted by earlier research.

PERSONAL EXPERIENCE OF THE CARD SORT AND IN-DEPTH INTERVIEW IN TRUST-BASED RESEARCH

In some of my work on trust, particularly that undertaken with Adrian Thornhill, a structured card sort of possible responses to change has been integrated with a subsequent audio recorded in-depth interview to explore and explain the reasons for each participant's categorization of responses and interpretation of the associated contexts. To date the approach has been used to research the strength of trust relative to other feelings (Saunders and Thornhill, 2003); whether trust and distrust are symmetrical – the occurrence of one precluding the other (Saunders and Thornhill, 2004) – and, currently, whether trust and distrust judgments entail conceptually different expectations and anticipated independent outcomes and the reasons for these. This research has been undertaken with participants selected using either probability or non-probability sampling.

In its most recent incarnation, the card sort involves each participant sorting 50 cards that expressed a possible feeling in the active voice; for example 'sceptical' rather than 'scepticism'. Feelings include 'trusting' and 'distrustful', 13 expressions and manifestations of trust and distrust identified by Lewicki et al. (1998) and 35 emotions identified and used by Saunders and Thornhill (2004), derived from literatures relating to psychology and stress. Whilst these responses have been used successfully when the focus has been on trust and internal change, my colleagues and I have also used a card sort followed by an in-depth interview (with a variation in the cards sorted) to explore external organizational change situations, for example mergers and acquisitions in the hospitality industry (Saunders et al., 2009a).

Within the card sort participants are asked to sort a randomly presented set of cards, each recording one of the feelings that might be experienced in relation to the organizational situation. Prior to this, assurances of confidentiality and anonymity are offered and the research purpose explained to the participant, for example to establish and understand her or his 'feelings in relation to the managed change at the organization', it being stressed there were no wrong answers. By not explicitly referring to trust, participants are not sensitized to either trust or distrust.

For the first sort each participant is given the complete set of cards and asked to categorize the possible feelings by physically placing each card under either the heading 'do not feel' or the heading 'feel to some extent' (Figure 11.1). During sorting, participants are allowed to change their mind, moving cards between the two headings. Following the completion of the first sort, those cards that contain a 'feeling' categorized as 'do not

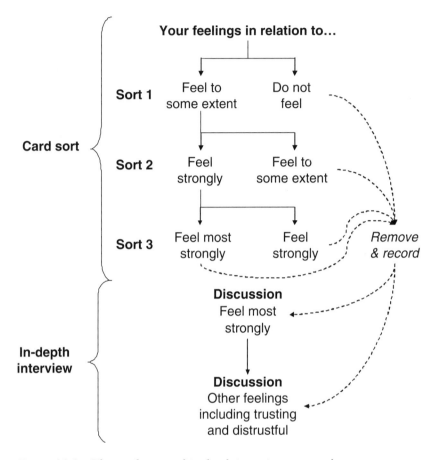

Figure 11.1   The card sort and in-depth interview approach

feel' are removed and recorded. Each participant is then asked to undertake two further sorts of the remaining cards. In the second sort, participants are asked to categorize the remaining cards under the heading either 'feel to some extent' or 'feel strongly'. Those cards that have been categorized as 'feel to some extent' are removed and recorded. In the third sort participants identify the three cards which they 'feel most strongly' from those they categorized as 'feel strongly'. These cards are subsequently removed and recorded. Although the cards are presented at random, the recording sheet design places those feelings that earlier research suggested were likely to be related in close proximity. This helps potential patterns in the rankings that emerge to be seen more easily, thereby aiding subsequent interviews.

The quantitative data are derived from each participant's categorization of each feeling using a four-point ordinal scale. These ranked feelings draw directly on the change experience of each participant, providing not only a sense of validity but, through the card sort data collection sheet, a means to ground and explore these feelings through the in-depth interview. Each interview flows seamlessly from the card sort, commencing with the participant discussing their reasons for categorizing the three feelings 'felt most strongly' (Figure 11.1). Where not among those categorized as felt most strongly, the selection and relative positions of feelings of 'trusting' and 'distrustful' is introduced using the question 'I've notice that you categorized . . . can we talk about this?' This allows the structure for each interview to be grounded in each participant's categorization of the emotions that he or she has experienced because of organizational change, involving a form of participant validation during the interview (Pidgeon, 1996). Participants are encouraged to discuss and explain their response in the context of their own perceptions of the changes. This allows their trust reactions to be described and explored from a grounded and subjective perspective. Because the relative rankings of each participant's feelings are introduced in a manner that is precisely related to their own responses, reasons for the selection and relative positions of seemingly contradictory feelings can be explored. Within such explorations additional insights are often gained as the interviews progress.

DISCUSSION

This chapter has outlined how a card sort can, in combination with an in-depth interview, be used to ask questions about sensitive issues such as trust. Initially I have outlined the purpose of research as establishing and understanding the participant's 'feelings in relation to the managed change', it being stressed there were no wrong answers. Within my accompanying explanation I have tried to provide sufficient information to enable each participant to decide whether or not to consent to take part, offering further clarification as requested without sensitizing them to issues of trust and distrust. Subsequently the use of the card sort provides an opportunity to build rapport with each participant and gain her or his trust through an exercise which, my experience suggests, is actively enjoyed. The physical sorting of feelings into different categories appears to break down barriers between the researcher and participant, responses to participants' questions about the process such as 'Can I change my mind?' and 'What do you mean by . . .?' allowing the researcher to emphasise further the focus on each participant's views and the meanings they attribute to individual feelings. Where participants are reluctant to categorize a feeling or are having difficulties, this is usually apparent through non-verbal cues such as hesitation or moving a card between categories. Here I have found that reassurances to take as much time as necessary are helpful, where necessary suggesting they might consider leaving the card until others have been categorized within the sort.

The card sort draws directly on the experience of each participant, providing not only a sense of validity but also a subsequent means of exploring these through the in-depth interview. As participants undertake their sort, they often provide a short commentary to support their categorizations, which can offer clues regarding possible subsequent interview questions. The concurrent in-depth interviews allow these categorizations to be explored and understood in the contexts from which they are derived, building on these data to ground each participant's feelings of trust. By focussing initially on categorizing feelings through a card sort, participants are not sensitized to trust. Consequently, it has been possible to collect data on the strength of trust relative to other feelings and, in particular, to explore whether trust and distrust are symmetrical, occurrence of one precluding the other. As outlined above, recent incorporation of theoretically derived expressions and manifestations of trust and distrust (Lewicki et al., 1998) as additional cards to be sorted has enabled the testing of whether trust and distrust judgments entail conceptually different expectations and anticipated outcomes.

Simultaneous collection of card sort and in-depth interview data reveals how the same highly ranked feelings can be selected for completely different reasons by different participants. This is important as, in addition to allowing the meanings attributed to each card to be compared, the interviews also provide insights concerning how a range of factors can affect trust. For example, the reasons for categorizing 'trusting' as 'most strongly felt' were, although diverse, related to how change had impacted positively on their working lives. Reasons given included improved job security, greater autonomy and a better understanding of what is happening (Saunders and Thornhill, 2004).

Combining data from the card sort with data from in-depth interviews is particularly beneficial to studying phenomena such as trust, which may be affected by equivocality (unclear meaning) or ambivalence (mixed feelings) among participants. The use of an in-depth interview alongside a card sort allows the researcher to ensure she or he has the same understanding of the words or phrases on the cards as the participant. Not sensitizing these participants to any particular feelings allows situations where what might be considered an unusual relationship of mixed feelings such as trust and distrust to surface. These can subsequently be explored in the in-depth interviews.

Invariably, if working within a pragmatist philosophy, the adoption of concurrent mixed method is dependent on its suitability to answer the research question. Hence, trust researchers first have to justify why their particular research question would benefit from this method. In addition trust researchers need to demonstrate how the data can be integrated to provide fuller understandings and additional insights. Both aspects are important as the use of a card sort and in-depth interview requires considerable preparation. In addition, my experience and that of my colleagues indicates that undertaking one card sort with an associated in-depth interview takes between 60 to 90 minutes with each participant. Finally, it is important to be mindful that asking questions about sensitive topics such as trust or distrust can cause stress to the participant. As researchers we need to be aware of this and plan accordingly, ensuring that, where necessary, counselling support can be made available for participants.

REFERENCES

Arksey, H. and P. Knight (1999), *Interviewing for Social Scientists*, London: Sage.

Bryman, A. (2006), 'Editor's introduction: mixed methods research', in A. Bryman (ed.), *Mixed Methods Volume 1*, London: Sage, pp. XXV–LII.

Creswell, J.W., V.L. Plano Clark and A.L. Garrett (2008), 'Methodological issues in conducting mixed methods research designs', in M.M. Bergman (ed.), *Advances in Mixed Methods Research*, Thousand Oaks, CA: Sage, pp. 66–83.

Crowne, D.P. and D. Marlowe (1964), *The Approved Motive: Studies in Evaluative Dependence*, New York: Wiley.

Dalton, D.R., C.M. Daily and J.C. Wimbush (1997), 'Collecting sensitive data in business ethics research: a case for the unmatched count technique', *Journal of Business Ethics*, **16**, 1049–57.

Edmondson, A.C. and S.E. McManus (2007), 'Methodological fit in management field research', *Academy of Management Review*, **32** (4), 1155–79.

Fincher, S. and J. Tenenberg (2005), 'Guest editorial: making sense of card sorting data', *Expert Systems*, **22** (3), 89–93.

Hammersley, M. (2008), 'Troubles with triangulation', in M. Bergmann (ed.), *Advances in Mixed Methods Research*, Thousand Oaks, CA: Sage, pp. 22–36.

Kelly, G.A. (1955), *A Theory of Personality: The Psychology of Personal Constructs*, New York: W.W. Norton.

Kvale, S. and S. Brinkmann (2009), *Interviews: Learning the Craft of Qualitative Research Interviewing*, Los Angeles: Sage.

Lee, R.M (1993), *Doing Research on Sensitive Topics*, London: Sage.

Lewicki, R.J., D.J. McAllister and R.J. Bies (1998), 'Trust and distrust: new relationships and realities', *Academy of Management Review*, **23**, 438–58.

Pidgeon, N. (1996), 'Grounded theory: theoretical background', in J.T.E. Richardson (ed.), *Handbook of Qualitative Research Methods for Psychology and the Social Sciences*, Leicester: BPS Books, pp. 75–85.

Rugg, G. and P. McGeorge (2005), 'The sorting techniques: a tutorial paper on card sorts: picture sorts and item sorts', *Expert Systems*, **22** (3), 94–107.

Saunders, M.N.K. and A. Thornhill (2003), 'Organisational justice, trust and the management of change: an exploration', *Personnel Review*, **32** (3), 360–74.

Saunders, M.N.K. and A. Thornhill (2004), 'Trust and mistrust in organisations: an exploration using an organisational justice framework', *European Journal of Work and Organisational Psychology*, **13** (4), 492–515.

Saunders, M.N.K., L. Altinay and K. Riordan (2009a), 'The management of post-merger cultural integration: implications from the hotel industry', *Service Industries Journal*, **29** (10), 1359–75.

Saunders, M.N.K., P. Lewis and A. Thornhill (2009b), *Research Methods for Business Students*, Harlow: FT-Prentice Hall.

Scandura, T.A. and E.A. Williams (2000), 'Research methodology in management: current practices, trends, and implications of future research', *Academy of Management Journal*, **43** (6), 1248–64.

Tashakkori, A. and C. Teddlie (2003), *Handbook of Mixed Methods in Social and Behavioral Research*, Thousand Oaks, CA: Sage.

Van Der Heijden, P.G.M., G. Van Gils, J. Bouts and J.J. Hox (2000), 'A comparison of randomized response, computer-assisted self-interview, and face-to-face direct questioning: eliciting sensitive information in the context of welfare and unemployment benefit', *Sociological Methods and Research*, **28** (4), 505–37.

Whaley, A.L. and R.A. Longoria (2009), 'Preparing card sort data for multidimensional scaling analysis in social psychological research: a methodological approach', *Journal of Social Psychology*, **149** (2), 105–15.

Annotated Further Reading

Butt, T. (2008), *George Kelly: The Psychology of Personal Construct*, Basingstoke: Palgrave Macmillan. A useful introduction to Kelly's work on personal construct theory.

Rugg, G. and P. McGeorge (2005), 'The sorting techniques: a tutorial paper on card sorts: picture sorts and item sorts', *Expert Systems*, **22** (3), 94–107. Paper offering one of the few overviews of sorting techniques along with practical advice regarding conducting a sort.

Saunders, M.N.K. and A. Thornhill (2004), 'Trust and mistrust in organisations: an exploration using an organisational justice framework', *European Journal of Work and Organisational Psychology*, **13** (4), 492–515. Paper using a card sort and in-depth interviews concurrently to explore perceptions of trust and distrust in an organizational setting.

12 Mixed method applications in trust research: simultaneous hybrid data collection in cross-cultural settings using the board game method
Miriam Muethel

INTRODUCTION

Cross-cultural studies on trust often face problems due to culture-dependent differences in the understanding of what trust actually is. In this situation, simultaneous collection of qualitative and quantitative data can help the researcher to examine the underlying issues. The board game method introduced in this chapter supports such data collection.

Mixed method application, that is the collection and analysis of qualitative and quantitative data, enables complementary data use (Yauch and Steudel, 2003). The combination of both types of data supports a more profound understanding of trust, particularly in cross-cultural settings (Pearsall, 1998: 623). Cross-cultural trust comparisons, for example, might suffer from culturally driven differences in underlying definitions. Such differences have been shown, for example with regard to trustworthiness, and more particularly honesty (Meglino et al., 1992). Although honesty has been shown to be a universal value, cultural influences lead to either an absolute understanding of honesty where there is just one truth that is not bound to any contextual influences (Locke and Woiceshyn, 1995); or a relative understanding where social relations primarily determine social behavior, so that truth becomes relative to the contextual influences (Muethel and Hoegl, 2007).

In dealing with such culture-bound differences in the understanding of trust, researchers may wish to discover not only how evaluations of trustworthiness are made but also why. Enhanced insights about the interpretation of trustworthiness can then aid our understanding of variances in the evaluation and, in particular, whether they stem from real or from spurious discrepancies. Real discrepancies are likely to occur when all participants have the same understanding of the investigated construct, but differ in their evaluation. Spurious discrepancies are based upon different underlying interpretations of the phenomenon, indicating that the variance does not necessarily stem from different evaluations but could also have arisen from different understandings of the same phenomenon. To be able to identify real concordances and discrepancies and to distinguish them from spurious ones, researchers can simultaneously collect both qualitative and quantitative data (rather than first collecting qualitative data and then, after a certain period of time, quantitative data). This way, researchers can analyse a person's evaluation while considering the same person's interpretation of trust.

In the following, I will describe how researchers can simultaneously collect both qualitative and quantitative data using the board game method.

MIXED METHODS IN TRUST RESEARCH: USING THE BOARD GAME METHOD

The board game supports the analysis of culture-dependent differences in the understanding and interpretation of trustworthiness in different cultures. Thus, it is particularly aimed at analysing trustworthiness measurement models (that is, it does not target at hypothesis testing). In the following, I will explain its application on a German–Chinese sample.

The board game method comprises a board with 12 fields, four fields outside the board and a set of 16 trustworthiness-related values depicted on triangular prisms (see Figure 12.1).

The 16 values were derived from earlier studies on trustworthiness and included honesty, credibility, morality, benevolence, carefulness, goodwill, competence, expertness, reliability, responsiveness, predictability, dependability, openness, shared understanding, dynamism, and personal attraction (for a comprehensive review see Mayer et al., 1995).

As pre-tests have shown that on average four values are not perceived to be related to trustworthiness at all (such as physical attractiveness and dynamism), German and Chinese participants were first asked to exclude four values and then to rank the remaining 12 values. This also facilitated the starting phase of the analysis as the exclusion of non-related values was easier for participants than the rank order building at that time. After participants had completed the rank order, I asked them to define each single value ('How do you define value honesty?'), to operationalize the value ('How do you see that somebody is behaving honestly?') and to explain the rank order ('Why is honesty ranked first?') or the exclusion from the rank order ('Why did you exclude personal attraction?').

The combination of ranking and operationalization was chosen in order to identify potential cultural differences in the perceived importance due to different definitions and ways of operationalization. Simultaneous data

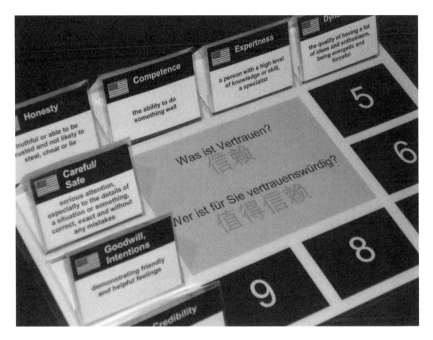

Figure 12.1   The board game

collection of qualitative data (definitions, operationalization, and reasons for rank order) and quantitative data (ranking places) allowed the supplementing of the Chinese and German rank order of trustworthiness-related values with value interpretations.

The board game is particularly useful to study cross-cultural differences as the triangular prism used to represent each value enabled the English, Chinese, and German translation of that value to be stated on one side. Each value was translated from German by native speakers into English and Chinese and then translated back into German. Inconsistencies and deviations from the original formulation that appeared after the back translations were discussed in the research team. As all participants were advanced English speakers, an English translation was also added. The multitude of languages was chosen to consider the fact that translations rarely reflect the precise meaning of a term, so that there will always be slight differences in meaning (Welch and Piekkari, 2006). Hence, reading all translations served as a method of diminishing differences in meaning and therefore aided the creation of a common understanding about the terms. The triangular prisms allowed an easy way of displaying all three translations of each value (Figure 12.2).

Figure 12.2   The triangular prism

Simultaneous data collection in studying cross-cultural differences holds further advantages. None of the participants in the study reported to have ever deliberately and systematically reflected on trust and trustworthiness before. Hence, this study aimed to analyse a phenomenon that did not lie at the surface of the individual perception, but remained an unconscious part of individual perception (Muethel, 2006). As such, directly asking for a rank order did not seem to lead to acceptable results. In fact, I wanted to give the participants the opportunity for an individual self-revealing process by allowing the participants to reflect and amend the position of the values in the rank order. The open board game design was thus explicitly chosen to allow respondents to change their mind. The process of ranking the prisms and explaining the reasons for the rank order (quantitative and qualitative data) was designed to support the individual in her or his thinking and re-thinking process. Interviewer questions such as 'Are you sure that this is your personal rank order?' and 'Can you tell me why?' supported this reflection process.

DATA ANALYSIS

Having collected qualitative and quantitative data concurrently the next is step to integrate both types of data for complementary data analysis.

However, according to Bryman (2007), it is challenging to integrate two different types of data in a meaningful way. Moreover, constructionists (assuming humans generate knowledge and meaning from their experiences) even argue that the two types of data may not provide different kinds of information about the same object, but constitute the world differently (Flick, 2004). Nevertheless, I adopt the so-called methodological pragmatism perspective. This perspective rejects the either/or choices often associated with different paradigms. Alongside a recognition of the role of the researcher's values in data interpretation, pragmatism asks what possible difference the combination of methods can make for the meanings of the research questions raised (Maxcy, 2003).

For the qualitative analysis of value definitions and operationalizations, I used an inductive approach (Strauss and Corbin, 1990), gathering individual definitions of the individual values and their behavioral indicators from respondents and classifying them into a number of categories by content analysis (Miles and Huberman, 1994). Initially, I developed a coding scheme for each value definition and operationalization. The analysis was iterative, going back and forth between the interview notes and the categories (Gibson and Zellmer-Bruhn, 2001). The final coding scheme consisted of three to five definitions and operationalizations for each of the 16 values. I only added a new definition or operationalization if supportive statements from at least three different persons were found.

Investigating the importance of each value, I analysed the rankings of Chinese and Germans. As data was non-parametric (each value was ranked between 1 and 12, sorted out values were ranked 13), I considered grouped medians and applied Kruskal-Wallis-H tests (Kruskal and Wallis, 1952) to determine the statistical significance of differences between Chinese and German rankings. The qualitative data of value definitions and operationalizations in combination with the quantitative results were then used to interpret rank and meaning of the 16 values for Chinese and German assessments of trustworthiness.

DATA INTERPRETATION

The board game allows us to collect both qualitative and quantitative data to be integrated and used complementarily for interpretation. The particular contribution of the board game method lies in its capacity to identify universal and culture-dependent operationalizations of constructs. As such, the use of board games can offer solutions of how to overcome the 'etic–emic dilemma' (Peng et al., 1991: 99) in cross-cultural research. While emic models describe behaviors as seen from the perspective of the cultural insider by using constructs drawn from their self-understanding, etic models describe phenomena in constructs that apply equally well to other cultures (Morris et al., 1999). The board game therefore facilitates the distinction between culture-specific and universal constructs by offering additional information on definitions and operationalizations of evaluated terms. As such, the study makes it possible to identify universal factors of trustworthiness, such as integrity, which might be used for cross-cultural studies (Wasti et al., 2007), as well as culture-dependent factors of trustworthiness, (for example, shared understanding for China) which are particularly valid in one country, but potentially not in other countries. Using the board game method therefore allows for the identification of universally applicable constructs which support high levels of national level validity in cross-cultural studies.

RESEARCH VALIDITY CAVEATS

To analyse validity in mixed methods, Tashakkori and Teddlie (2003) recommend the evaluation of interpretive rigor and design quality. With the board game method being a specific design for mixed method data collection, I will focus on design quality. To evaluate design quality, Tashakkori and Teddlie propose three criteria: within-design consistency, design suitability, and design fidelity.

Within-design consistency focuses on the consistency of procedures of the study. The board game method follows a strict set of procedures. First, non-trustworthiness related values are excluded. Second, the other 12 values are ranked. Third, values are defined, operationalized and their ranking (exclusion) is explained. Furthermore, qualitative data analysis also follows clearly defined procedures. Here, particularly the minimum nomination of a single definition to be included as content category increases the focus on core definitions. As concerns data interpretation, single values serve as matching units for qualitative and quantitative data. Thus, there is a clear definition how different types of data are used complementarily.

Design suitability refers to whether the methods of the study are appropriate for addressing the research question. The research question I targeted when applying the board game method focuses at the identification of culture-dependent differences in the interpretation and evaluation of trustworthiness-related values between Germans and Chinese people. Simultaneously collecting data on value ranks (exclusion), their definitions and operationalizations, as well as on value-rank decision explanations, the board game method especially supports the complementarity of data.

Design fidelity hints as to whether the procedures are capable of capturing meaning, associations, or effects. The open design of the board game method allows the participants physically to see her/his evaluation at a glance and to change the rank order easily. Taking into account that participants probably never reflected on trustworthiness-related aspects before, the process of (1) value rank order building, (2) value definition, operationalization, and rank-order explanation, and (3) a potentially second round of rank ordering facilitates the self-revealing process needed for participants to develop an opinion of which value is more important than another.

PERSONAL EXPERIENCE

My personal experience with the board game methods underlines the crucial role of the researcher. For most participants, it was easy to decide which values are not related to trustworthiness at all, but it became much harder to rank order the remaining values. In this situation it would have been easy to manipulate the game. To avoid this situation, I explained that there is no preferred order and that any value could potentially be the most important one. Moreover, I presented the game from the very beginning as a tool for people to learn more about themselves than for me to gather data. As such I framed the data collection as a 'discovery journey' for participants to learn more about why they trust some people and others not. In consequence, the atmosphere was less about me collecting data, but more about the participant reflecting on his or her own subjective trust theory. At the end of the collection phase I asked whether or not they had learned something they did not know before about their own subjective trust theory – all participants agreed that they had.

DISCUSSION

When deciding on whether or not to apply the board game method, researchers should take into account the effort required for the preparation of the board game and for the process of data collection. One execution of the board game takes approximately 60 to 90 minutes. I believe that the necessary effort can be justified by the specific interpretative power of the method to solve research questions dealing with equivocality. However, it is necessary to consider when and how to integrate the board game method into the research process. When studying trust in a cross-cultural context, the board game method facilitates the identification of universal constructs, which are understood in the same way by the countries under investigation. As such, applying the board game method in the early stages of the research process can help to strengthen construct validity for quantitative analysis in later stages.

REFERENCES

Bryman, A. (2007), 'Barriers to integrating quantitative and qualitative research', *Journal of Mixed Methods Research*, **1** (1), 8–22.
Flick, U. (2004), 'Triangulation in qualitative research', in U. Flick, E. von Kardorff and I. Steinke (eds), *A Companion to Qualitative Research*, London: Sage, pp. 178–83.
Gibson, C.B. and M.E. Zellmer-Bruhn (2001), 'Metaphors and meaning: an intercultural analysis of the concept of teamwork', *Administrative Science Quarterly*, **46** (2), 274–303.
Kruskal, W.H. and W.A. Wallis (1952), 'Use of ranks in one-criterion variance analysis', *Journal of the American Statistical Association*, **47**, 583–621.
Locke, E.A. and J. Woiceshyn (1995), 'Why businessmen should be honest: the argument from rational egoism', *Journal of Organizational Behavior*, **16** (5), 405.
Maxcy, S.J. (2003), 'Pragmatic threads in mixed methods research in the social sciences: the search for multiple modes of enquiry and the end of the philosophy of formalism', in A. Tashakkori and C. Teddlie (eds), *Handbook of Mixed Methods in Social and Behavioral Research*, Thousand Oaks, CA: Sage, pp. 51–89.
Mayer, R.C., J.H. Davis and F.D. Schoorman (1995), 'An integrative model of organizational trust', *Academy of Management Review*, **20** (3), 709–34.
Meglino, B.M., E.C. Ravlin and C.L. Adkins (1992), 'The measurement of work value congruence: a field study comparison', *Journal of Management*, **18** (1), 33.
Miles, M.B. and A.M. Huberman (1994), *Qualitative Data Analysis*, 2nd edn, Thousand Oaks, CA: Sage.
Morris, M.W., K. Leung, D. Ames and B. Lickel (1999), 'Views from the inside and outside: integrating emic and etic insights about culture and justice judgment', *Academy of Management Review*, **24** (4), 781.
Muethel, M. (2006), *Successful Teamwork in German–Chinese Project Teams (German: Erfolgreiche Zusammenarbeit in Deutsch-Chinesischen Teams)*, Wiesbaden: Deutscher Universitätsverlag.
Muethel, M. and M. Hoegl (2007), 'Initial distrust: on the role of perceived dishonesty in international innovation teams', *Zeitschrift für Betriebwirtschaft (ZfB)*, special issue, **4**, 103–24.
Pearsall, J. (1998), *The New Oxford Dictionary of English*, Oxford: Oxford University Press.
Peng, T.K., M.F. Peterson and S. Yuh-Ping (1991), 'Quantitative methods in cross-national management research: trends and equivalence issues', *Journal of Organizational Behavior*, **12** (2), 87–107.
Strauss, A.L. and J. Corbin (1990), *Basics of Qualitative Research: Grounded Theory Procedures and Techniques*, Newbury Park, CA: Sage.
Tashakkori, A. and C. Teddlie (2003), *Handbook of Mixed Methods in Social and Behavioral Research*, Thousand Oaks, CA: Sage.
Wasti, S.A., H.H. Tan, H. Brower and C. Oender (2007), 'Cross-cultural measurement of supervisor trustworthiness: an assessment of measurement invariance across three cultures', *Leadership Quarterly*, **18** (5), 477–89.
Welch, C. and R. Piekkari (2006), 'Crossing language boundaries: qualitative interviewing in international business', *Management International Review*, **46** (4), 417–38.
Yauch, C.A. and H.J. Steudel (2003), 'Complementary use of qualitative and quantitative cultural assessment methods', *Organizational Research Methods*, **6**, 465–81.

Annotated Further Reading

Cheung, F.M., Shu Fai Cheung, Jianxin Zhang, K. Leung, F. Leong and Kuang Huiyeh (2008), 'Relevance of openness as a personality dimension in Chinese culture: aspects of its cultural relevance', *Journal of Cross-Cultural Psychology*, **39** (1), 81–108 – an empirical example of culture-dependent differences in the interpretation of constructs.

Muethel, M. and M. Hoegl (2007), 'Initial distrust: on the role of perceived dishonesty in international innovation teams', *Zeitschrift für Betriebwirtschaft (ZfB)*, special issue, **4**, 103–24 – a detailed description of method.

13 Utilising repertory grids in macro-level comparative studies
Reinhard Bachmann

INTRODUCTION

This chapter argues that Repertory Grids are a powerful method which can help transcend the current limitations of trust research. Moving away from the conventional one-questionnaire-fits-all approach, many new insights into the nature of trust can be gained by utilising this method. Repertory Grids allow for a high level of context-sensitivity while ensuring comparability of results between individual interview sessions. Although not initially designed to produce aggregated data, I will argue that repertory grids are especially useful for international comparative research on trust.

Trust research has become a relatively established field within management studies. Much conceptual and empirical work has been done in the past two decades to understand what is arguably one of the most important and efficient coordination mechanisms in contemporary business relationships. Apart from a myriad of journal and book publications, a *Handbook of Trust Research* has been published (Bachmann and Zaheer, 2006), and even a *Journal of Trust Research* has been launched. These are clearly signs that – despite persisting different views and controversies – this research field has reached a certain degree of maturity.

The research community has come up with various definitions of trusting behaviour which converge on the notion of making oneself vulnerable under conditions of limited knowledge and risk. It has managed to develop an understanding of different types of trust relevant in business contexts. For example, Mayer et al. (1995) suggested that competence-based trust, integrity-based trust and benevolence-based trust are the major types of trust that occur in business relationships, and many scholars orient their ideas towards such classifications. There is some common ground as to how trust can be created and how it may be ruined or repaired. Kim et al. (2006) as well as Gillespie and Dietz (2009) found that a breakdown of integrity-based trust has different effects from a breach of competence-based trust, thus requiring different approaches to repairing it. Such insights are valuable and confirm that today we indeed understand the relevance and role of trust in business much better than in the 1970s, when Dale Zand introduced this concept to management research (Zand, 1972).

However, there are still many unsolved problems and there is no reason for the research community to rest in their efforts to refine our knowledge of trust. Much work lies ahead of us if we really want to get to grips with it. What we now have are conceptual frameworks and empirical results which explicitly or tacitly claim universal validity. We have not bothered much, and perhaps this is so in any newly developing research field, about the fact that '*sinroi*', '*guanxi*', '*vertrauen*', or whatever we may find as translations of the word 'trust' in other languages, are to a large extent culture-specific concepts. We should take this seriously now and, as a next step, become more ambitious, abandoning the idea that trust is a universal concept that remains the same at any time and everywhere. As is the case with other phenomena of the social world, trust is an inherently context-bounded concept.

Take, for example, the study of power or risk. Here, we look back on a longer research tradition in management studies and it seems that we have already arrived at a point where simplifications rooted in a positivist epistemology are widely recognised as naive and inappropriate. Trust research will simply have to catch up with this insight. Arguably, more established research on social concepts sometimes goes a bit too far in their constructivist attempts to counter positivism where it dissolves its object of study into purely subjective contributions to – for example – power discourses or risk perceptions. But, at least, most scholars who research power or risk would hardly step back from the fundamental insight that there is no universal order of phenomena and relations to be revealed in the social sciences, as is the case in the natural sciences, and that our theoretical approaches as well as our empirical research methods should reflect that. Thus we may conclude that more sophisticated concepts, specifically context-sensitive methods, are needed in trust research in order to deepen our understanding of trust in various management and business contexts.

In the following, I will discuss repertory grids and their potential as a method for studying trust in business relationships. While this method has proven useful to analyse individual perceptions and the collective views in small groups, I will suggest utilising this method for macro-level comparative research on trust. I believe that this method has no leaning towards positivist universalism and yet escapes the dangers of constructivist relativism. It provides the chance to keep the research instrument constant so that it allows for comparisons between culturally and institutionally different contexts, and yet is context sensitive enough to provide room for different meanings and understandings of trust in different cultural settings and under conditions of different institutional arrangements in different business systems.

DESCRIPTION OF METHOD

As there exist instructive guides on how to use repertory grid techniques (for example Jankowicz, 2003) as well as another chapter by Ashleigh and Meyer on this method in this handbook (Chapter 14), I will be brief in describing how this method works. Generally, the method is based on the idea of giving a minimal input by the interviewer and receiving a maximum of output from the interviewee in the interview session. If a questionnaire is put together, the researcher will inevitably make many substantial assumptions about potential behaviours, interests and preferences on the part of the interviewee and what these might indicate with regard to the research question. These assumptions are implied in the questions that are to be asked in the interview session (Saunders et al., 2009). By contrast, collecting primary data by means of repertory grid-based interviews allows the researcher to make considerably fewer and weaker assumptions about what might be important issues in the eyes of the interviewee. So, for example, where a question in a conventional questionnaire may ask for the frequency of meetings between actors, this would typically build on the assumption that frequent face-to-face contacts between two managers indicates a high level of trust in a relationship. The repertory grid method neither requires nor allows the researcher to make such strong assumptions. With this method one would only need to assume that frequent face-to-face contacts may in some way or another be relevant for the interviewee with regard to trust building in a relationship. But in what way these might be relevant is not pre-decided by the researcher.

Rather than a list of questions (such as 'How often do you meet face-to-face?', 'What is the average length of your contracts?'), repertory grid-based interviews draw on a list of elements (for example face-to face contact, lengthy detailed contracts, and so on) deemed important for the interviewee(s) with regard to trust processes. These elements are given as input by the researcher and it is up to the interviewee to attach meaning to these elements. Thus, it is not a priori assumed by the researcher that, for example, frequent face-to-face contacts or lengthy contracts indicate a certain level of trust, as this would be the underlying assumption when a questionnaire is constructed. Repertory grid-based interviews are more cautious; if these elements do indicate something specific in terms of trust, the interviewee will tell us and, if so, in what way this might be the case.

What the interviewer will do with a prepared list of – let's assume – 20 elements is the following. Pairs of elements are picked randomly and the interviewee will be asked if – with regard to trust – these elements are in his or her mind similar or dissimilar. When the interviewee has made his or her decision, the immediate next question will be: 'In what respect are these elements "similar" (or "dissimilar", respectively)"? The interviewee will now come up with one or two of what we call 'constructs'. For example, the two elements 'lengthy contracts' and 'membership in the same professional association' could be seen as similar in that they are both classified as 'anonymous'; or 'frequent face-to-face contacts' and 'lengthy contracts' may be viewed by the interviewee as dissimilar, one of these elements being felt to be 'transparent' and the other as 'bureaucratic'. It does not matter whether the interviewee's answers make sense to the interviewer or whether there is a clear logical opposition if two elements are described as dissimilar. The only important issue is that this procedure is continued for some time to allow for the creation of a list of constructs. Only when (almost) no new constructs are produced by the interviewee and old ones are frequently repeated to describe the similarities and dissimilarities between pairs of elements, does this procedure end. What we have now is a list of 20 elements and a list of – let's just guess – 25 constructs.

As the next and final phase of the interview, all elements are tested against all constructs. This means that the interviewee will, for example, be asked whether 'lengthy contracts' (as an element) can be associated with constructs such as 'bureaucratic', 'transparent', 'abstract', and so on. The answer will always be 'yes' or 'no', or in some rare cases 'neither-nor'. If this procedure is continued long enough, every element receives a construct-based profile (a 'yes', a 'no', or a 'neither-nor' for each construct).

Depending on the degree of the similarity of acquired profiles, the elements can be depicted on a map where they will appear in different proximity to each other. For example, if two elements appear on such a map in close proximity to one another that would be due to the fact that these elements have received similar construct profiles, whereas they would appear further apart from each other if their profiles are less similar.

The following graphical representation (the 'global meaning space') may give an idea of what such a cognitive map could look like (Figure 13.1). It was created in the context of research on virtual organisations that I was involved in some time ago (Clases et al., 2003). Here, the content of this map is not part of my argument and serves only illustrative purposes. The varying sizes of the depicted elements are merely due to the three-dimensional representation mode that the specific software used to produce this map uses. The latter can be ignored in the present context.

The creation of these cognitive maps as well as the data collection procedures can be widely supported by software that is available in different variants. These software packages can be tremendously helpful in speeding up the processes of producing such cognitive maps that are to be created for each and every individual interviewee. What makes the repertory grids specifically interesting for management researchers, however,

Global meaning space

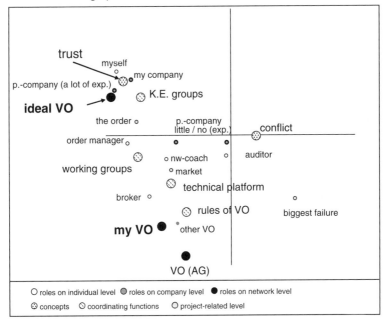

Figure 13.1   Global meaning space/cognitive map (illustration)

is not that individual maps can be produced, discussed and evaluated but that data can be aggregated to allow for the creation of 'ideal-typical' firm-specific, industry-specific and even country-specific maps. Clearly, the greatest insights are to be expected when one then analyses these maps in a comparative perspective.

Repertory grids are a method which – in terms of context sensitivity – has some significant advantages over conventional questionnaire-based techniques to collect data. Interviewees from different contexts will produce different cognitive maps, where the elements are kept constant but the location of the elements in the cognitive maps will vary according to the meaning that the interviewees attach to them. The first is necessary to ensure comparability between individual interviewees' answers; the latter reflects the high level of context-sensitivity of this method. Another important feature of the repertory grid method is that, while it can be seen as a qualitative instrument in the phase of data collection, it becomes a tool for quantitative measurements when the location of the elements and the distances between them have been determined. The latter allows for various forms of quantitative analysis, including, for example, cluster analysis.

THE POTENTIAL FOR COMPARATIVE RESEARCH

While repertory grids have occasionally been used in management research and consultancy, the focus of these efforts has invariably been on how individuals and sometimes small groups of organisational actors make sense of the environment in which their actions are embedded (Easterby-Smith et al., 1996). The reason for this seems to be that the repertory grid method was originally developed by a psychologist (Kelly, 1955) and it is still mostly organisational psychologists who are familiar with this method. From my point of view, however, there is much scope to utilise this method in larger organisational contexts within but also across organisational boundaries, and for comparative research on inter-organisational relationships across cultures and national institutional settings.

By way of aggregating data gathered in individual interview sessions, firm-specific, industry-specific and indeed country-specific cognitive maps can be generated and compared to each other. The latter can reveal a variety of country-specific meanings of trust and country-specific ways to develop, ruin and repair trust in business relationships. Thus national contexts can be shown to influence not only the concept of trust but also the context-specific conditions and consequences of trust processes in single-country and international relationships. If repertory grid-based research should reveal that the comparison between country-specific cognitive maps does not show great differences – which in my eyes would be surprising – the conclusion would be that the meaning of trust and the processes surrounding this phenomenon would indeed have more or less universal characteristics. This would also of course be a valuable finding of context-sensitive research which we would not know for sure before such research is carried out. If we have a large number of repertory grid-based cognitive maps we could sort them according to different criteria and thus find out which context-dependent variable – whether its size, industry, country and so on – matters most and what is the relative weight of all these factors when different forms of trust are to be explained. Currently, research is prepared to go exactly through this procedure (for details see Bachmann, 2010). This, in my view, is exciting and likely to contribute to putting trust research on a new level.

DISCUSSION

What we did in the past was certainly not all wrong. Questionnaire-based research of the kind that I myself was involved in could reveal some fundamental differences of trust development in countries so close to one another as Germany and the UK (for example, Bachmann, 2001; Lane and Bachmann, 1996). I simply think that we have developed our field of research up to the point where we can now take on more complexity and take into account that there appear to be many different nuances of trust in many different cultural and institutional settings. This, in my view, calls for the utilisation of more sophisticated methods, such as repertory grids, in future trust research.

As shown above, collecting data by means of the repertory grid method has the advantage of getting very close to the interviewees' own conceptualisations of trust, trust development, trust ruining and trust repair processes. While the elements need to be kept the same over different contexts, the constructs that the interviewees attach to them change from one individual interview to the next and can, for example in international comparative research, even remain in the native language of the interviewee. What is important for the location of the elements is solely determined on the basis of similarities between construct profiles that each element receives by the interviewee.

The analysis of repertory grid-based data can draw on very exact measurements of the distances between the elements in the generated cognitive maps. Thus, the usual quantitative techniques, such as cluster analysis, can be performed and combined with more interpretative techniques. This is a notable advantage because quantitative techniques are usually strong in the phase of data analysis, while having their downside mainly in the data collection phase. Admittedly, repertory grids – like any single research method – also have their limitations. For example, the necessary pre-decided input in the form of a list of relevant elements may still be seen as crucially dependent on the researcher's subjective judgment. This may be true but, at least in comparison to questionnaire-based interviews, these influences are strongly reduced. Of course, repertory grids can also be used in parallel with other methods in both the data collection and the data analysis processes, thus allowing 'methodological triangulation' to verify the validity and reliability of research results. In sum, I believe that repertory grids can provide a very powerful method that should have its place in the toolbox of any organisational trust scholar who is ambitious to transcend the near-exhausted paradigm of context-*in*sensitive trust research.

REFERENCES

Bachmann, R. (2001), 'Trust, power and control in trans-organizational relations', *Organization Studies*, **22** (2), 341–69.
Bachmann, R. (2010), 'Towards a context-sensitive approach to researching trust in

inter-organizational relationships', in M.N.K. Saunders, D. Skinner, G. Dietz, N. Gillespie and R.J. Lewicki (eds), *Organizational Trust: A Cultural Perspective*, Cambridge: Cambridge University Press, pp. 87–106.
Bachmann, R. and A. Zaheer (eds) (2006), *Handbook of Trust Research*, Cheltenham, UK and Northampton, MA, USA: Edward Elgar.
Clases, C., R. Bachmann and T. Wehner (2003), 'Studying trust in virtual organizations', *International Studies of Management and Organization*, **33** (3), 7–27.
Easterby-Smith, M., R. Thorpe and D. Holman (1996), 'Using repertory grids in management', *Journal of European Industrial Training*, **20** (2), 3–30.
Gillespie, N. and G. Dietz (2009), 'Trust repair after an organization-level failure', *Academy of Management Review*, **34** (1), 127–45.
Jankowicz, D. (2003), *The Easy Guide to Repertory Grids*, Chichester: Wiley.
Kelly, G.A. (1955), *The Psychology of Personal Constructs, A Theory of Personality*, New York: Norton and Co.
Kim, P., K. Dirks, C. Cooper and D. Ferrin (2006), 'When more blame is better than less: the implications of internal vs. external attributions for the repair of trust after a competence- vs. integrity-based trust violation', *Organizational Behaviour and Human Decision Processes*, **99**, 49–65.
Lane, C. and R. Bachmann (1996), 'The social constitution of trust: supplier relations in Britain and Germany', *Organization Studies*, **17** (3), 365–95.
Mayer, R., J. Davis and D. Schoorman (1995), 'An integrative model of organizational trust', *Academy of Management Review*, **20** (3), 709–34.
Saunders, M.N.K., P. Lewis and A. Thornhill (2009), *Research Methods for Business Students*, 5th edition, Harlow: FT Prentice-Hall.
Zaheer, S. and A. Zaheer (2006), 'Trust across borders', *Journal of International Business Studies*, **37**, 21–9.
Zand, D.E. (1972), 'Trust and managerial problem solving', *Administrative Science Quarterly*, **17** (2), 229–39.

Annotated Further Reading

Bachmann, R. (2010), 'Towards a context-sensitive approach to researching trust in inter-organizational relationships', in M.N.K. Saunders, D. Skinner, G. Dietz, N. Gillespie and R.J. Lewicki (eds), *Organizational Trust: A Cultural Perspective*, Cambridge: Cambridge University Press – a more detailed discussion of the problem of comparative research which should ensure both the comparability of data as well as a high level of context-sensitivity of data.
Clases, C., R. Bachmann and T. Wehner (2003), 'Studying trust in virtual organizations', *International Studies of Management and Organization*, **33** (3), 7–27 – an article which reports on research carried out by means of repertory grid-based interviews. Two Swiss virtual organisations were studied and the results are presented in the form of cognitive maps.

14 Deepening the understanding of trust: combining repertory grid and narrative to explore the uniqueness of trust
Melanie J. Ashleigh and Edgar Meyer

INTRODUCTION

Historically, much of the research on trust has been viewed through a positivist lens, where scholars have been consumed with attempting to extract rational functionality from this complex and intangible concept. For example the contentious issue of definition is still being debated several decades after Deutsch's (1958) first ideas that trust consisted of 'confident expectation' in others based on co-operative interdependence that would lead to favourable outcomes. Nearly half a century later trust is still being researched as a commodity one can use or analyse to extract a favourable outcome. It has been subjected to various categorisation analyses for example cognitive-based or affective-based trust (McAllister, 1995) and calculus-based, knowledge-based and identification-based trust (Lewicki and Bunker, 1996).

Research, however, has brought 'the functionality' of trust into question, arguing for promoting a move towards 'hermeneutic frameworks and methods' (Möllering, 2001: 404) and the aim of this chapter therefore is to encourage trust researchers to adopt more integrative and inductive approaches when measuring trust. This was achieved by using some parts of two inductive theories – repertory grid and narrative. These two methods both emanate from a research paradigm that promotes the grounding of findings in the situated nature of the research context. Used together they are compatible as well as complimentary to each other. Repertory grid can be used at a surface level (for example to generate bottom-up constructs), whilst narrative can be used to explore beneath the surface and reflect on trust as a unique concept. Following Möllering's rationale, the combination of these two approaches addresses the unique nature of trust; narrative helps to elicit a deeper meaning of the constructs developed through repertory grid. This can help to understand how people develop and articulate their constructs. Thus combining such approaches allows a deeper reflection of what individual constructs mean and how they are formed.

This chapter discusses the benefits of trying to capture trust by combining two inductive approaches, which may be more appropriate in certain working contexts. The methodologies of repertory grid and narrative[1] will be discussed and indicative evidence presented to show how such methods may improve the measurement of such a complex and intangible variable. Narrative approaches have now become an accepted and widely used method to investigate a range of issues. The anecdotal link between narrative/storytelling and trust can be found, for example, in Grisham (2006). Repertory grid uses interview data to elicit trust categories (Ashleigh and Nandhakumar, 2007), narrative can then be used to contextualise and expand on the construct and meaning of trust. Using examples from the qualitative components of repertory grid, we will show that qualitative, narrative interview data can usefully be employed to characterise trust (for example Harwood and Ashleigh, 2005; Wang et al., 2006), and demonstrate the value that a combined approach of narrative studies and repertory grid can bring to trust research.

DESCRIPTION OF METHOD

By taking an integrative approach and combining two methods that allow a different conceptual understanding of trust, a predetermined view is eliminated, which in effect defines trust within a specific and unique 'context'. We believe this contributes to the theoretical debate in both conceptualising and measuring trust. Through the repertory grid technique, participants can freely define their constructs based on their contextual experiences (cf. Chapter 13 in this volume). Furthermore, by using narrative we can explore the meaning of their unique constructs, as well as comprehending the reasoning structure underlying construct development.

Repertory Grid

Repertory grid (rep grid) is an interview technique originally developed as a methodological tool by Kelly (1955), based on his personal constructs theory (PCT). The principle of the theory grew from Kelly's belief that individuals cannot and should not be fitted into 'boxes' based on others' value or belief systems. In order to make sense of the world, individuals actively construe a network of constructs that are representations of their own truth of the world as they (and only they) understand it. Over time these constructs are built into a repertoire which forms a construct system. For example the construct of 'honest' only exists in relation to its bipolar opposite which may be 'dishonest' – or it may be 'doesn't always tell the truth'. What such a construct means to one individual will never be identical to another; this similarly applies to one's unique conceptualisation of trust. Therefore the way that we view our world is by comparing things as similar to some but different from others.

The grid is developed using concrete and discrete representations of the domain one wants to explore, known as elements (Stewart and Stewart, 1981). For example nouns such as desk or names such as John or Southampton are elements. However certain rules exist for selecting elements. First, elements must always be real, and observable (people, objects, activities or events). Second, an element set should be homogeneous (Easterby-Smith, 1980), that is, drawn from the same category, for example, an appropriate set would be John, Edgar, Mel, whereas Edgar, desk, Southampton would not be homogeneous. Finally elements must not be evaluative – that is having meaning that may be individual (Stewart and Stewart, 1981). Whereas John is an element, the concept of motivation is evaluative as it carries different individual meanings and thus it is a construct. Once the elements are set, a series of questions are asked relevant to the field of inquiry to allow the interviewee to elicit their own bipolar constructs by comparing elements in a triangular rotation, known as triading. In relation to trust, where we are comparing Mel, Edgar and John, one may ask, how are Mel and Edgar similar but different to John (Stewart and Stewart, 1981). Therefore the construct is elicited by participants directly comparing two elements that are similar with one that is different and then the constructs are linked to each element to make a grid. Depending on the purpose of the analyses, rep grid can be used to quantify or qualify constructs. For the former this may be done either via a tick box grid or a rating using a Likert scale. This gives the process a standardised scoreability, enabling replicability and reliability of results. For the latter, elements can be ranked against each construct qualitatively, with some studies having used cognitive mapping (for example Senior, 1997).

Narrative

Narrative is less clearly defined as a method and authors suggest that research in and on narrative is a melting pot with a 'state of near-anarchy in the field' (Kreiswirth, 2000; Pentland, 1999). One of the reasons for the multiplicity of approaches is how narrative has been applied across various disciplines; each discipline borrowing and adapting narrative forms and usage. There has been a recent increase in the use of narrative which may be due to the recognition that narrative is the primary means by which people make sense of the world and how individuals inhabit it. Narrative is often described as a particular form of cognition (Wagner,

2002) through which we perceive reality (Andrews et al., 2003). Narrative has the property to frame encounters into a coherent experience (Kohler-Riessman, 1993); it depicts events, situations, or experiences, as well as containing references to individual belief systems and social categorisation processes. The meaning created from an experience is the result of the organisation of non-systematic encounters (the observations of events, situations, or experiences) into a coherent whole which takes a narrative, or storied, form (McCane et al., 2001). This form is then used to communicate an individual's experience to others. This reflects the ideas behind personal construct theory and repertory grid, as it mirrors the sense-making capability of individuals to develop constructs that are tightly bound to their frame of reference.

Narratives can be found in texts, as oral communication, or as a visual representation (Connell et al., 2003). Narrative theories have often ignored forms such as practices of history, newspaper stories, police reports, or everyday gossip – all of which can be seen as narratives. This breadth of what could constitute a narrative indicates the challenge in defining the concept. Andrews et al. (2003) argue that it is almost impossible to arrive at a robust shared definition of what constitutes a narrative. A narrative is when activities are brought together and are then organised into a 'temporally organized whole'. Comparing different approaches (for example Barthes, 1977; Pentland, 1999), we argue that the basic features of a narrative are time, sequence, voice, and point of view. Abma summarises narrative with the purpose of producing meaning in mind: 'A narrative creates meaning through a certain (temporal or causal) sequence (plot line) by highlighting certain people (characters), and through a moral endpoint' (2002: 7). This definition, we believe, seems relevant to repertory grid, as narrative unearths the uniqueness of a trust construct. Narrative is described here as a tool that helps to give meaning to individual behaviours at a given time whilst allowing for some form of subjective judgement. This resonates with the development of individual constructs through triads, as in repertory grid interviews individuals recount a narrative and judge behaviour of individuals. For the context of this research, narrative is valued predominantly for its usefulness in understanding the construction of meaning and its ability to allow individuals to make sense of observed situations, events, and experiences.

RESEARCH VALIDITY AND CAVEATS

Using a repertory grid has benefits over other interpretive approaches as it allows a deep exploration of a topic. It is especially successful for exploring intangible and ill-defined concepts (such as trust). The interviewer can probe and abstract someone's 'real perception' of a concept through understanding how their experiences have brought them to their current evaluation of something or someone, rather than giving an answer that they 'think' the interviewer wants to hear. The technique is therefore valid as the interviewee drives the process; this eliminates any interviewer bias and so enhances validity of the data. As no two elicited constructs are usually identical, the technique also gives a large amount of context-rich data without researchers being concerned about self-serving biases or 'interviewer pleasing', which therefore helps reliability (Rogers and Ryals, 2007). A process of laddering is often used, where participants are asked for more explanation about their constructs or to try and articulate them better; this is where narratives are being elicited. In regards to narrative, its validity as a research method can only be demonstrated through its wide use across a range of disciplines in a number of different ways. The ambiguity of narrative as a concept and as a research tool requires researchers to create their own understanding and method to analyse the gathered data. This means there is no standardised comparator to verify the approach taken. However, by basing one's use of narrative on existing frameworks and describing the steps undertaken this problem can be somewhat diminished.

Caveats that apply to both repertory grid and narrative approaches exist. The issue of reliability and validity sits awkwardly in phenomenological research, as the paradigm itself is unconvinced by absolute truths. Various authors support this argument (McKinnon, 1988; Russell, 1996). They argue that these concepts are usually used within a positivist framework and may therefore be considered inappropriate for interpretive research. Because this research investigates a phenomenon in specific instances, traditional concepts of generalisability also tend to be problematic, as in all interpretive research (Atkinson et al., 1994; Cassell and Symon, 1994). However, this type of research never aimed at deriving some general, universal laws, but was much more concerned with learning about the individual meanings given to trust in a specific setting.

For some purists repertory grid is not strictly a phenomenological approach, as it has an element of scoreability and standardisation if the researcher needs to quantify the data. However, as mentioned earlier, the development of the grid can take a qualitative form and by combining it with narrative the focus shifts towards the inductive development of constructs such as trust. Other limitations are that repertory grid and narrative can be very time consuming (Easterby-Smith et al., 1996). We found both methods to be most meaningful and valid for smaller populations where the need for individual, group insight and shared meaning systems are key factors in the research.

PERSONAL EXPERIENCE OF USING INDUCTIVE METHODS ON TRUST-BASED RESEARCH

An example of combining these two approaches for measuring trust was a study exploring the concept of trust within and between teams working in a highly volatile, secure and controlled domain (Ashleigh and Nandhakumar, 2007). The research was to be used in an attempt to restructure operator and technological processes and develop robust systems for more effective control of energy distribution. Due to the complexity and volatility of the domain the concept of trust was difficult for engineers to articulate, which was the main reason for choosing these inductive approaches. The elements were set via observed interactions and talking with the participant cohort and so were bespoke; they therefore held meaning for those involved (see Appendix). The repertory grid interviews were carried out by asking operators to compare a triad of elements within each section, enabling them to elicit their bipolar constructs. The interview was conducted along the lines of 'Can you tell me a way in which two of these people/systems are similar to each other but different from the third in terms of . . .?' The qualifier – 'in terms of' – allows the interviewee to consider the elements in relation to the purpose of inquiry (in this case, trust). Examples of the constructs elicited are shown in the Appendix. It is interesting to note that bipolar opposites that operators gave were not necessarily the 'logical' or agreed antonym of the given word. For example, the given opposite of 'honesty' was not 'dishonesty', but when discussing 'intra-team' elements was 'is not always open'. In order to induce the participant to attach value and meaning to that construct it was often necessary to ask for clarification of what they meant by their opposite construct. Very often the participant would give an example by relating a narrative of what happened between two elements. The following two examples from the study provide an insight into our approach.

Example 1

> . . . Well it's like when I talk to my best friend – he's someone I've worked with for the last 25 years, then I know that he's being honest with me. Even though I'm at a higher level than him in terms of status and he could say things to make himself look good sometimes I totally believe that he has an inborn integrity and basic honesty. It's like when he left a shift and forgot to reset the alarms – he could have said it was the system/software, but he was totally honest and said, 'John, I forgot, I made a mistake – can you fix it for me?' On the other hand, there's my team-mate who I work on shift with most of the time and I just get the feeling that he's not always open with me. It's often a gut feeling but it feels like he's holding out on me or holding something back and I then always recheck what he's done – for instance in a shift handover – or when he gives me

the figures for the predictions. Does that mean I don't trust him? I don't know, but it's the difference between knowing someone is honest and therefore totally trusting them and having a doubt, not quite knowing if they are telling you the whole story – but it's not dishonest if you know what I mean.

Using repertory grid as a sole method, this vignette would serve to clarify the participant's elicited bipolar constructs of 'honesty' versus 'not always open' in terms of qualifying his definition of trust within a team context. Although seeking to understand how and why these constructs were given, the researcher is not particularly interested in the richness or detail of the story, as it only pertains to the confirmation of the construct and not the value associated with it.

Narrative, on the other hand, is very much interested in the way this story has been told and the emphasis the teller places on certain aspects. If we look at the structure of the quote, we can identify the main aspects of a narrative as outlined previously. The narrative has a clear voice; that of the interviewee. It also locates an event in time. The interesting aspect about the sequencing of time is that the anecdotes and examples retold did not necessarily happen in the told order, but the interviewee structures them in a way that make sense to him and helps him to tell a convincing story. Furthermore, we learn many things about the point of view of the interviewee. For instance, he relates the word 'trust' to his own feelings. He considers 'gut feelings' and length of friendship as an indicator for openness and trustworthiness – notice that he did not mention the length of time he has been working with his team-mate. Therefore, we can appreciate that for this individual trust is a concept that relies on feelings and perceptions based on experience, rather than on measurable behaviours. This is further emphasised by his reference to his status within the organisation. The comparison between his friend, who holds lower status, and his team-mate suggests that organisational structures of team work or hierarchy are insignificant in determining and defining trust, but that the feelings developed towards an individual are the important definitional aspects.

What can be gleaned from this brief exemplary analysis is that we are not only able to understand the bipolar concepts that define trust for an individual (the construct), but we can also see where these constructs are located in respect to individual frames of reference. By comparing different narratives, the researcher can develop a richer picture of the underlying factors and characteristics determining trust; thus explaining how individuals define trust. This in turn may lead to further insights into possible measures that could be applied to capture trust between individuals.

Another example is taken from a supervisor who had been an engineer for 30 years. The bipolar constructs here were elicited as 'commitment' versus 'uninterested.' This is an extract from a transcript of how the engineer explained why he thought these constructs were appropriate.

Example 2

> You just never know what to expect in these youngsters coming from university these days. Yes they may have good degrees and are so smart but they don't seem to share the same work ethic these days – do you know what I mean? Take the last one [graduate] we had who is on my shift as an operator. Seems totally uninterested in going that extra mile or putting himself out to get better or for the team or something. It's like he's got the job now and he's just cruising – there's not the drive in the same way I remember being a novice in this game! When I was a young apprentice (I never went to university), we were totally in awe of our supervisor, who had so much knowledge of the system and knew how every pipe and holder worked. We would ask him loads of questions and want to do a great job always trying to do better and impress – like John, he's been here nearly as long as me – he's the controller of the other team. He's first on site when there is a problem and is always committed to his junior operators. If anyone doesn't understand anything he takes time out after a shift and runs workshops for his boys or he'll come in on his day off. He'll always ask how it's going or try and find better ways of working for his team. He is so committed, not only to the job but to his staff as well.

Taking a narrative view, the constructs of 'commitment' and 'uninterested' are located within a wider web of assumptions. For instance, the teller of the story – the interviewee – situates his narrative in the past and in the present, identifying that things were different back then. By sequencing his plot or story line in this way, the teller provides us with a value judgement about age and relationships. He does not easily trust younger individuals who have undergone a different training route. However, he trusts his colleague, whom he has known most of his working life. Besides the tenure of the relationship, it is the nature of these relationships that we can explore using a narrative approach. For instance, mentioning the 'extra mile' or the working outside of hours indicates that individuals who show total devotion to improving the performance and the team are trustworthy – not those that 'just' do their job. Whilst not referring directly to it, the mentioning of the recent graduate compared with another controller suggests some aspect of hierarchy and/ or ageism. One may argue that a new graduate cannot undertake some of the tasks assigned to the controller as he is likely to be less experienced. By not qualifying his remarks, the story alludes to scepticism towards younger, less-experienced colleagues.

DISCUSSION AND EVALUATION

The arguments and analyses presented here highlight the possibilities that exist when combining these two methodological approaches. By examining these two short narratives, we can identify some different measures for trust. For instance, tenure of relationship features strongly in both narratives. This additional measure would have been lost had we purely applied the repertory grid method. Furthermore, organisational status and experience also seem to be important aspects to be considered when conceptualising trust; in the first narrative status was insignificant, whereas in the second narrative status seemed to matter somewhat more. Both narratives imply that the tellers perceive a certain level of experience in their 'heroes'; thus experience may be an additional construct of trust.

By examining the underlying sense-making structures that lead to these constructs, we believe that a richer, more contextualised, explanatory and valid measure of trust is achieved. Combining these two inductive methods helps us to capture the complexity of trust and reinforces just how socially and subjectively constructed – that is, unique – trust is and how attitudes, values, and experiences can affect and change our perception of it. By using a robust method of construct development with a meaning-focused narrative analysis, we anticipate the development of more descriptive and meaningful measures of trust across a range of contexts.

NOTE

1. Narrative has often been used in conjunction with storytelling or stories more generally. The distinction, whilst relevant in some contexts, is seen of less importance for the argument presented in this chapter. Coste (1989) posits that the concepts of narrative, story, and genre are often tightly bound, making their identification difficult. In addition, the distinctions tend to be derived from an abstract discussion mainly concerned with the adequacy of narrative models that analyse fictional narrative. The distinctions have paid little attention to narratives that emanate from the 'real' world (Kreiswirth, 2000). Therefore, we will refer to the term 'narrative' throughout.

REFERENCES

Abma, T.A. (2002), 'Emerging narrative forms of knowledge representation in the health sciences: two texts in a postmodern context', *Qualitative Health Research*, **12** (1), 5–27.
Andrews, M., S. Day-Sclater, C. Squire and M. Tamboukou (2003), 'Stories of narrative research', in C. Seale, G. Gobo and J. Gubrium (eds), *Qualitative Research Practice*, London: Sage, pp. 109–24.
Ashleigh, M.J. and J. Nandhakumar (2007), 'Trust and technologies: implications for technology supported engineering working practices', *Decision Support Systems*, **43** (2), 607–17.

Atkinson, P. and M. Hammersley (1994), 'Ethnography and participant observation', in N.K. Denzin and Y.S. Lincoln (eds), *Handbook of Qualitative Research*, Thousand Oaks, CA: Sage, pp. 248–61.

Barthes, R. (1977), *Image Music Text*, London: Fontana.

Cassell, C. and G. Symon (1994), 'Qualitative research in work context', in G. Symon (ed.), *Qualitative Methods in Organisational Research*, London: Sage, pp. 1–13.

Connell, N.A.D., J.H. Klein and E. Meyer (2003), '"Are you sitting comfortably? Then I'll begin (. . . to transfer some knowledge?)": narrative approaches to the transfer and interpretation of organisational knowledge', KMAC2003, Aston University, Birmingham.

Coste, Didier (1989), *Narrative as Communication*, Minneapolis: University of Minnesota Press.

Deutsch, M. (1958), 'Trust and suspicion', *Journal of Conflict Resolution*, **2**, 265–79.

Easterby-Smith, M. (1980), 'The design, analysis and interpretation of repertory grids', *International Journal of Man-Machine Studies*, **13** (3), 24.

Easterby-Smith, M., R. Thorpe and D. Holman (1996), 'Using repertory grids in management', *Journal of European Industrial Training*, **20** (3), 3–30.

Grisham, T. (2006), 'Metaphor, poetry, storytelling and cross-cultural leadership', *Management Decision Making*, **44** (4), 486–503.

Harwood, I. and M.J. Ashleigh (2005), 'Unravelling the dichotomy between "trust and confidentiality" in mergers, acquisitions and other strategic organisational change programmes', *Strategic Change*, **14** (2), 63–75.

Kelly, G. (1955), *The Psychology of Personal Constructs*, New York: Norton.

Kohler-Riessman, C. (1993), *Narrative Analysis*, London: Sage.

Kreiswirth, M. (2000), 'Merely telling stories? Narrative and knowledge in the human science', *Poetics Today*, **21** (2), 293–318.

Lewicki, R.J. and B.B. Bunker (1996), 'Developing and maintaining trust in working relationships', in R.M. Kramer and T.R. Tyler (eds), *Trust in Organisations: Frontiers of Theory and Research*, London: Sage, pp. 99–132.

McAllister, D.J. (1995), 'Affect- and cognition-based trust as foundations for interpersonal cooperation in organisations', *Academy of Management Review*, **38**, 24–59.

McCane, T.V., H.P. McKenna and J.R.P. Boore (2001), 'Exploring caring using narrative methodology: an analysis of the approach', *Journal of Advanced Nursing*, **33** (3), 350–56.

McKinnon, J. (1988), 'Reliability and validity in field research: some strategies and tactics', *Accounting, Auditing and Accountability*, **1** (1), 34–54.

Möllering, G. (2001), 'The nature of trust: from Georg Simmel to a theory of expectation, interpretation and suspension', *Sociology*, **35** (2), 403–20.

Pentland, B.T. (1999), 'Building process theory with narrative: from description to explanation', *Academy of Management Review*, **24** (4), 711–24.

Rogers, B. and L. Ryals (2007), 'Using repertory grid to access the underlying realities in key account relationships', *International Journal of market Research*, **49** (5), 595–612.

Russell, J.D. (1996), 'An approach to organizational ethnographic research: strategy, methods and processes', *Families and Social Captial ESRC Research Group Departmental Discussion Paper*, London: South Bank University, p. 36.

Senior, B. (1997), 'Team performance: using rep grid technique to gain a view from the inside', *Team Performance Management*, **3** (1), 33–9.

Stewart, V. and A. Stewart (1981), *Business Applications of Repertory Grid*, London: McGraw-Hill.

Wagner, E.L. (2002), 'Interconnecting information systems narrative research: an end-to-end approach for process-oriented field studies', in *Global and Organisational Discourse About Information Technology*, Barcelona: Kluwer Academic Publishers, pp. 419–35, is2.lse.ac.uk/wp/pdf/wp105.pdf.

Wang, J.K., M.J. Ashleigh and E. Meyer (2006), 'Knowledge sharing and team trustworthiness', *Knowledge Management Research and Practice* **4**, 175–86.

APPENDIX

Repertory Grid Sheet

Similar	Intra-team								Inter-team						Technology							Different
	The Team member I work most with	Another engineer on my shift	Somebody I totally trust	Person I am physically closest to in my team	Somebody I don't trust at all	My best friend	My immediate supervisor	My departmental manager	Someone with my job on another team	Someone who works in another control room	An outside agent (e.g. recs/maintenance/districts)	A member of the technical support team	A member of the planning team	The overall boss	The email system	Logging system	Video/TV monitor/conferencing	SCADA system	Demand forecasting system	Alarm management system	Telephone system	
Honesty																						Not always open
Shared goals																						Self interest
Understanding																						Little knowledge
Commitment																						Disinterested
Quality of interaction																						Rarely gives feedback

15 Hermeneutic methods in trust research
Gerard Breeman

INTRODUCTION

The hermeneutic method is often implicitly applied in historical research. This chapter shows explicitly how the hermeneutic method can help us to understand trust relations in unique historical cases, and how it helps us to discern general patterns of gaining and losing trust.

It is sometimes amazing why people trust other persons or organizations. A great deal of trust research focuses on listing all the different reasons people have for trusting and correlating them with various independent variables. My fascination, though, is with the reasons behind these reasons: why do people give specific reasons for trusting someone or something? Not only do I want to know how much trust is out there and what the reasons for trusting are, but also why people give those particular reasons for trusting.

In my experience the hermeneutic approach is a good method for finding out how and why people trust other people. The method is particularly useful to gain insights into the different intentions of all the parties involved. It connects the actual human interactions with intentions. The strong asset of the hermeneutic method is that it aims not only to understand a specific event, but also to identify general, objective patterns of human interaction. Scholars who use the hermeneutic method construct abstract patterns of interaction, in which they highlight specific features and disregard other observations. The economic-sociologist Max Weber referred to these patterns as '*Ideal Typen*' (Weber, 1972). These general patterns, in turn, are used to understand specific historic incidents. By analysing the discrepancy between the abstracted patterns and the historic events, one is able to better understand social and cultural behaviour.

In the following section I describe the hermeneutic method and illustrate the different parts of the method with the help of a specific case study. I will show how the method has helped me to construct a general pattern about the trust-establishing process and how, in turn, this has helped me to understand the specifics of this particular case. Moreover, the abstracted pattern helped me to understand other case studies as well.

The case study presented in this chapter is part of a larger research project and consists of the analysis of more than 100 texts (Breeman, 2006). It tells us how in the nineteenth century a Catholic priest, Gerlacus Van den Elsen (1853–1925) tried to establish trust among Dutch farmers for a cooperative banking system, the Raiffeisen bank. At that time an economic crisis had hit the Netherlands hard, especially the small farmers in the south (Sneller, 1943: 90). Poor credit facilities was one of most important problems and Van den Elsen wanted to solve this by establishing cooperative banks in all small villages. This cooperative banking system was inspired by the ideas of a German mayor, Friedrich Wilhelm Raiffeisen. Van den Elsen preferred the Raiffeisen system over the liberal shareholder system, which was also being introduced at the time. In his eyes, only the rich would benefit from a shareholder system and it would lead to usury. In contrast, the Raiffeisen banks would be based on cooperation between farmers guaranteed by the liability of every individual participant. Van den Elsen recognized some Christian values in the Raiffeisen banking system. Establishing trust for this system, however, turned out to be more difficult than he had anticipated.

DESCRIPTION OF THE METHOD

The hermeneutic method is particularly suitable for studying trust because it gives the scholar a certain empathy with the trustee (*Einfühlung*). Through close and careful analysis of texts and acts, the researcher is able to internalize the situation of the persons they study, to 'relive' and experience what the object has experienced before, and, hence, to understand the acts of the trustee (Habermas, 1969: 226). Once a scholar has observed and 'relived' a number of these cases, he will get a fuller understanding of the specific cases, and discern general patterns of trust building that cut across all the cases.

The basic hermeneutic method aims to understand small pieces of text by referring to a larger piece of text, and to understand a whole text by analysing small pieces of text. 'The part can only be understood from the whole, and the whole only from the parts [. . .]; you begin, for example, in some part, try tentatively to relate it to the whole, upon which new light is shed, and from here you return to the part studied, and so on' (Alvesson and Sköldberg, 2000: 54). Figure 15.1 illustrates the basic hermeneutic procedure.

Scholars have applied hermeneutics to much more than written texts. German scholars in particular expanded the boundaries of the art of hermeneutic interpretation. Dilthey, for example, saw all human life as 'text'. In his *Lebensphilosophie als Hermeneutik des Lebens* he argued that

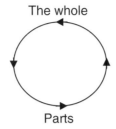

Figure 15.1   The original hermeneutic circle

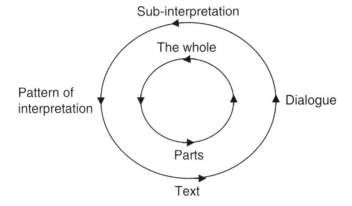

Source: Alvesson and Sköldberg (2000).

Figure 15.2   The elaborated hermeneutic circle

we constantly interpret our words and acts in order to come to an understanding of them (see Schüz, 2001: 58). Hermeneutics is applied to written
texts, spoken words, interview reports, and (historical) acts in general.

In *Reflexive Methodology*, Alvesson and Sköldberg specify the hermeneutic procedure (2000: 58–67). They identify four steps that a scholar
of hermeneutics must consider: (1) the pattern of interpretation, (2) the
text, (3) the dialogue, and (4) the sub-interpretation. The ultimate goal
of this procedure is to discern a general pattern which leads us to a better
understanding of the event at hand, and which can also help us to understand other events as well. Figure 15.2 illustrates this specification of the
hermeneutic circle. In the following sub-sections these four aspects of the
hermeneutic circle are further explained.

Step 1: The Pattern of Interpretation

The pattern of interpretation consists of the initial interpretation of the texts at the very start of a hermeneutic exercise. These early interpretations are based on so-called extra-hermeneutic sources such as preconceptions, propositions, partial theories, and the presumptions of the scholar. The pattern of interpretation thus 'refers to the overarching set of interpretations of a certain text, that is, the coherent whole of partial interpretations' at the start of an analysis (Alvesson and Sköldberg, 2000: 61). In line with the hermeneutic procedure, these preconceptions and concepts are constantly reflected on, discussed, and adjusted while studying and analysing the smaller parts of the text.

My initial framework of the trust-building process is based on various theories. With a background in public administration studies and theology, I reviewed both philosophical, public policy and management literature (Blackburn, 1998; Castaldo, 2002; Holton, 1994; Searle, 1983, 1996; Seligman, 1997). This interdisciplinary approach has led me to define trust as an intentional status of favourable expectations (Breeman, 2006).

I chose this initial pattern of interpretation and these theoretical approaches because my research question is focused on how trust is established rather than on measuring the amount or intensity of trust. Based on the theory of this trust-establishing process (Möllering, 2001; Searle, 1983, 1996), I argue that intentional states are obtained through experiences and interpretations (Breeman, 2006). Individuals continually interpret the behaviour of others, the qualities of objects, and the features of events. They are constantly developing various intentional states through this interpretative activity. Intentional states only function though, 'in relation to numerous other intentional states' (Searle, 1983: 141).

This means that building trust is a rather subjective activity, and usually takes place in interactions with other persons. The reasons for justifying one's trust, however, do not depend on the consent of others. For trusting there is no need that others agree with the reasons provided (Blackburn, 1998). It is also not necessary that one's reasoning is based on rational argument (though it could be). Initially, only the person involved believes that he has good reasons to trust (Möllering, 2001).

Establishing trust, however, needs more than just good reasons. Möllering argues that people only come to trust if they also suspend uncertainties, ignorance, and risks. Trust involves situations in which persons are not entirely certain, but act as if they are certain. 'Suspension, then, can be defined as the mechanism that brackets out uncertainty and ignorance, thus making interpretative knowledge momentarily "certain"

Reasons

Intentional States   Suspension of
                      Risks/uncertainties   **Trust**

Figure 15.3   The trust-establishing process

and enabling the leap to favourable (or unfavourable) expectations'
(Möllering, 2001: 414). Hence, besides good reasons for trusting, the
trustee needs also some kind of encouragement to take the leap to trust.

In sum, the trust-establishing process involves both interpretation and
suspension (Möllering, 2001). Through interpretation, a trustee attains
reasons for trusting. A precondition for these reasons is that they should
relate fruitfully to the many other intentional states a trustee already has;
they have to fall on fertile grounds. In addition the trustee also needs
encouragement to suspend uncertainties and risks to take the leap to trust.
Figure 15.3 summarizes this process.

Step 2: Interpreting Texts and Actions

The next step in the hermeneutic process consists of the reading and interpretation of the texts. The purpose is to find 'facts' such as words, textual
fragments, or actions that either support or weaken the trust-building
process. The interpreter reads the text first while seeking 'facts' about
how the trust-building process has evolved over time. He or she should,
however, also deliberately look for new 'facts' which teach about the concepts, and the results may entail adjustments or the making of entirely new
concepts. 'The text can be literal, consisting of written or spoken words.
It can also be figurative, in that social acts are regarded as meaningful
symbols' (Alvesson and Sköldberg, 2000: 61).

In practical terms I extract 'facts' from the texts by categorizing words,
acts, events and other social phenomena that can possibly contribute to
the hermeneutic interpretation. The use of a software program for qualitative analysis, such as Atlas.ti, can be useful here. I first underline words
and textual fragments that refer to intentional states, encouragements of
suspension, and utterance of trust (see the underlined words in the texts
below). The underlined words are then grouped together in categories.

In my case study, for instance, I observed that the priest Van den Elsen was using both religious (text 1) and financial (text 2) arguments to win trust for the Raiffeisen banking system.

Text 1

'the bank is foremost a tool for the <u>religious and zealous </u>elevation of the farmers: the true motivation of all social action.' (Van Campen et al., 1949: 40).
  '<u>Christian</u> in the true sense.' (ibid.: 41)
  'every village would become one large <u>Christian family</u>, in which the strong would reach out to the weak, until they would be able to stand up to the struggle of life. Or, to put it in even better words, then everyone would reach out to each other to bear the financial burdens and overcome them. <u>Christianity</u> in its true meaning!' (ibid.: 41)

Text 2

He [Van den Elsen] indicated that the basis of the Raiffeisen-system, the <u>unlimited liability</u>, was supported by different <u>insurances</u>: 'in practice, only the <u>notables</u> of a community would <u>control</u> the bank's board [. . .] in the last 37 years that these types of co-operative banks have existed (in Germany), <u>not</u> one single member due to this liability has had the smallest <u>financial damage</u>. This means that the bourgeois class would <u>not</u> run any <u>dangers</u>, even concerning their capital, if they would take part in these institutions' (ibid.: 41–2).

To me these texts indicate that Van den Elsen was addressing different groups of people, with different reasons, because he had to appeal to different sets of intentional states. A collection of these types of quotes was finally grouped together in the categories: 'Christian values' and 'financial securities'. Note also that Van den Elsen was explicitly encouraging the notables to take part – to take the leap of trust.

Step 3: The Dialogue

The third step is the hermeneutic dialogue. This is a 'dialogue' between the initial understanding, based on the theoretical concepts, and the new facts and findings that were extracted from the texts. This third step is the hermeneutic method's core activity. Hermeneuticians 'use the procedure of asking questions to the text, and listening to it, in a dialogic form', they 'glide back and forth between the "old" aspect imposed on the text in the shape of pre-understanding, and the new understanding' (Alvesson and Sköldberg, 2000: 62). During the reading of the texts, the interpreter initially asks questions which are directly derived from his preconceptions. Concurrently, however, the interpreter should also look for new 'facts' that contradict the preconceptions and push him to specify or adjust his conceptions.
  Obviously, in my case study the hermeneutic dialogue began with

the question of whether or not trust was established and, if so, how it was established and, if not, why not. I tried to understand the trustor's interpretation by asking questions such as: What reasons did the trustor provide for his trust? Why these reasons? How did he communicate these reasons? Did others also communicate these reasons? What is the background of the one who tried to establish trust? What were the reactions of the persons whose trust was desired? What were their backgrounds? Did other individuals have a similar reaction?

In my dialogue with the texts I found that Van den Elsen encouraged people to establish Raiffeisen banks by praising new initiatives, using local trustworthy persons (such as other priests, schoolteachers and mayors) to set up a new local bank, and by continually referring to the Christian character of the banking system (Text 3).

Text 3

> When in 1897 the first initiatives were taken, he was quite excited: 'Hear hear, a small rural bank is functioning! Our compliments to the founder. (Van Campen et al., 1949: 43)
>
> When he visited a community, he arrived early in order to 'secure the co-operation of the local priest and notables (such as schoolteachers) as well as to establish a temporary bank board. By doing so, success was almost always guaranteed. (ibid.: 69)
>
> 'Liability with all one's property for the debts of a bank, is a deed of love, which is incomprehensible for those who are not raised Christians.' (ibid.: 46)

At the same time, however, I also observed that especially rich farmers, who had to provide the money, were not convinced by the religious reasoning. At a national meeting of farmer representatives, one said, for example: 'I do not know Christian money' (ibid.: 46). The consequence was that the priest had to win the trust of different types of people, using different types of arguments. So, besides religious reasoning, Van den Elsen also prepared model statutes to reduce the risks and uncertainties among the rich farmers, and reduce their suspicions.

These observations gave support to my initial trust-establishing theory, because they showed that the use of good reasons is essential to winning trust. I also observed that encouragements were necessary to suspend risks and uncertainties. What was new in these observations, though, was the ambiguous effect of the use of religious arguments. Many found Van den Elsen's appeal to Christian values convincing, but others, especially the rich farmers, were suspicious exactly because of these arguments. Apparently, the same arguments in the trust-building process may trigger opposite reactions at the same time.

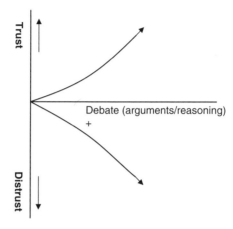

Figure 15.4   The ambiguous trust effect

Step 4: Sub-interpretations

The observations in Step 3 affected my initial theoretical framework. Alvesson and Sköldberg argue that 'In the course of the process of interpretation we continually formulate sub-interpretations' (2000: 62). These new interpretations are a reflection on the initial patterns of interpretation and discuss the modifications to the concepts. They improve our understanding of the way trust is established.

In my case study the sub-interpretation delivered new insights about the fragility of the trust-establishing process and its ambiguity. The same argument intended to win trust may trigger both a reaction of trust or distrust: trust from the general farmer, but distrust from the rich farmer. In other parts of my analysis, I discovered that the more arguments and reasons were given that did not fit within the set of intentional states, the more suspicious and distrustful people became. Figure 15.4 summarizes this effect. This shows that the trust-establishing process is a delicate activity.

RESEARCH VALIDITY CAVEATS

Hermeneutics is mainly used to understand social phenomena in a specific case study. However, as I have illustrated above, the hermeneutic method also helps to discern some modest general patterns (see Figures 15.3 and 15.4). In my larger analysis, I found a couple of such 'social mechanisms'

(Hedström and Swedberg, 1998) – that is, small modular theories, or theories of the middle range (Merton, 1967). They help us to make modest generalizations about observed patterns in specific cases. Thinking in terms of social mechanisms is a 'way out' of using 'only' thick description while not pretending to develop abstract social laws. This is a strength but also a weakness: social mechanisms are modest in their claims, they cannot predict future developments because they 'are triggered under generally unknown condition[s] and they have indeterminate consequences' (Elster, 1999).

Furthermore, the hermeneutic method starts with preselected concepts, partial theories, and some ideas about causal relations. This starting point implies a bias and could result in a sub-optimal understanding of the case at hand. It is therefore necessary to present the initial theoretical concepts beforehand, and to give a good argument about why one has chosen these. My choice for the Möllering 'leap of trust' scheme was based on my research question. I wanted to know more about the trust-establishing process and therefore looked for theories that presented trust as a kind of activity, such as taking a leap.

PERSONAL EXPERIENCE OF USING THE HERMENEUTIC METHOD

Through my case study I obtained a better understanding of the trust-establishing process. At least, I have learned that establishing trust in any individual requires good reasons and encouragements so that he may take the leap of trust, and that this trust-establishing process is delicate and not straightforward. Through the hermeneutic method I now understand better how the trust-building process could develop.

With hermeneutics the test of a good theory is in its heuristic use. In other words, does the theory 'work'? Does it help to explain a situation better than without it? I have been using my trust-building theory in my scholarly work and as a management consultant. For instance, in one case I used my theory to explain why more of the same arguments would be more harmful to winning trust for a policy plan rather than it would be to stop arguing about it (see Figure 15.4). In this particular case, a governor wanted to gain trust from the citizens for a spatial development plan with massive barns for pigs and chickens. He tried to win trust by referring to various scientific reports that supported his plans in terms of economics, animal welfare, and environment. The citizens, however, simply did not want these barns in their backyard, and they became increasingly suspicious of all the extra research the governor was conducting. Once he understood the ambiguity of his conduct, he was able to adjust his behaviour and address the citizens in a different manner. As for myself, I tried to gain more insight into how the spiral of distrust between the governor and the citizens was developing, with the hermeneutic approach. (Termeer et al., 2009). The presentation of this spiral of distrust was recognized by the actors and it helped them further to change their behaviour. And I gained a more detailed theory about how distrust could increase.

DISCUSSION

It is not easy to find trust studies that explicitly use a hermeneutic approach. I believe there are two reasons for this. First, trust research is quantifiable. The competition between research methods is strong, and quantitative methods usually win over the more qualitative ones. Analysing why people trust is easily done by setting up a survey, resulting in long lists or reasons, which in turn is correlated with various variables (Cummings and Bromiley, 1996).

A second reason for not easily finding hermeneutic analyses is that this approach is not always spelled out as a method, when it is applied. In *Trust and Rule*, for instance, Tilly (2005) uses different historical events to analyse how small communities generate interpersonal trust relations and how governments affect these trust relations. Based on his analysis, Tilly argues that democracy benefits from a sound balance between interpersonal trust and governing. Hence, Tilly uses small empirical examples to understand a general pattern of behaviour. Gambetta and Hamill (2005), to give another example, analyse how taxi drivers judge the trustworthiness of their customers. They use informal conversations with taxi drivers and interviews to discern general patterns (Gambetta and Hamill, 2005). Here again, they analyse small pieces of texts (conversations, interviews) to understand a bigger picture. In other words, both these studies clearly employ a hermeneutic approach, but neither of them does so explicitly.

Another realm of trust research in which (parts of) the hermeneutic approach is (are) implicitly being applied, so I believe, is in the literature on social capital. Here scholars try to find ways to increase the level of trust by studying different types of citizen interactions. They ground their analysis on various observations, case analyses, and anecdotes. In *Better Together*, Putnam and Feldstein (2003) describe, for instance, a dozen projects in which local governments seek to win citizens' trust. Based on these specific analyses, the authors present a list of ways to restore trust. Again, their work typifies the hermeneutic approach, because they are using small experiences to understand a general pattern better.

Perhaps the only field in which one can easily find the explicit use of hermeneutic methods to study trust is religious studies. Theologians use the hermeneutic method frequently, and how trust is established is one of their core concerns. A nice example is von Sinner's 'Trust and convivência: contributions to a hermeneutics of trust in communal interaction' (2009). In this article, he analyses first how trust is established, by using specific (biblical) texts and stories, and then applies his findings to building trust in an ecumenical community.

REFERENCES

Alvesson, M. and K. Sköldberg (2000), *Reflexive Methodology: New Vistas for Qualitative Research,* London: Sage.

Blackburn, S. (1998), 'Trust, cooperation, and human psychology', in V. Braithwaite and M. Levi (eds), *Trust and Governance,* New York: Russell Sage Foundation, pp. 28–45.

Breeman, G. (2006), *Cultivating Trust: How Do Public Policies become Trusted?* Rotterdam: Optima Grafische Communicatie.

Castaldo, S. (2002), 'Meanings of trust: a meta-analysis of trust definitions', paper presented at the 2nd Annual Conference on Innovative Research in Management, 9–12 May, Stockholm, European Academy of Management.

Cummings, L.L. and P. Bromiley (1996), 'The organizational trust inventory (OTI): development and validations', in R.M. Kramer and T.R. Tyler (eds), *Trust in Organizations: Frontiers of Theory and Research,* Thousand Oaks, CA: Sage, pp. 302–30.

Elster, J. (1999), *The Alchemies of the Mind: Rationality and the Emotions,* Cambridge: Cambridge University Press.

Gambetta, D. and Hamill, H. (2005), *Streetwise: How Taxi Drivers Establish Their Customers' Trustworthiness,* New York: Russell Sage Foundation.

Habermas, J. (1969), *Protestbewegung und Hochschulreform,* Frankfurt: Suhrkamp.

Hedström, P. and R. Swedberg (eds) (1998), *Social Mechanisms: An Analytical Approach to Social Theory,* Cambridge: Cambridge University Press.

Holton, R. (1994), 'Deciding to trust, coming to believe', *Australasian Journal of Philosophy,* **72** (1), 63–76.

Merton, R.K. (1967), 'On sociological theories of the middle range', in R.K. Merton, *On Theoretical Sociology: Five Essays, Old and New,* New York: The Free Press.

Möllering, G. (2001), 'The nature of trust: from Georg Simmel to a theory of expectation, interpretation and suspension', *Sociology,* **35** (2), 403–20.

Putnam, R.D. and L.M. Feldstein (2003), *Better Together: Restoring the American Community,* New York: Simon and Schuster.

Schüz, G. (2001), *Lebensganzheid und Wesensoffenheid de Menschen: Otto Friedrich Bollnows Hermeneutische Anthropologie,* Würzburg: Königshausen and Neumann.

Searle, J.R. (1983), *Intentionality: An Essay in the Philosophy of Mind,* Cambridge: Cambridge University Press.

Searle, J.R. (1996), *The Construction of Social Reality,* London: Penguin.

Seligman, A.B. (1997), *The Problem of Trust,* Princeton: Princeton University Press.

Sneller, Z.W. (ed.) (1943), *Geschiedenis van den Nederlandschen Landbouw 1795–1940,* Groningen: Wolters.

Termeer, C.J.A.M., M. van Lieshout, G. Breeman and W. Pot (2009), *Politieke besluitvorming over het Landbouwontwikkelingsgebied Witveldweg in de Gemeente Horst aan de Maas,* Wageningen: Leerstoelgroep Bestuurskunde.

Tilly, C. (2005), *Trust and Rule,* Cambridge: Cambridge University Press.

Van Campen, P.C.M, P. Hollenberg and F. Kriellaars (1949), *Landbouw en Landbouwcrediet*

1898-1948: Vijftig jaar Geschiedenis van de Coöperatieve Centrale Boerenleenbank, Eindhoven: Coöperatieve Centrale Boerenleenbank.
von Sinner, R. (2009), 'Trust and convivência: contributions to a hermeneutics of trust in communal interaction', *Ecumenical Review*, **57** (3), 322–41.
Weber, M. (1972), *Wirtschaft und Gesellschaft*, Tübingen: J.C.B. Mohr (Paul Siebeck).

Annotated Further Reading

Alvesson, M. and K. Sköldberg (2000), *Reflexive Methodology: New Vistas for Qualitative Research*, London: Sage. This book gives a general introduction of different kinds of qualitative research methods. In particular chapter 3 provides a nice overview of the hermeneutic method.
Sinner, R. von (2009), 'Trust and convivência: contributions to a hermeneutics of trust in communal interaction', *Ecumenical Review*, **57** (3), 322–41. This article is a good example of how the hermeneutic method can be applied on historic texts and how the findings, in turn, may be applied to new events.

16 Using critical incident technique in trust research
Robert Münscher and Torsten M. Kühlmann

INTRODUCTION

The critical incident technique provides a number of advantages for researching trust and trust dynamics in specific contexts or relationships, and for realising comparative (including cross-cultural) studies on trust. In this chapter we show that it is especially suited to collecting data on the behaviours involved in creating, strengthening or destroying trust.

Trust is not easy to research empirically. Trust phenomena, like the development of trust or the assessment of trustworthiness, are often not reflected on or take place subconsciously in everyday life. A well-tried and sound way to collect and analyse rich data on such phenomena is the critical incident technique (CIT). Since its introduction by Flanagan (1954), CIT has proven valuable in quite a number of research disciplines, and has become increasingly important for trust research. Focusing on behavioural sequences in specific contexts, CIT helps to avoid researching subjects' folk psychological theories about trust, but instead collects detailed descriptions of real-life situations in which trust is created, strengthened or destroyed. To date, few methodological reflections on CIT are available, but with the method being adapted more and more to new research contexts, the literature is slowly growing (Chell, 1998; Gremler, 2004; Kemppainen, 2000).

DESCRIPTION OF THE METHOD

Basics of the Approach

When deciding whether to trust someone, the partner's behaviour is a most valuable source of information. From a research point of view, it thus appears promising to ask respondents for a report of those incidents involving their own or their partner's behaviour that they take to be critical for creating, strengthening or destroying trust. This means applying a method to trust research that was originally developed by US psychologist

John F. Flanagan in a number of studies, starting back in the 1940s. Flanagan's aim 'to obtain valid information regarding the truly critical requirements for success in a specific assignment' (Flanagan, 1954: 329) still adequately describes the core of the method. More specifically, CIT serves to determine those requirements 'which have been demonstrated to have made the difference between success and failure in carrying out an important part of the job assigned in a significant number of instances' (ibid.).

Following Flanagan, CIT is traditionally used to collect and analyse incidents in order to determine the critical requirements for effective behaviour. From a more general point of view, analysing critical incidents, or CIs, is a way to determine triggers and other influencing factors regarding different sorts of phenomena. Recent applications also use CIT in order to determine critical factors of cognitive processes like developing decisions or forming attitudes (Chell, 1998; Roos, 2002). This keeps the focus on situated behaviours, but criticality refers not to the actor realising an activity, but to the one observing the behaviours of the actor. Respondents are asked to describe which behaviours of their partner were critical for their developing a decision or forming an attitude. For example, customers are asked to report incidents they consider to be critical for their decision to change their service provider (Keaveney, 1995). In the same vein, in our research we asked managers to report incidents that were critical for them to trust (or not to trust) their partner (see below).

Application Contexts

Much of Flanagan's use of CIT for determining critical requirements for job performance basically aimed at selection and training of personnel (Flanagan, 1954; for this application of CIT also see Krause and Gebert, 2003). In other studies CIT served to understand how workplace design may handicap job performance, and thus help to implement design changes (Flanagan, 1954; Maguire, 2001). CIT has also been used to address performance measurement (for example White and Locke, 1981), assessment of intercultural competence (for example McAllister et al., 2006) and development of intercultural training tools (for example Brislin and Cushner, 1986). In recent years much CIT research has been realised in nursing (for example Norman et al., 1992), education (e.g. Copas, 1984) and services marketing and management (for example Bitner et al., 1990; Keaveney, 1995). In summary, the general nature of the CIT framework allows for a wide range of application contexts in trust research and elsewhere.

Sampling

Obviously, CIT studies need to assure that the respondents selected have experienced CIs and are able and willing to report on them. As for defining sample size, it should be taken into account that it is generally difficult to get respondents to provide usable CIs. In his analysis of CIT studies in service research, Gremler (2004: 73) found that the average number of incidents collected per respondent was only 1.3. In other research contexts, higher numbers are possible, but the number of CIs per person is unlikely to exceed 10. If the researcher chooses to sample CIs directly (as opposed to sampling research subjects), and collects more than one CI per person, it has to be considered in data analysis that the elements of the sample are not independent (for sampling strategies see Chapter 8 in this volume).

Data Collection

Different methods are used to collect data for CIT studies. Flanagan (1954: 326ff.) trained observers to report CIs according to clear specifications. If it is possible for researchers to observe the activities of their research subjects and record CIs, they gain direct access to their actions, and the data will not suffer from memory biases. However, this presupposes Flanagan's (1954: 327) CI definition as an 'observable human activity that is sufficiently complete in itself to permit inferences and predictions to be made about the person performing the act'. The research subjects' interpretation of observable behaviours cannot be investigated this way. Furthermore, many research contexts might not allow for participant observers at all (for example trust development in foreign companies), and if they do, the observers' presence might influence the research subjects' behaviours, thus challenging data validity. Flanagan himself, over time, switched to collecting CI reports provided by research subjects. This is the usual approach in current usage of CIT. In some studies, respondents are asked to write down their CIs in paper and pencil or online questionnaires (Neale et al., 2000). The main data collection tool in CIT studies, however, is the interview (Gremler, 2004). Respondents are asked to describe CIs, allowing the interviewer to ask questions of clarification or request the interviewee to go into detail at certain points of the report.

Data Analysis

CIT yields mainly unstructured data. This creates a need for a classification system to provide insights regarding the structure and the dynamics of the phenomenon of interest (Gremler, 2004: 66). The basic distinction here is that between a deductive approach, which applies classification categories deduced from a theoretical model (content analysis, Krippendorff, 2004), and inductive approaches, which are used to develop the classification system by using inductive interpretation techniques (for example grounded theory, Strauss and Corbin, 1990, or qualitative content analysis, Mayring, 2004). When the data has been coded by help of the classification system, frequency analyses become possible (Srnka and Köszegi, 2007). For category development as well as coding so-called qualitative data analysis (QDA) software packages are of invaluable assistance to the researcher (for example Atlas.ti®, NVivo® or MAXqda®).

Study Designs

CIT is predominantly used for exploratory research aiming at theory development, but it has also been used in hypothesis-testing designs (Chell, 1998; Gremler, 2004). Generally speaking, CIT-generated data can be used both qualitatively – allowing for narrative analysis and inductive category building – and quantitatively, aiming at assessing 'the type, nature and frequency of incidents which when linked with other variables . . . can provide important insights into general relationships' (Chell and Pittaway, 1998: 26).

Furthermore, CIT can be used in different combinations with other methods. Following the typology of Teddlie and Tashakkori (2006), study designs can be classified according to the number of research strands. For example, researchers can employ CIT and other methods as a sequential mix. CIT might help to develop a quantitative survey instrument that is put to use as a second step (for example Miller et al., 2000). Alternatively, CIT results might assist in creating realistic scenarios for a subsequent experiment (for example Swanson and Kelley, 2001).

A different approach is the conversion mix: there is no two-step data collection, but the data type from one data collection process is converted into another type in order to allow for further analyses. As for CIT studies, this usually means what the literature refers to as 'quantitising' (Teddlie and Tashakkori, 2006: 17). Qualitative data types (such as narratives of CIs) are converted into numerical codes that can be analysed statistically (Miles and Huberman, 1994). This may be done by rating CIs according to aspects that are relevant to the research question (for example conditions, criticality, effect). Another option is coding the CI data by assigning categories to text passages, thereby obtaining frequency data (Srnka and Köszegi, 2007) for further analysis. Given a (quasi-)experimental sample structure, these frequency data can be used for comparative analyses of subgroups like in our project (see below).

RESEARCH VALIDITY CAVEATS

While offering a way to collect rich data on trust phenomena, CIT none-theless presents a number of challenges to reliability and validity in both data collection and analysis. In this section we describe ways to meet these challenges and illustrate them by drawing on our own research.

Assuring Quality in Data Collection

In CIT data collection it is key to obtain detailed and realistic descriptions of trust-related CIs. In this section, we present strategies for assuring that the method actually yields such data concerning the trust phenomena to be investigated. They primarily address the most promising data collection technique, that is, face-to-face interviews.

Focus on details and process orientation
It is advisable to ask interviewees to report CIs in as much detail as possible, and to encourage them to follow the chronological development of the incident strictly (Franke and Kühlmann, 1985). As a visual aid, the researcher can offer the interviewee a sheet of paper containing a time line (Chell, 1998). These measures support the recollection process of the interviewee and facilitate structuring the data afterwards. It also counter-acts interview bias phenomena, such as social desirability (Crowne and Marlow, 1964).

Combination of perspectives
In CIT data collection it can be advisable to look for both positive and negative CIs, that is, to collect incidents both where 'it worked' and where 'it didn't work'. In trust research, a joint look at CIs enhancing trust and CIs destroying trust can help to give a better understanding of the nature of trust development (Butler, 1991). In our research we even took one step further and also combined the perspective of assessing the trustworthiness of others with the perspective of demonstrating one's own trustworthiness towards others ('trust-building measures'). This double combination of perspectives served as a way of data triangulation (Denzin, 1977), enhancing validity by addressing trust development from different perspectives.

Memory-enhancing techniques
Interview data may generally suffer from memory distortions (Loftus, 1991; Pohl, 2004). This is especially true if they address processes which do not necessarily take place consciously – such as trust dynamics. However,

scholars in forensic psychology have applied insights from memory research to interviewing (Fisher and Geiselman, 1992). Interviewees should be urged to report details that they take to be insignificant because recalling context information improves recollection of more important aspects. Interviewers should also flexibly track and support the recollection process of the interviewees, allowing them to switch between positive and negative CIs and to violate the principle of chronological reporting. A third technique we used was to ask interviewees who had difficulties recalling details to take a different point of view for describing the incident. For example, we asked them to imagine being in court and justifying their trusting (or not trusting) attitude.

Neutral interview behaviour

Especially in non-standardised interviews on sensitive issues such as trust, interviewers run the risk of involuntarily influencing their interviewees (Salazaar, 1990). It is therefore advisable to restrict interviewing to the use of neutral prompts and clarifying questions (Arksey and Knight, 1999). Examples include: who was involved? What happened next? What was the result? Could you explain this in detail?

Assuring Quality in Data Analysis

In CIT data analysis the different analytical steps imply different quality requirements. Since CIT yields unstructured data, a basic quality requirement is the intersubjective transparency of the analytical process. Researchers should report the rules and procedures for transcription, data structuring, identifying units of analysis, developing categories, coding the data and running reliability tests (Flick, 2008; Münscher, 2011).

The process of identifying units of analysis in an unstructured CI data set may be biased. In order to assure the validity of deriving units, that is, 'unitisation', researchers need to define clear rules for identifying which text passages are to be considered relevant to the question of analysis (Krippendorff, 2004). Furthermore, researchers should control for *reliability* in applying these rules. One should check whether independent coders, according to the previously defined rules for identifying relevant text passages, concur in defining units of analysis within the data (Srnka and Köszegi, 2007).

When using trust-related categories to code the units of analysis (content analysis), the researcher generally aims at mapping some structure of meaning (text) onto a formal structure (numbers). Accordingly, assuring validity of coding in CIT data analysis means taking care that the categories are well suited to describe the relevant aspects of the CIs according to the research question. Additionally, the categories should be well defined, mutually exclusive and exhaustive (Krippendorff, 2004).

This relates to the issue of reliability of coding. When the researcher inductively develops the coding categories, intercoder tests help to check whether the categories actually enable trained and independent coders to reproduce the same coding (for an overview of intercoder reliability indices see Gremler, 2004: 74). In research projects with large time horizons it may also be necessary to check for intracoder reliability repeatedly, in order to ensure that the coding scheme is applied consistently over time by one and the same coder.

PERSONAL EXPERIENCES USING CIT TO RESEARCH INTERCULTURAL MANAGEMENT

In the following we report experiences from using CIT in our own research on trust. Particularly, we discuss the methods of data collection and analysis that we chose to realise CIT according to our research context and questions.

In a research project we investigated how cultural difference can influence trust development and the assessment of trustworthiness (Münscher, 2008, 2011). Since the German and French economies are highly interrelated and the extant literature reports German–French cultural differences (Pateau, 1998; Pill, 2006), we chose to analyse trust in German–French business interactions. Our principal research question was: do managers from both nations weigh trust development factors differently? Given such differences, we were interested in how they could possibly lead to misattributions of trustworthiness.

CIT appeared well-suited for the project. Cross-cultural research on trust development requires a fairly differentiated account of trust development factors, that is the different aspects that play a role in the decision to trust others. This is because in different cultures people possibly weigh and interpret behavioural trust cues differently. Given the same behavioural cue, a manager from one culture might clearly interpret it as a certain trust building factor while a manager from another culture may not do so. Since the literature did not provide such a detailed account, our first step was to apply CIT in order to develop one. CIs of trust development in management relationships were collected and served to determine inductively the trust factors used by German and French managers. Our sample consisted of 100 hour-long interviews with German and French middle- and upper-level executives who worked for multinational companies and reported CIs in a total of 850 different management relationships. The resulting classification system covered a total of 60 trust development factors organised in 12 fields of management activity (Münscher, 2011).

Advantages of Using Interviews for Data Collection

One challenge of collecting trust development CIs is that the corresponding psychological processes in daily life are most often not reflected on or take place subconsciously (Greenwald et al., 2006). Our research on trust clearly showed that it is difficult for respondents to recall detailed and observable aspects of incidents that were critical for trust development. For different reasons, respondents may also just not be willing to go into detail when describing trust-related incidents (Edvardsson and Roos, 2001). We therefore chose to employ an open interview method (Kvale and Brinkmann, 2009) and conducted face-to-face interviews. In our experience this also helped to build trust with the interviewees, and at the beginning of the interviews we could explain in detail why and how we worked with the CI method. This enhanced the interviewees' willingness to report detailed CIs. Moreover, we could use memory-enhancing techniques to support the respondents in selecting CIs and recalling important details.

Even though we asked them to report CIs, we found that managers tended to describe trust development factors on a rather abstract level. Clarifying questions and the insistence on behavioural details revealed that managerial trust terminology is considerably plurivalent. For example, our interviewees used the term 'openness' to refer to quite a number of different behaviours (including 'share knowledge', 'manage conflicts proactively', 'talk about private affairs', 'reveal goals or assessments').

Different Steps in CIT Data Analysis

We used the CI data for developing a classification system of trust development factors. To do so, we ran an inductive category-building process using qualitative content analysis (Mayring, 2004) which involved the following steps.

Transcribing the interviews was necessary due to the plurivalence of trust terminology. Transcripts facilitate the comparing of statements and clarifications given at different sections of the interview in order to ensure that the interviewees' accounts are interpreted correctly.

Furthermore, we found that interview-based CIT data collection tends to yield fragmented CIs, especially if the interviewer flexibly tracks and supports the recollection process of the interviewee. Information concerning a given CI is found at different sections of the interview. Bringing those pieces together facilitated and enhanced data analysis. Another reason for data structuring was that our interviewees tended to comment on the CIs they reported, developing hypotheses or elaborating folk psychological theories on trust development. It was thus necessary to isolate the genuine trust-development CIs (observational level) from those comments (more abstract level).

We first marked all descriptions of behavioural cues that the interviewees referred to in order to justify why they built or lost trust ('units of analysis', Krippendorff, 2004). The second step was category building. We did not use a predefined conceptual framework but rather followed an exploratory study design in order to develop a differentiated account of trust development factors inductively. To do so, we processed the units of analysis one by one, looking for repetition of patterns and grouping similar units into categories and subcategories (Mayring, 2004). As more and more units were processed, category definitions were developed and refined, rules of category differentiation established, and sample units collected. As a result, a coding manual of trust-development factors emerged which we could use to code the data. Nearly all units of analysis could be assigned to categories of the classification system – thus getting 'from words to numbers' (Srnka and Köszegi, 2007). We then used the resulting frequency distributions of trust development factor codings for statistical cross-cultural comparisons.

DISCUSSION

CIT is a method of data collection and analysis that presents a number of advantages for researching trust. First, the creation, strengthening or destruction of trust in a partner depends in many ways on the behaviour of this partner. Collecting CI reports on trust development is a promising way of understanding how situated behaviour affects trust decisions. Second, CIT is especially suited for exploratory approaches. It can help to investigate trust in new or very specific contexts or relationships. As an exploratory tool, CIT can be combined with other approaches. 'CIT can be particularly effective when used in developing the conceptual structure (that is, hypotheses) to be used and tested in subsequent research' (Gremler, 2004: 67). However, one can also use CIT in mixed methods designs, such as for determining a set of domain-specific trust development factors and using them afterwards to code data and run frequency analyses as we did in our research project. Third, given the multiple meanings of the trust concept and the 'conceptual morass' of trust definitions (Barber, 1983: 1), CIT helps researchers as well as respondents to focus. It 'facilitates the revelation of those issues which are of critical importance to the interviewee' (Chell, 1998: 68). CIT 'often results in useful information that is more rigorously defined than many other qualitative approaches' because it forces researchers 'to define the "specific aim" of their study and helps identify important thematic details, with vivid examples to support their findings' (Gremler, 2004: 68). The method is well tried and has been found to be both reliable and valid for generating comprehensive insights into specific content domains (Andersson and Nilsson, 1964). Finally, trust development is a subject of practical relevance, for example in management, and CIT 'provides relevant, unequivocal, and very concrete information for managers' and 'can suggest practical areas for improvement' (Gremler, 2004: 67).

While there are many benefits of using CIT in trust research, some drawbacks need to be considered. For a number of reasons CIT data collection may be difficult. Respondents may hesitate to disclose critical experiences concerning trust development, or not be willing to participate at all. Furthermore, 'the CIT interview is not easy to conduct well. It requires a skilled and mature researcher who can manage the respondent, directing the interview to achieve clarity of understanding, and who can handle the expression of emotion including distress' (Chell, 1998: 69). In addition, data analysis (including transcription, category development and coding) is very time consuming. All this brings about that CIT projects usually work with much smaller numbers of respondents than do large quantitative sample surveys. Researchers therefore need to adopt different generalisation strategies or use CIT in addition to other methods.

Altogether, CIT offers a most valuable and versatile approach to gain a better understanding of trust and trust dynamics in specific contexts or cultures. It can be used to determine how a partner's behaviour affects the creation, strengthening or destruction of trust. CIT can be used to analyse trust development through individual incidents or interrelated series of CIs within one and the same relationship ('critical threads') (Carroll et al., 1993).

REFERENCES

Andersson, B.E. and S.G. Nilsson (1964), 'Studies in the reliability and validity of the critical incident technique', *Journal of Applied Psychology*, **48** (6), 398–403.
Arksey, H. and P. Knight (1999), *Interviewing for Social Scientists: An Introductory Resource with Examples*, Thousand Oaks, CA: Sage.
Barber, B. (1983), *The Logic and Limits of Trust*, New Brunswick, NJ: Rutgers University Press.
Bitner, M.J., B.H. Booms and M.S. Tetreault (1990), 'The service encounter: diagnosing favorable and unfavorable incidents', *Journal of Marketing*, **54** (1), 71–84.
Brislin, R.W. and K. Cushner (1986), *Intercultural Interactions: A Practical Guide*, Thousand Oaks, CA: Sage.

Butler, J.K. (1991), 'Toward understanding and measuring conditions of trust: evolution of a conditions of trust inventory', *Journal of Management*, **17** (3), 643–63.

Carroll, J.M., J. Koenemann-Belliveau, M.B. Rosson and M.K. Singley (1993), 'Critical incidents and critical themes in empirical usability evaluation', in J.L. Alty, D. Diaper and S. Guest (eds), *People and Computers VIII. Proceedings of the HCI '93 Conference, September 1993*, Cambridge: Cambridge University Press, pp. 279–92.

Chell, E. (1998), 'Critical incident technique', in G. Symon and C. Cassell (eds), *Qualitative Methods and Analysis in Organizational Research: A Practical Guide*, Thousand Oaks, CA: Sage, pp. 51–72.

Chell, E. and L. Pittaway (1998), 'A study of entrepreneurship in the restaurant and café industry: exploratory work using the critical incident technique as a methodology', *International Journal of Hospitality Management*, **17** (1), 23–32.

Copas, E.M. (1984), 'Critical requirements for cooperating teachers', *Journal of Teacher Education*, **35** (6), 49–54.

Crowne, D.P. and D. Marlow (1964), *The Approval Motive: Studies in Evaluative Dependence*, New York: Wiley.

Denzin, N.K. (1977), *The Research Act: A Theoretical Instruction to Sociological Methods*, 2nd edition, New York: McGraw-Hill.

Edvardsson, B. and I. Roos (2001), 'Critical incident techniques: towards a framework for analyzing the criticality of critical incidents', *International Journal of Service Industry Management*, **12** (3), 251–68.

Fisher, R. and R.E. Geiselman (1992), *Memory Enhancing Techniques for Investigative Interviewing: The Cognitive Interview*, Springfield, IL: C.C. Thomas.

Flanagan, J.C. (1954), 'The critical incident technique', *Psychological Bulletin*, **51** (4), 327–58.

Flick, U. (2008), *Managing Quality in Qualitative Research*, Thousand Oaks, CA: Sage.

Franke, J. and T.M. Kühlmann (1985), 'Erkunden: Zur Handhabung einer variantenreichen Führungsaufgabe', *Zeitschrift Führung und Organisation*, **54**, 337–41.

Greenwald, A.G., M.R. Banaji, L.A. Rudman, S.D. Farnham, B.A. Nosek, and D.S. Mellott (2006), 'A unified theory of implicit attitudes, stereotypes, self-esteem, and self-concept', *Psychological Review*, **109** (1), 3–25.

Gremler, D.D. (2004), 'The critical incident technique in service research', *Journal of Service Research*, **7** (1), 65–89.

Keaveney, S.M. (1995), 'Customer switching behaviour in service industries: an exploratory study', *Journal of Marketing*, **59** (2), 71–82.

Kempppainen, J.K. (2000), 'The critical incident technique and nursing care quality research', *Journal of Advanced Nursing*, **32** (5), 1264–71.

Krause, D.E. and D. Gebert (2003), 'A comparison of assessment center practices in organizations in German-speaking regions and the United States', *International Journal of Selection and Assessment*, **11** (4), 297–312.

Krippendorff, K. (2004), *Content Analysis: An Introduction to Its Methodology*, 2nd edition, Thousand Oaks, CA: Sage.

Kvale, S. and S. Brinkmann (2009), *Interviews: Learning the Craft of Qualitative Research Interviewing*, 2nd edition, Los Angeles: Sage.

Loftus, E.F. (1991), 'Made in memory: distortions in recollection', in G.H. Bower (ed.), *The Psychology of Learning and Motivation*, San Diego, CA and New York, NY: Harcourt Brace Academic Press, pp. 187–216.

Maguire, M. (2001), 'Methods to support human-centred design', *International Journal of Human-Computer Studies*, **55** (4), 587–634.

Mayring, P. (2004), 'Qualitative content analysis', in U. Flick, E.V. Kardorff, and I. Steinke (eds), *A Companion to Qualitative Research*, Thousand Oaks, CA: Sage, pp. 266–9.

McAllister, L., G. Whiteford, B. Hill, N. Thomas and M. Fitzgerald (2006), 'Reflection in intercultural learning: examining the international experience through a critical incident approach', *Reflective Practice*, **7** (3), 367–81.

Miles, M.B. and M.A. Huberman (1994), *Qualitative Data Analysis*, 2nd edition, Thousand Oaks, CA: Sage.

Miller, J.L., C.W. Craighead and K.R. Karwan (2000), 'Service recovery: a framework and empirical investigation', *Journal of Operations Management*, **18** (4), 387–400.

Münscher, R. (2008), 'Relationship management für Führungskräfte. Ein Modul für das interkulturelle Training deutscher und französischer Manager', in E. Jammal (ed.), *Vertrauen im interkulturellen Kontext,* Wiesbaden: VS Verlag für Sozialwissenschaften, pp. 151–92.

Münscher, R. (2011), *Vertrauensentwicklung im interkulturellen Management. Ein empirischer Beitrag am Beispiel der deutsch-französischen Zusammenarbeit*, Wiesbaden: Gabler.

Neale, D.C., D.R. Dunlap, P.L. Isenhour and J.M. Carroll (2000), 'Collaborative critical incident development', in *Proceedings of the 44th annual meeting of the Human Factors and Ergonomics Society*, Santa Monica: Human Factors and Ergonomics Society, pp. 598–601.

Norman, I.J., S.J. Redfern, D.A. Tomalin and S. Oliver (1992), 'Developing Flangans's critical incident technique to elicit indicators of high and low quality nursing care from patients and their nurses', *Journal of Advanced Nursing*, **17** (5), 590–600.

Pateau, J. (1998), *Une Etrange Alchimie. La Dimension Interculturelle dans la Cooperation Franco-Allemande*, Levallois-Perret: Circac.

Pill, S.D. (2006), *Germans and French in Business Life: Intercultural Differences Between the Neighbouring Countries,* Saarbrücken: Dr Müller.

Pohl, R.F. (ed.) (2004), *Cognitive Illusions: A Handbook on Fallacies and Biases in Thinking, Judgement and Memory*, London: Psychology Press, pp. 363–78.

Roos, I. (2002), 'Methods of investigating critical incidents', *Journal of Service Research*, **4** (3), 193–204.

Salazaar, M.K. (1990), 'Interviewer bias: how it affects survey research', *American Association of Occupational Health Nurses Journal*, **38** (12), 567–72.

Srnka, K.J. and S.T. Köszegi (2007), 'From words to numbers: how to transform qualitative data into meaningful quantitative results', *Schmalenbach Business Review*, **59** (1), 29–57.

Strauss, A. and J.M. Corbin (1990), *Basics of Qualitative Research: Grounded Theory Procedures and Techniques*, Thousand Oaks, CA: Sage.

Swanson, S.R. and S.W. Kelley (2001), 'Service recovery attributions and word-of-mouth intentions', *European Journal of Marketing*, **35** (1–2), 194–211.

Teddlie, C. and A. Tashakkori (2006), 'A general typology of research designs featuring mixed methods', *Research in the Schools*, **13** (1), 12–28.

White, F.M. and E.A. Locke (1981), 'Perceived determinants of high and low productivity in three occupational groups: a critical incident study', *Journal of Management Studies*, **18** (4), 375–87.

Annotated Further Reading

Flanagan, J.C. (1954), 'The critical incident technique', *Psychological Bulletin*, **51** (4), 327–58. The seminal paper which, drawing on a huge number of studies, set the foundations for CIT research and is still a most valuable introduction to the method.

Gremler, D.D. (2004), 'The critical incident technique in service research', *Journal of Service Research*, **7** (1), 65–89. A good overview paper which undertakes a systematic methodological review of a total of 141 recent CIT studies in service marketing and management publications.

PART III

QUANTITATIVE APPROACHES

17 Measuring trust in organizational contexts: an overview of survey-based measures
Nicole Gillespie

INTRODUCTION

The organizational trust literature has burgeoned over the past two decades. Whilst this expanding research has produced increasing coherence on the conceptualization and definition of trust, the same cannot be said about the psychometric measurement of trust. Rather, the measurement of trust has received scant attention, resulting in a highly fragmented and idiosyncratic use of trust measures, and a confusing array of instruments that vary widely in construct validity and the number and type of trust dimensions (McEvily and Tortoriello, 2011).

This chapter aims to provide researchers with insights into the issues and challenges involved in measuring trust in organizational settings through survey measures. Drawing on existing reviews, as well as my own review of the literature, I discuss the strengths and limitations of the psychometric measurement of trust, and provide recommendations for choosing appropriate trust instruments. I conclude by reflecting on my experience of searching for an appropriate trust scale and how this led to the development of a new scale, the Behavioral Trust Inventory. The rationale, methodology and challenges involved in developing this inventory are described, along with its validity and appropriate application.

Before discussing the measurement of trust, it is essential first to clarify what we mean by trust. In the organizational literature, there has been increasing convergence on the defining conceptual features of trust. Since the seminal work of Mayer et al. (1995), organizational researchers have increasingly defined trust as 'the willingness to be vulnerable to the actions of another party.' In a cross-disciplinary collection of trust research and theory, Rousseau and colleagues, identified convergence around this definition, and proposed their own closely related definition: 'Trust is a psychological state comprising the intention to accept vulnerability based upon positive expectations of the intentions or behavior of another' (1998: 395). These two definitions have been cited extensively: based on the Web of Science, McEvily and Tortoriello (2011) report over 1,300 and 650 citations for each of these definitions, respectively.

In addition to the view that vulnerability is central, there is considerable agreement on two other conditions required for trust to exist. These are risk and interdependence (for example Bigley and Pearce, 1998; Hosmer, 1995; Rousseau et al., 1998; Zand, 1972). As many scholars note, risk creates the opportunity for trust (for example Hosmer, 1995; Lewis and Weigert, 1985; Luhmann, 1988). Zand (1972) states that trusting behavior occurs in situations where the penalty if the other abuses trust is greater than the benefit one gains if the other does not abuse trust. Uncertainty regarding how the other will act is a key source of risk.

In line with Mayer and colleagues' (1995) model, and a recent meta-analysis of the trust literature (Colquitt et al., 2007), the distinction is made between trust, perceived trustworthiness and trusting behavior. Perceived trustworthiness refers to perceptions and beliefs about the trustworthy character of another. Several dimensions of trustworthiness have been proposed in the literature, including ability, integrity, benevolence, predictability, openness and loyalty (Butler, 1991; Dietz and den Hartog, 2006; Mayer et al., 1995). While beliefs on trustworthiness, along with other antecedent factors such as disposition to trust, are understood to inform the decision to trust (see Colquitt et al., 2007; Mayer et al., 1995), trust often requires a 'leap of faith' that goes beyond such assessments (Lewis and Weigert, 1985; Möllering, 2006). Trusting behavior is the behavioral manifestation or enactment of trust (for example a leader delegating an important task or confiding confidential information to a follower).

Given the adopted definition of trust as a psychological state, this chapter focuses on the measurement of trust at the individual-level. However, the referent or target of trust may be an individual (interpersonal trust) or a collective (such as a team, group or organization). The focus of this chapter is restricted to intra-organizational relationships, excluding measures of trust between organizations, as well as measures of the disposition to trust that reflect a person's generalized tendency to trust others. On the basis of conceptual work suggesting that trust and distrust are distinct constructs (Lewicki et al., 1998; Sitkin and Roth, 1993), this chapter also excludes discussion of distrust measures and the related mechanisms of suspicion, control, surveillance and monitoring.

DESCRIPTION OF THE METHOD

The psychometric measurement of trust refers to the use of a multi-item survey of questions designed to capture one or more dimensions of trust.

This approach is arguably the dominant method for assessing trust in the organizational sciences. Its popularity can be understood through three major strengths of this technique. First, given the conceptualization of trust as a psychological state, confidential survey questions are well suited to capture individuals' perceptions and intentions. Second, pre-existing trust instruments can be used across studies, enabling the replication of results. Third, the construct validity of psychometric instruments can be assessed through rigorous, transparent and well-accepted methods, providing the researcher with confidence that the measures tap the intended constructs.

Unfortunately, these potential strengths of the psychometric approach are rarely realized in the organizational trust literature. Rather, recent reviews of trust measurement in the organizational sciences (Dietz and den Hartog, 2006; McEvily and Tortoriello, 2011) collectively reveal three serious limitations:

1. *The fragmented and idiosyncratic use of trust instruments.* Rather than adopting pre-existing measures, and hence deriving the benefits that replication affords, trust measurement in the organizational sciences is highly fragmented. In a recent detailed review of organizational trust measures, McEvily and Tortoriello (2011) analysed 171 trust papers published over the past 48 years, identifying a total of 129 unique measures of trust. Of these measures, more than half were newly developed rather than replications of previously validated instruments, and only 22 instruments had been replicated more than once. Further analysis revealed that the accuracy of replication was also low, with changes in wording and/or number of items so substantial as to question whether they represent the original measure.

2. *Construct validity.* The construct validity of many trust measures is a further cause for concern. For example, McEvily and Tortoriello (2011) identify that for most studies, the information reported was insufficient for evaluating how accurately trust had been measured, with most measures only reporting reliability statistics. Where construct validity is provided, this typically takes the form of exploratory or confirmatory factor analysis only, with few measures displaying evidence of convergent or discriminant validity. Furthermore, although trust is widely conceptualized as a multifaceted construct, recent reviews reveal that the vast majority of measures treat trust as a unidimensional construct (Dirks and Ferrin, 2002; McEvily and Tortoriello, 2011). This may, in part, reflect the lack of validated multidimensional measures historically available.

3. *The gap between the conceptualization and measurement of trust.* Most

research on trust in organizations has neglected to link the conceptual definition of trust with its operational definition (Currall and Judge, 1995; Gillespie, 2003). Despite widespread use of the Mayer et al., (1995) and Rousseau et al. (1998) definitions of trust, researchers rarely adopt trust instruments that directly measure the 'willingness to be vulnerable' or 'intention to accept vulnerability.' Rather, as three recent reviews identify, the large majority of studies use measures of perceived trustworthiness rather than trust (Dietz and den Hartog, 2006; Dirks and Ferrin, 2002; McEvily and Tortoriello, 2011).

Gillespie (2003) identifies several reasons why measures of perceived trustworthiness should not be used as a proxy for trust. First, holding beliefs and judgments about another's trustworthiness does not involve risk, vulnerability or interdependence, features that discriminate trust from related concepts such as confidence and cooperation (for example Luhmann, 1988; Mayer et al., 1995; Rousseau et al., 1998).

Second, empirical research suggests that whilst trustworthiness is an important and significant determinant of trust, it does not equate to trust. Rather trust and trustworthiness are distinct factors with distinct relationships with other constructs. For example, Mayer and Davis (1999) show that trust in management, but not the perceived trustworthiness of management, was enhanced through the implementation of a fairer performance appraisal system. Davis et al. (2000) report that trustworthiness accounts for only 46 percent of restaurant employees' trust in their general manager. In their meta-analysis, Dirks and Ferrin (2002) report that trustworthiness is more strongly associated with intentions to quit, commitment, job satisfaction and procedural justice, whereas overall trust has a stronger relationship with civic virtue, performance and quality of the leader–member relationship. In their analysis of 132 samples, Colquitt et al. (2007) report that trust only partially mediates the relationship between perceived trustworthiness and the outcomes of risk-taking behaviors, task performance, citizenship behavior and counterproductive behavior.

Third, several scholars have noted that the practical significance of trust is in its action (Lewis and Weigert, 1985; Mayer et al., 1995). From a measurement point of view, a willingness to be vulnerable by engaging in trusting behavior is proximally closer to trust behavior than perceptions of another's trustworthiness, and therefore better able to predict actual trust behavior. For these reasons, several researchers advocate measuring trust in addition to perceived trustworthiness (see Dietz and den Hartog, 2006; Gillespie, 2003; Schoorman et al., 2007).

Our knowledge of trust from survey-based, quantitative research is only as good as the psychometric scales used to measure trust. The limitations in trust measurement hinder our ability to compare and integrate results across studies meaningfully in a way that optimizes a cumulative body of knowledge.

RESEARCH VALIDITY AND CAVEATS

The current state of trust measurement in part reflects the limited number of well-validated trust scales, coupled with the challenges involved in measuring the concept of trust in organizational research. These challenges include: the diversity of organizational trust targets; the referent- and context-specific nature of trust; and the multidimensional nature of trust. Each is discussed in turn.

Survey measures have been used to assess trust in a broad variety of targets. At the interpersonal level, common targets include immediate managers, subordinates, peers and team members. At the group level, targets include the team or working group, department, middle or senior management, and the 'employer' or organization. Several scholars have noted that, to be valid, trust instruments need to make the referent of trust specific and identifiable (Dietz and den Hartog, 2006; Mayer and Davis, 1999).

Most trust scales are designed and validated to assess trust in a particular referent. Yet often it is assumed that the same instrument can be adapted directly for use across targets, without any check of the validity of the instrument for the new target. Given the different types of interdependences, vulnerabilities and expectations underlying different forms of relationships, it is not apparent that instruments designed to assess trust in upward relationships will be valid for assessing trust in lateral and downward relationships. Yet, few measures have been specifically validated across multiple targets. Even when instruments are designed to assess a range of targets, often items are worded in a way that makes translation to other targets difficult. For example, consider an item from Mayer and Davis' (1999) four-item trust measure: 'I would be willing to let . . . have complete control over my future in this company.' While this may be a valid question for assessing trust in one's leader or management, one may ask to what extent this is a meaningful question to assess trust in subordinates or peers. A related concern is that some trust instruments switch between a variety of targets within the one measure (such as management, the organization, subordinates), rendering the referent of trust unclear.

Given that trust is a psychological state, many scholars agree that it is most appropriately assessed at the individual level. However, some trust instruments require the respondent to make judgments on behalf of the target of trust or others in the relationship, or appraise the collective assessment of trust in another group. For example, an item from McAllister's (1995) scale is: 'We have a sharing relationship. We can both freely share our ideas, feelings and hopes.' Similarly, an item from Cummings and Bromiley's (1996) scale is: 'We think that the people in . . . tell the truth in negotiations.' Dietz and Den Hartog (2006) argue that it is unclear whether respondents would be sufficiently experienced and informed to make such complex judgments.

Trust is also context specific, as the nature and forms of interdependence and vulnerability change according to the context and type of relationship. There is an inherent tension between creating an instrument that is sufficiently sensitive to the unique research context in which it is developed, and one that is sufficiently generalizable and applicable across a range of contexts to enable replication. Some trust instruments include items that are worded so specifically to the particular context that they have limited applicability to other settings. For example, Currall and Judge's (1995) instrument assessing trust between boundary role persons was developed in the context of school district superintendents and presidents. While the items for some dimensions of trust (communication, for example) are applicable across a range of contexts, many of the items tapping 'task coordination' are specific to the relationship and context (for example 'Ask the superintendent to try to persuade the district's administrators to lend their support to a newly initiated cooperative program between teachers and administrators').

The applicability of instruments across national cultural contexts is another important consideration. Recent research by Tan and her colleagues suggests there are limitations in the transferability of dominant western conceptualizations and scales of trust to Confucian settings (see Tan and Chee, 2005; Wasti et al., 2007). For example, in a test of the measurement equivalence of the trust scales developed by Mayer and Davis (1999) in three countries (the US, Turkey and Singapore), they found that the trust scale had poor psychometric properties across the board, and several items of the ability and benevolence scales appeared to be interpreted differently by respondents from collectivist-high power distant versus individualist-low power distant cultures (Wasti et al., 2007). The authors call for the development of scales which reflect not a single culture but are more applicable across multiple cultures.

Collectively these issues limit the applicability, and hence replication, of trust instruments across targets and studies, as well as the ability to compare trust dimensions and processes across referents and contexts. These issues directly contribute to the fragmented and idiosyncratic use of trust instruments. However, the fragmentation is also due in part to the lack of well-validated trust measures. McEvily and Tortoriello (2011) identify only five measures appropriate to organizational settings that have been developed and tested with care. Of these, only three instruments assess trust per se, as opposed to perceived trustworthiness. These are Currall and Judge (1995), Mayer and Davis (1999) and the Behavioral Trust Inventory (Gillespie, 2003). Currall and Judge's (1995) 15-item measure was specifically designed to assess trust in boundary role persons. Mayer and Davis' (1999) four-item unidimensional trust measure was designed to be relevant to a variety of relationships, and has predominately been used to assess trust in top management. The Behavioral Trust Inventory is a 10-item measure designed to assess trust in manager, subordinate and peer relationships. It has two factors: reliance-based trust and disclosure-based trust. The validation and appropriate application of this most recent trust measure is described further in this chapter.

STRATEGIES AND CAVEATS ON THE VALID USE OF PSYCHOMETRIC TRUST INSTRUMENTS

How can we as organizational scholars collectively advance and strengthen the psychometric assessment of trust? Clearly one way is to use existing validated instruments where ever possible, rather than developing new measures. This will help us move toward a set of commonly accepted and well-validated instruments, and ultimately facilitate a more integrated body of trust literature. The following questions and guidelines are provided to assist researchers in the choice of an appropriate existing trust measure:

1. *Does the instrument match the chosen definition and theoretical conceptualization of trust?* The key issue here is to ensure that the operationalization of trust fits with the theoretical conceptualization and definition of trust. This requires first deciding on the key constructs under investigation. Is it trust, perceived trustworthiness, trusting behavior, distrust, or a combination? As low *distrust* does not necessarily equate to high *trust* (see Lewicki et al., 1998; Sitkin and Roth, 1993), care should be taken to avoid using reverse-scored distrust items as indicators of trust (for example, 'I really wish I had a good way to keep an eye on top management'
2. *Is the instrument well-validated and psychometrically sound?* A rigorous evaluation of an instrument's validity includes assessment of its construct, divergent and convergent validity, as well as the instrument's

reliability and stable factor structure across studies (Hinkin and Schriesheim, 1989; Landy, 1986). Researchers often adopt trust measures that have been published in earlier empirical studies, without examining evidence of the instrument's validity. Yet publication does not necessarily mean it is well validated. Fortunately, there now exist several excellent recent reviews of trust measures, to help identify and compare well-validated instruments (see Dietz and den Hartog, 2006; McEvily and Tortoriello, 2011).

3. *Is the instrument applicable to the chosen referent and context?* Key issues here include: does the measure clearly and consistently identify the target of trust? Has the instrument been validated for use with the chosen referent group? Are items worded in a manner that is applicable to the chosen research context? Do they have face validity in the eyes of respondents? Researchers using instruments in countries that differ markedly from the culture in which the instrument was developed, need to consider the validity of the instrument in their chosen context.

Unfortunately, trust researchers rarely can answer 'yes' to each of these questions. In order for this to become commonplace, further development and validation of trust instruments is warranted. In particular, further research is required to evaluate the applicability and validity of existing measures across different targets and levels, as well as across different cultural contexts (for reviews of trust across cultures see Dietz et al., 2010; Ferrin and Gillespie, 2010). Another fruitful area for future research is assessing the extent to which survey measures predict actual trust behavior. This type of validation work requires the use of mixed methodologies that validate survey measures with qualitative, observational and experimental methods.

PERSONAL EXPERIENCE OF DEVELOPING AND VALIDATING A NEW TRUST MEASURE

When embarking on my PhD studies in the late 1990s, I conducted a thorough search of the literature to identify a validated instrument for assessing trust in leader, member and peer relationships. While I found several appropriate instruments for assessing perceived trustworthiness, no such measure was available that adequately assessed trust as the 'willingness to be vulnerable.' The closest instrument was the four-item measure developed by Mayer and Davis (1999). However, I had concerns over the applicability of these items to leader, member and peer relationships, the low reported reliability, and mix of trust and distrust items. Therefore, I developed a new trust scale, subsequently called the Behavioral Trust Inventory (BTI). The full inventory (see Appendix) has been reviewed in Dietz and den Hartog (2006) and McEvily and Tortoriello (2011) and used or cited in a number of publications (for example Lam et al., 2011; Lau and Liden, 2008; Lee et al., 2010; Lewicki et al., 2006; Schoorman et al., 2007). The full validation paper is available from the author upon request.

In developing the BTI, I had two aims in mind. First, to devise an instrument that captured a person's willingness to be vulnerable in a relationship with a specified other. Second, to measure trust sensitively in leader–member and peer relationships in a team setting. Hence, the inventory needed to capture the essential features of these typically complex and highly interdependent work relationships. I commenced by reviewing the existing trust literature and trust scales to identify common behavioral expressions of trust in work relationships. To examine whether these domains were appropriate and important to leader–member and peer relations, 96 interviews were conducted with project leaders and two of their team members drawn from a large Australian research and development (R&D) organization. Interviewees were asked to identify trust behaviors in their relationship with their leader, peer and/or team member(s). Examination of the interview transcripts revealed two domains of trust behavior: (1) reliance: that is, relying on another's skills, knowledge, judgments or actions, including delegating and giving autonomy; and (2) disclosure: that is, sharing work-related or personal information of a sensitive nature.

Next, an initial pool of 50 items tapping reliance and disclosure behaviors was generated from the interviews, the trust literature and existing instruments. Care was taken to word the items in a way that made them generalizable to both leader–member and peer relations, and work relationships beyond the field of research and development. Two pilot studies were then conducted. The first used a sample of people working in project teams across a range of different organizations and industries. After deleting poor-performing items, a pool of 39 items remained. A second pilot study was conducted on R&D project leaders and team members. Respondents were asked to rate each trusting behavior using three response scales: how willing they would be to engage in each of the behaviors with the referent, whether there had been an opportunity to engage in the behavior with the referent, and if so, whether they had actually engaged in the behavior. Respondents were also asked to describe any additional behaviors not covered by the questionnaire that showed they trusted their leader and/or team member(s), and to rate their overall trust

184 Handbook of research methods on trust

in these relationships. After deleting uncommon trusting behaviors and items that failed to distinguish between high and low trust relationships, 15 items remained.

The validation sample comprised 77 project leaders and 234 team members drawn from two divisions of a large Australian R&D organization, and the cross-validation sample consisted of 67 managers and 214 of their direct reports drawn from a medium-sized transportation company and an energy company. Participation in the research was voluntary. Paper and pencil surveys were administered to all staff in these organizations, with an overall response rate of 64 percent. Exploratory and confirmatory factor analytic techniques revealed a two-factor structure, and after cross-loading items were deleted, this resulted in a final 10 items. The two factors had high reliability, ranging from .90 to .93 across the samples, and correlated between .61 and .71 across the samples.

For the validation study, a hypothesis-testing approach to establishing construct validity was adopted (Landy, 1986; Nunnally, 1978) to test whether the measure behaved as hypothesized in relation to other variables within the nomological network (Chronbach and Meehl, 1955). Analyses revealed strong support for the hypothesized associations using cross-sectional, longitudinal and matched dyad samples, providing evidence of the convergent validity of the reliance and disclosure scales. Evidence of the divergent validity of the BTI came from confirmatory factor analyses showing that reliance and disclosure were constructs distinct from trustworthiness and distrust, as well as from each other. Predictive validity was supported by the finding that the BTI significantly contributes to the prediction of important leadership outcomes, beyond existing measures of trustworthiness. The content validity of the BTI was further examined by assessing responses to the open-ended survey question: 'list two or three key behaviors that show you trust your . . . leader, peer/team member.' The behaviors identified fell within the two dimensions of reliance and disclosure.

DISCUSSION

As evidenced by the process described above, the rigorous development and validation of a trust inventory takes considerable time and investment. The outcome, however, can be very rewarding. The BTI contributes to the literature by offering a valid, reliable and multidimensional measure of trust applicable to leader–member and peer relationships. Establishing construct validity is an ongoing process and there is research that would strengthen the validity of the BTI further. For example, whilst the cross-validation study suggests the BTI is applicable to non-team contexts and other industries and organizations, further research examining the applicability and validity of the BTI in a range of work settings is warranted, as is research examining the BTI in non-western cultural settings. In this regard, the instrument has now been used in over 20 independent studies, spanning a range of countries and organizational contexts, providing a broader base of evidence upon which to evaluate its validity and generalizability. I am currently in the process of developing a norm base across professionals, industries and referents to facilitate the interpretation of mean scores on the BTI factors.

The excellent recent reviews of survey-based trust measures have clarified the range, validity, strengths and limitations of existing measures, and provide a valuable resource to guide researchers in the choice of an appropriate scale. Armed with these reviews, it is anticipated that we will witness greater adoption of well-validated trust measures that are clearly aligned with the chosen conceptualization and referent of trust. However, given the inherent tensions between the accurate replication of trust measures and the need for context- and referent-sensitivity, some tailoring of items from existing trust measures is likely to continue as a necessary practice in the organizational sciences. I hope this chapter helps guide the thoughtful use of trust scales, as well as stimulates further research on trust measurement.

REFERENCES

Bigley, G.A. and J.L. Pearce (1998), 'Straining for shared meaning in organisation science: problems of trust and distrust', *Academy of Management Review*, **23**, 405–21.
Butler, J.K. (1991), 'Toward understanding and measuring conditions of trust: evolution of a conditions of trust inventory', *Journal of Management*, **17** (3), 643–63.
Chronbach, L. and P. Meehl (1955), 'Construct validity in psychological tests', *Psychological Bulletin*, **52**, 281–302.
Colquitt, J.A., B.A. Scott and J.A. LePine (2007), 'Trust, trustworthiness, and trust propensity: a meta-analytic test of their unique relationships with risk taking and job performance', *Journal of Applied Psychology*, **92** (4), 909–27.
Currall, S.C. and T.A. Judge (1995), 'Measuring trust between organisational boundary role persons', *Organisational Behavior and Human Decision Processes*, **64** (2), 151–70.
Davis, J.H., F.D. Schoorman, R.C. Mayer and H.H. Tan (2000), 'The trusted general manager and business unit performance: empirical evidence of a competitive advantage', *Strategic Management Journal*, **21** (5), 563–76.
Dietz, G. and D. den Hartog (2006), 'Measuring trust in organisations', *Personnel Review*, **35** (5), 557.
Dietz, G., N. Gillespie and G. Chao (2010), 'Unravelling the complexities of trust across cultures', in M.N.K. Saunders, D. Skinner, G. Dietz, N. Gillespie and R. J. Lewicki (eds), *Organisational Trust: A Cultural Perspective*, Cambridge: Cambridge University Press, pp. 3–41.

Dirks, K.T. and D.L. Ferrin (2002), 'Trust in leadership: meta-analytic findings and implications for research and practice', *Journal of Applied Psychology*, **87** (4), 611–28.
Ferrin, D. and N. Gillespie (2010), 'Trust differences across national-societal cultures: much to do, or much ado about nothing?', in M.N.K. Saunders, D. Skinner, G. Dietz, N. Gillespie and R.J. Lewicki (eds), *Organisational Trust: A Cultural Perspective*, Cambridge: Cambridge University Press, pp. 42–87.
Gillespie, N. (2003), 'Measuring trust in work relationships: the Behavioural Trust Inventory', paper presented at the Academy of Management Conference, Seattle.
Hinkin, T.R. and C.A. Schriesheim (1989), 'Development and application of new scales to measure the French and Raven (1959) bases of social power', *Journal of Applied Psychology*, **74** (4), 561–67.
Hosmer, L.T. (1995), 'Trust: the connecting link between organisational theory and philosophical ethics', *Academy of Management Review*, **20** (2), 379–403.
Lam, L.W., R. Loi and C. Leong (2011), 'Reliance and disclosure: how supervisory justice affects trust in supervisor and extra-role performance', *Asia Pacific Journal of Management*, www.springerlink.com/content/f8416979w31r7281.
Landy, F.J. (1986), 'Stamp collecting versus science: validation as hypothesis testing', *American Psychologist*, **41**, 1183–92.
Lau, D.C. and R.C. Liden (2008), 'Antecedents of coworker trust: leaders' blessings', *Journal of Applied Psychology*, **93** (5), 1130–38.
Lee, P., N. Gillespie, L. Mann and A. Wearing (2010), 'Leadership and trust: their effect on knowledge sharing and team performance', *Management Learning*, **41** (4), 473–91.
Lewicki, R.J., D.J. McAllister and R.J. Bies (1998), 'Trust and distrust: new relationships and realities', *Academy of Management Review*, **23** (3), 438–58.
Lewicki, R.J., E.C. Tomlinson and N. Gillespie (2006), 'Models of interpersonal trust development: theoretical approaches, empirical evidence, and future directions', *Journal of Management*, **32** (6), 991–1022.
Lewis, D.J. and A. Weigert (1985), 'Trust as a social reality', *Social Forces*, **63** (4), 967–85.
Luhmann, N. (1988), 'Familiarity, confidence and trust: problems and alternatives', in D. Gambetta (ed.), *Trust: Making and Breaking Cooperative Relationships*, New York: Basil Blackwell, pp. 94–107.
Mayer, R.C. and J.H. Davis (1999), 'The effect of the performance appraisal system on trust for management: a field quasi-experiment', *Journal of Applied Psychology*, **84**, 123–36.
Mayer, R.C., J.H. Davis and F.D. Schoorman (1995), 'An integrative model of organisational trust', *Academy of Management Review*, **20** (3), 709–34.
McEvily, B. and M. Tortoriello (2011), 'Measuring trust in organisational research: review and recommendations', *Journal of Trust Research*, **1** (1), 23–63.
Möllering, G. (2006), *Trust: Reason, Routine, Reflexivity*, Oxford: Elsevier Science.
Nunnally, J.C. (1978), *Psychometric Theory*, New York: McGraw-Hill.
Rousseau, D.M., S.B. Sitkin, R.S. Burt and C. Camerer (1998), 'Not so different after all: a cross-discipline view of trust', *Academy of Management Review*, **23** (3), 393–404.
Schoorman, F.D., R.C. Mayer and J.H. Davis (2007), 'An integrative model of organisational trust: past, present and future', *Academy of Management Review*, **32** (2), 344–54.
Sitkin, S.B. and N.L. Roth (1993), 'Explaining the limited effectiveness of legalistic "remedies" for trust/distrust', *Organisation Science*, **4** (3), 367–92.
Tan, H.H. and D. Chee (2005), 'Understanding interpersonal trust in a Confucian-influenced society: an exploratory study', *International Journal of Cross Cultural Management*, **5** (2), 197–212.
Wasti, S.A., H.H. Tan, H.H. Brower and Ç.Önder (2007), 'Cross-cultural measurement of supervisor trustworthiness: an assessment of measurement invariance across three cultures', *Leadership Quarterly*, **18** (5), 477–89.
Zand, D.E. (1972), 'Trust and managerial problem solving', *Administrative Science Quarterly*, **17** (2), 229–39.

Annotated Further Reading

Dietz, G. and D. den Hartog (2006), 'Measuring trust in organisations', *Personnel Review*, **35** (5), 557. This paper reviews and content analyses 14 recently published survey measures of intra-organizational trust, highlighting where measures match theory and also a number of limitations and 'blind-spots.'

McEvily, B. and M. Tortoriello (2011), 'Measuring trust in organisational research: review and recommendations', *Journal of Trust Research*, **1** (1), 23–63. These authors analysed 131 papers on trust published over the past 45 years, only to conclude that trust measurement is currently rudimentary and highly fragmented. The framework for selecting a trust measure and the rich description of the few well-validated measures are particularly valuable.

APPENDIX: THE BEHAVIORAL TRUST INVENTORY

Note: Items 1–5 tap reliance-based trust and items 6–10 tap disclosure-based trust.

Please indicate how willing you are to engage in each of the following behaviors with *your Leader/Team Member/Follower*, by circling a number from 1 to 7.

		Not at all willing				Completely willing		
1.	Rely on your leader's task related skills and abilities.	1	2	3	4	5	6	7
2.	Depend on your leader to handle an important issue on your behalf.	1	2	3	4	5	6	7
3.	Rely on your leader to represent your work accurately to others.	1	2	3	4	5	6	7
4.	Depend on your leader to back you up in difficult situations.	1	2	3	4	5	6	7
5.	Rely on your leader's work-related judgments.	1	2	3	4	5	6	7
6.	Share your personal feelings with your leader.	1	2	3	4	5	6	7
7.	Discuss work-related problems or difficulties with your leader that could potentially be used to disadvantage you.	1	2	3	4	5	6	7
8.	Confide in your leader about personal issues that are affecting your work.	1	2	3	4	5	6	7

		Not at all willing			Completely willing			
9.	Discuss how you honestly feel about your work, even negative feelings and frustration.	1	2	3	4	5	6	7
10.	Share your personal beliefs with your leader.	1	2	3	4	5	6	7

18 The actor–partner interdependence model: a method for studying trust in dyadic relationships
Donald L. Ferrin, Michelle C. Bligh and Jeffrey C. Kohles

INTRODUCTION

Dyadic trust research typically focuses on trustee behaviours and charac-teristics that earn, maintain, or repair another's trust, and/or on trustor perceptions, beliefs, and intentions toward a trustee. This approach of understanding trust as a dyadic trustor–trustee phenomenon can be seen in trust's foundational literatures of game theory (Deutsch, 1958) and close relationships (Rempel et al., 1985), and in more contemporary research on leader–follower trust (Dirks and Ferrin, 2002), trust between work colleagues (McAllister, 1995), trust between groups (Serva et al., 2005), relationships between participants in laboratory studies (Schweitzer et al., 2006), and negotiation studies (Maddux et al., 2008), among others.

In most real-life dyadic relationships, each party acts simultaneously as both trustor and trustee. For instance, in a leader–follower dyad, the leader will typically behave in ways that earn or damage the follower's trust while at the same time forming his or her own beliefs about the fol-lower's trustworthiness. And the follower will behave in ways that earn or damage the leader's trust while at the same time forming beliefs about the leader's trustworthiness. In contrast to this simultaneous reality of trust, empirical studies typically assign one party to report as trustor and the other as trustee. For instance, a typical field study might measure fol-lowers' trust in their leader and assess whether that can be predicted with leader behaviours and characteristics.

Why is there such a disconnect between trust as a real-life phenom-enon and trust as studied in field and laboratory research? One reason is analytical: because trust tends to be reciprocated within dyads, trust measures within a dyad are naturally correlated. Consequently, studying the development of trust in a sample that includes both members of each dyad would violate the independence assumption of ordinary least square methods. The independence assumption requires that, after controlling for variation due to the independent variable, the data from each individual in a study are unrelated to the data from every other individual in the study (Kenny et al., 2006: 3). Nonindependence among dyad members can occur because of voluntary linkages (for example, friends, coworkers, or couples), experimental linkages (relationships created in the laboratory), or yoked linkages (two individuals are exposed to the same experiences or environmental stimuli, such as a common leader). And within such linked pairs, individual scores may also become interdependent due to partner effects, mutual influence, and common fate. Partner effects occur when one person's behaviour affects his or her partner's outcomes. Mutual influence occurs when both persons' behaviours and outcomes directly affect one another. For example, the behaviours of negotiating partners ultimately contribute to the outcomes that they both share (that is, the size and split of the negotiating surplus). Finally, common fate effects occur when both dyad members are exposed to the same causal factor, such as environmental, cultural, or structural elements, or shared experiences.

Concerns about nonindependence often lead researchers to use simplified designs in which only one party of a dyad reports as trustor. However, these simplified designs prevent us from examining some trust-related phenomena that are practically important and theoretically interesting. For instance, attribution theory is one of the more frequently used perspectives for understanding trust formation (Ferrin and Dirks, 2003). Core attribution theories would suggest that a leader's trust towards a follower could be influenced by the follower's behaviour (Heider, 1958), and also by the leader's own behaviour towards the follower (Bem, 1972). Simultaneously and by the same logic, the follower's trust towards the leader could be influenced by the leader's behaviour towards the follower (Heider, 1958) and also the follower's trust towards the leader (Bem, 1972). A researcher interested in testing these effects could readily collect trust and behaviour data from leaders and followers. However, if the researcher wished to study how leader and follower trust form simultaneously based on leader and follower behaviour, the inherent nonindependence in the data would represent a significant impediment to using ordinary least square (OLS) methods.

What is needed is a method that can model the interdependence that occurs naturally within dyads. Over the last decade or so, scholars have developed a range of dyadic designs that can model such interdependence (Kenny et al., 2006). One of these designs, the actor–partner interdependence model (APIM; Kashy and Kenny, 2000; Kenny et al., 2006), is especially relevant to the study of interpersonal trust because of its flexibility: it can accommodate dyads in which the parties are distinguishable (leader–follower) or indistinguishable (peer–peer), and it can accommodate independent and outcome variables that vary both within (for example, party A's trust toward B is greater than party B's trust toward A) and between (for example, dyad 1's mean level of trust differs from dyad 2's) dyads. The APIM has the same assumptions as OLS methods, except that it models interdependence rather than assuming independence. Using dyadic data, the APIM allows the researcher to disaggregate actor effects (such as the effect of an actor's behaviour on the actor's beliefs) from partner effects (for example, the effect of an actor's behaviour on a partner's beliefs) and test the significance and effect sizes of each.

In the following sections we discuss the features of the APIM that make it particularly useful for studying trust, the present use of the APIM, our own experience using the APIM to understand the spiralling of trust perceptions and cooperation between individuals and groups, and the potential for using the APIM to understand trust-related phenomena in field and laboratory settings.

FEATURES OF THE ACTOR–PARTNER INTERDEPENDENCE MODEL THAT ARE PARTICULARLY RELEVANT FOR STUDYING TRUST

Kashy and Kenny (2000: 451) describe the APIM as a 'simple yet compelling' model of dyadic behaviour. When two people interact or are involved in a relationship, each person's outcomes may be affected by both his or her own inputs and his or her partner's inputs. The APIM explicitly allows for the very real possibility that actor and partner effects may also co-occur, and that sometimes co-occurrence is the major research focus (Kenny et al., 2006). For instance, in a study of leader–follower dyads, the degree to which a person is dispositionally trusting can have actor and partner effects: being trusting may increase a person's own level of information disclosure, and may also increase the partner's level of information disclosure.

The APIM also permits analysis of independent variables that are mixed in nature (variables that vary both between and within dyads). For example, in studying behavioural determinants of trust within a dyad, a leader may perform more trust-earning behaviours than a follower, and between dyads some dyads may perform a higher mean level of trust-earning behaviours than others. The APIM enables the researcher to estimate actor and partner effects in a population of dyads where variance occurs within and between dyads.

Reciprocity represents a specific type of interdependence that can also be modelled with the APIM. In the context of trust, reciprocity often refers to 'tit-for-tat' behaviours as might be seen in positive or negative trust spirals (for example Ferrin et al., 2008). In the APIM, if a participant responds to a given action in kind, this response constitutes reciprocity (for example, company A is competitive so in response company B is competitive). However, if he or she responds in the opposite manner (company A is competitive so in response company B is overly cooperative), we would then have what Kenny et al. (2006) define as compensation. In addition, reciprocity is distinct from synchrony, in which the behaviour of two individuals or groups is coordinated (either simultaneously or sequentially) on the basis of the same temporal 'clock'.

The APIM can also be applied to group data (Kashy and Kenny, 2000; Kenny et al., 2002). For instance, a person's behaviour may be influenced by his or her own levels of trust (an actor effect) and by the other group members' trust (the partner effect). Because in this case the partner effect is the effect of an average of other group members' scores, with group data researchers can also consider weighting some members' scores more than others, essentially computing a weighted mean for the partner effect (see Kenny et al., 2006).

RESEARCH USING THE ACTOR–PARTNER INTERDEPENDENCE MODEL

The capability of modelling and testing both actor and partner effects has helped to propel the dyad into the mainstream study of relationships across several areas in the social sciences (Simpson, 2006). For example, researchers have used the APIM to explore interdependence in emotion and expressive suppression (Butler et al., 2003), health-related social influence (Butterfield and Lewis, 2002), leisure activities and satisfaction (Berg et al., 2001), communication and conflict strategies (Lakey and Canary, 2002), partner personality traits (Robins et al., 2000), relationship commitment in couples (Kurdek, 2000), interpersonal accuracy and bias in perception in couples (Kenny and Acitelli, 2001), relationship violence and abuse (Moffitt et al., 2001), social influence (Oriña et al., 2002), and attachment orientations (Campbell et al., 2001). The APIM has also been used in the study of families and family outcomes in nursing (Rayens and Svavardottir, 2003) and in exploring participation and control within small groups (Bonito, 2002).

Kenny et al. (2006; also see Kashy and Kenny, 2000) delineate three different methods to estimate the APIM: pooled regression, multilinear modelling (MLM), and structural equation modelling (SEM), and discuss the advantages, disadvantages, and appropriate uses of each. In a review of the empirical literature using the APIM, we found that 12 articles (33 per cent of the total articles found) utilised MLM, 10 (28 per cent) utilised SEM, and seven (19 per cent) utilised pooled regression. The remaining seven articles (19 per cent) utilised multiple approaches, either comparing APIM with other dyadic models or comparing the three analytical options available (that is, pooled regression, MLM, or SEM).

USE OF THE ACTOR–PARTNER INTERDEPENDENCE MODEL IN TRUST-BASED RESEARCH

Despite the prominence of studies using dyadic designs in other disciplines such as the close relationships literature, dyadic designs have hardly made their way into the study of trust by organisation scholars. (For a recent exception, see Yakovleva et al., 2010). In our own research (Ferrin et al., 2008), we wished to study how trust perceptions and cooperative behaviours spiralled between individuals and between groups. Our theoretical model suggested three alternatives: a perceived trustworthiness spiral model in which party A's trust perceptions influenced party B's trust perceptions and vice versa (as suggested by theories of verbal and nonverbal communication), a cooperation spiral model in which party A's cooperative behaviours influenced party B's cooperative behaviours and vice versa (which would be suggested by normative and evolutionary psychological perspectives on reciprocity), and a more complex perceived trustworthiness–cooperation spiral model in which trust perceptions were transmitted from actor to partner via actor cooperative behaviours, and cooperation was transmitted from actor to partner via partner trust perceptions (which would be suggested by trust and attribution theories) (Figure 18.1).

Our model hypothesized a series of actor and partner effects between members of isolated dyads. Given the dyadic nature of our theoretical model, it was necessary that we collect data from dyads in which both parties cooperated with each other and reported their trust towards each other. The APIM then allowed us to test for the significance of hypothesized actor and partner effects while also controlling for all non-hypothesized actor and partner effects. Using the APIM, we found strong support for the perceived trustworthiness–cooperation spiral in interpersonal interactions. In a second study, we found strong support for the perceived trustworthiness–cooperation spiral in intergroup interactions (Figure 18.2).

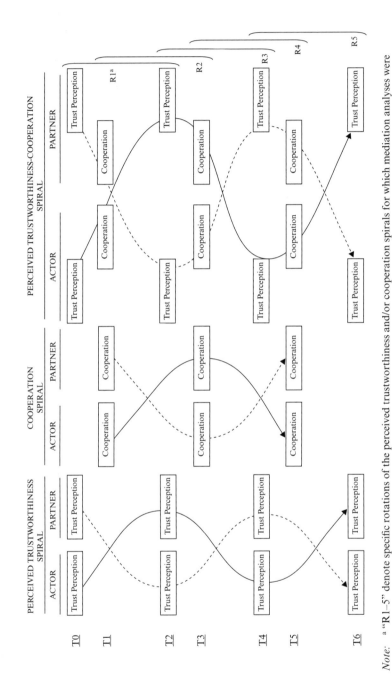

Note: [a] "R1–5" denote specific rotations of the perceived trustworthiness and/or cooperation spirals for which mediation analyses were conducted.

Figure 18.1 Perceived trustworthiness and cooperation spirals

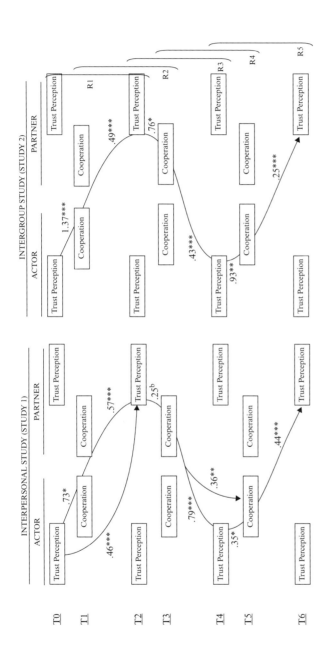

Note: Path coefficients summarize the mediation findings. Only significant hypothesized paths are shown. Specifically, indirect paths (e.g., cooperation (T1) → perceived trustworthiness (T2)) reflect the coefficient while controlling for the prior level of the criterion variable (e.g., perceived trustworthiness (T0)). Direct effects (e.g., perceived trustworthiness: (T0) → perceived trustworthiness (T2)) are shown as significant only if the predictor retained a significant predictor of the criterion when controlling for the mediator (e.g., cooperation (T1)). For clarity, only one "side" of the spiral is shown; in actuality, the spiraling is symmetric (as depicted in Figure 1).

[b] $p<.10$; *$p<.05$; **$p<.01$; ***$p<.001$

Figure 18.2 Summary of results

195

This study highlighted several research design and data collection considerations. First, the APIM is appropriate in dyadic studies where actor and partner effects are hypothesized to occur simultaneously, and it is also appropriate when one wishes to examine a partner effect while controlling for a non-hypothesized actor effect or vice versa. Thus, even in studies where the primary interest is in partner effects, it may still be useful to use the APIM to control for actor effects. Second, to conduct an APIM analysis, the study must be designed so that identical data are collected from both members of each dyad (that is, the researcher should administer identical instruments to both parties to measure behaviour, attitudes, demographics, and so on).

DISCUSSION

In our own experience, the APIM has been at least as valuable for its theoretical insights as its empirical functions. As researchers, we tend to focus our thinking on effects that can be tested. The APIM's ability to disaggregate partner effects from actor effects first forced us, then encouraged us, and eventually inspired us to think in a more theoretically nuanced way about the development and consequences of trust. We suspect, and indeed we have found (Ferrin et al., 2007), that some of the 'enigmas' of trust are considerably less enigmatic when one specifies whether it is actor or partner effects that are of interest. The APIM therefore provides a framework that helps one better appreciate the complexity of dyadic relationships, and also makes that complexity more tractable.

It is somewhat ironic that interdependence is recognised as a necessary condition of trust (Rousseau et al., 1998), yet independence is an assumption of the OLS methods that we use to study trust empirically. The primary advantage of the APIM is that it encourages researchers to gather and test dyadic data in their more natural, interdependent form. Importantly, the APIM and other dyadic methods are not limited to micro and laboratory studies of trust. The partners in an APIM analysis can as easily be coworkers, leader–followers, departments within an organisation, or even corporate partners in a joint venture.

ACKNOWLEDGEMENT

Figures 18.1 and 18.2 are reprinted from Ferris, D.L., M.C. Bligh and J.C. Kohles (2008), 'It takes two to tango: an interdependence analysis of the spiraling of perceived trustworthiness and cooperation in interpersonal and intergroup relationships', *Organizational Behavior and Human Decision Processes*, **107**, 161–78, with permission from Elsevier.

REFERENCES

Bem, D.J. (1972), 'Self-perception theory', in L. Berkowitz (ed.), *Advances in Experimental Social Psychology*, New York: Academic, vol. 6, pp. 1–62.

Berg, E.C., M. Trost, I.E. Schneider and M.T. Allison (2001), 'Dyadic exploration of the relationship of leisure satisfaction, leisure time, and gender to relationship satisfaction', *Leisure Sciences*, **23**, 35–46.

Bonito, J.A. (2002), 'The analysis of participation in small groups: methodological and conceptual issues related to interdependence', *Small Group Research*, **33**, 412–38.

Butler, E.A., B. Egloff, F.H. Wilhelm, N.C. Smith, E.A. Erickson and J.J. Gross (2003), 'The social consequences of expressive suppression', *Emotion*, **3**, 48–67.

Butterfield, R.M. and M.A. Lewis (2002), 'Health-related social influence: a social ecological perspective on tactic use', *Journal of Social and Personal Relationships*, **19**, 505–26.

Campbell, L., J.A. Simpson, D.A. Kashy and W.S. Rholes (2001), 'Attachment orientations, dependence, and behavior in a stressful situation: an application of the actor–partner interdependence model', *Journal of Social and Personal Relationships*, **18**, 821–43.

Deutsch, M. (1958), 'Trust and suspicion', *Journal of Conflict Resolution*, **2**, 265–79.

Dirks, K.T. and D.L. Ferrin (2002), 'Trust in leadership: meta-analytic findings and implications for research and practice', *Journal of Applied Psychology*, **87**, 611–28.

Ferrin, D.L. and K.T. Dirks (2003), 'The use of rewards to increase and decrease trust: mediating processes and differential effects', *Organization Science*, **14**, 18–31.

Ferrin, D.L., M.C. Bligh and J.C. Kohles (2007), 'Can I trust you to trust me? A theory of trust, monitoring, and cooperation in interpersonal and intergroup relationships', *Group and Organization Management*, **32**, 465–99.

Ferrin, D.L., M.C. Bligh and J.C. Kohles (2008), 'It takes two to tango: an interdependence analysis of the spiraling of perceived trustworthiness and cooperation in interpersonal and intergroup relationships', *Organizational Behavior and Human Decision Processes*, **107**, 161–78.

Heider, F. (1958), *The Psychology of Interpersonal Relations*, New York: John Wiley and Sons.

Kashy, D.A. and D.A. Kenny (2000), 'The analysis of data from dyads and groups', in H.T. Reis and C.M. Judd (eds), *Handbook of Research Methods in Social and Personality Psychology*, Cambridge: Cambridge University Press, pp. 451–77.

Kenny, D.A. and L.K. Acitelli (2001), 'Accuracy and bias in the perception of the partner in a close relationship', *Journal of Personality and Social Psychology*, **80**, 439–48.

Kenny, D.A., D.A. Kashy and W.L. Cook (2006), *Dyadic Data Analysis*, New York: Guilford Press.

Kenny, D.A., L. Mannetti, A. Pierro, S. Livi and D.A. Kashy (2002), 'The statistical analysis of data from small groups', *Journal of Personality and Social Psychology*, **83**, 126–37.

Kurdek, L.A. (2000), 'The link between sociotropy/autonomy and dimensions of relationship commitment: evidence from gay and lesbian couples', *Personal Relationships*, **7**, 153–64.

Lakey, S.G. and D.J. Canary (2002), 'Actor goal achievement and sensitivity to partner as critical factors in understanding interpersonal communication competence and conflict strategies', *Communication Monographs*, **69**, 217–35.

Maddux, W.W., E. Mullen and A.D. Galinsky (2008), 'Chameleons bake bigger pies and take bigger pieces: strategic behavioral mimicry facilitates negotiation outcomes', *Journal of Experimental Social Psychology*, **44**, 461–8.

McAllister, D.J. (1995), 'Affect- and cognition-based trust as foundations for interpersonal cooperation in organizations', *Academy of Management Journal*, **38**, 24–59.

Moffitt, T.E., R.W. Robins and A. Caspi (2001), 'A couples analysis of partner abuse with implications for abuse-prevention policy', *Criminology and Public Policy*, **1**, 5–36.

Oriña, M.M., W. Wood and J.A. Simpson (2002), 'Strategies of influence in close relationships', *Journal of Experimental Social Psychology*, **38**, 459–72.

Rayens, M.K. and E.K. Svavardottir (2003), 'A new methodological approach in nursing research: an actor, partner, and interaction effect model for family outcomes', *Research in Nursing and Health*, **26**, 409–19.

Rempel, J.K., J.G. Holmes and M.P. Zanna (1985), 'Trust in close relationships', *Journal of Personality and Social Psychology*, **49**, 95–112.

Robins, R.W., A. Caspi and T.E. Moffitt (2000), 'Two personalities, one relationship: both partners' personality traits shape the quality of their relationship', *Journal of Personality and Social Psychology*, **79**, 251–9.

Rousseau, D.M., S.B. Sitkin, R.S. Burt and C. Camerer (1998), 'Not so different after all: a cross-discipline view of trust', *Academy of Management Review*, **23**, 393–404.

Schweitzer, M.E., J.C. Hershey and E.T. Bradlow (2006), 'Promises and lies: restoring violated trust', *Organizational Behavior and Human Decision Processes*, **101**, 1–19.

Serva, M.A., M.A. Fuller and R.C. Mayer (2005), 'The reciprocal nature of trust: a longitudinal study of interacting teams', *Journal of Organizational Behavior*, **26**, 625–48.

Simpson, J.A. (2006), 'Foreword', in D.A. Kenny, D.A. Kashy and W.L. Cook, *Dyadic Data Analysis*, New York: Guilford Press, pp. vii–ix.

Yakovleva, M., R.R. Reilly and R. Werko (2010), 'Why do we trust? Beyond individual to dyadic perceptions', *Journal of Applied Psychology*, **95**, 79–91.

Annotated Further Reading

Ferrin, D.L., M.C. Bligh and J.C. Kohles (2008), 'It takes two to tango: an interdependence analysis of the spiraling of perceived trustworthiness and cooperation in interpersonal and intergroup relationships', *Organizational Behavior and Human Decision Processes*, **107**, 161–78. This paper demonstrates how the APIM can be used to model actor and partner effects related to trust; the paper includes an appendix providing details of the APIM, its use, and how it relates to other methods.

Kenny, D.A., D.A. Kashy and W.L. Cook (2006), *Dyadic Data Analysis*, New York: Guilford Press. This book provides a detailed discussion of three categories of dyadic designs: standard designs, social relations model designs, and one-with-many design, plus detailed guidance on how and when to use each.

19 Embedded trust: the analytical approach in vignettes, laboratory experiments and surveys
Davide Barrera, Vincent Buskens and Werner Raub

INTRODUCTION

In recent years, research programs on trust have been extremely numerous and diverse in terms of both theoretical and methodological approaches as well as empirical applications. In this chapter, we focus on one research stream, which we refer to as the 'analytical approach' (Hedström, 2005; Hedström and Bearman, 2009) and discuss complementary empirical strategies consistent with this approach.

In the framework of analytical sociology, what qualifies a sociological explanation is a focus on collective phenomena that result, often as unintended consequences, from the actions and interactions of individual actors who constitute the elementary units of the social system in which the collective phenomenon emerges. The analytical approach implies that trust is not studied as a property of social systems, but as the result of individual decisions made by interdependent actors. For example, most economic transactions imply a trust problem between sellers and buyers. Online transactions are an illustration: when purchasing online, the buyer has to trust that the seller will ship the good. A definition of trust which captures this interdependence has been proposed by Coleman (1990: ch. 5). Coleman characterizes a trust problem as a strategic interaction between two actors – a trustor and a trustee – and having four properties:

1. The trustor has the possibility of placing some resources at the disposal of the trustee, who has the possibility of either honouring or abusing trust.
2. The trustor prefers to place trust if the trustee honours trust, but regrets placing trust if the trustee abuses it.
3. There is no binding agreement that protects the trustor from the possibility that the trustee will abuse trust.

4. There is a time lag between the decision of the trustor and that of the trustee.

Making the individual decisions explicit, this approach to the study of trust has three advantages. First, the emphasis on the individual decisions allows the use of theoretical tools such as formal game theory and agent-based modelling to build theoretical models of trust (Buskens and Raub, 2010). Second, the empirical data used to test sociological theories typically have individuals, rather than collectivities, as units of observation. Therefore, theoretical models incorporating assumptions on the 'micro level' of individual actors are preferable. Third, the research results are often meant to be applied in designing policies to promote trust, or dissuade detrimental forms of cooperation (such as formation of oligopolies or cooperation between and within criminal organizations). A correct understanding of the mechanisms guiding individual trust choices will lead to more successful policies targeting individual behaviour.

In addition to this emphasis on the micro component of theoretical models, the analytical approach requires that the social conditions for individual choices are taken appropriately into account. As pointed out by Granovetter in his classic article on economic action and social embeddedness, economic transactions do not occur in an idealized perfect market with 'atomized interactions' but are embedded in complex systems of economic and social relations (Granovetter, 1985). Social embeddedness concerns restrictions and opportunities for the actors' choices. These restrictions and opportunities can be conceived as mechanisms affecting individual decisions and hence the emergence of trust relationships. For this reason, the analytical approach is often referred to as the analysis of social mechanisms (Hedström, 2005). An analytical approach to the study of embedded trust thus combines game-theoretically inspired analyses and formal tools of social network analysis. Empirical testing of theoretically grounded hypotheses is an essential ingredient of the approach.

THEORIES AND HYPOTHESES

The theories applied to study the social mechanisms of trust often consist of formal game-theoretical models (for example Buskens, 2002; Camerer and Weigelt, 1988; Dasgupta, 1988). In particular, the Trust Game and the Investment Game (Camerer, 2003) are two models of strategic interaction with incentive structures consistent with Coleman's informal definition of trust. In these models, the characteristics of the game – that is, alternative choices available to the actors, the sequence in which choices are made, and the information available to an actor when making a choice – represent opportunities and restrictions for the actors, while the ranking of the payoffs reflects what is assumed about the preferences of the actors.

The information available to the actors is particularly important because it can influence their expectations concerning the behaviour of their partner, that is, it can influence the trustor's assessment of the trustee's trustworthiness. In situations of embedded trust, information available to the trustor may include previous own experience, or vicarious experience acquired via third parties. The former situation is referred to as dyadic embeddedness, the latter as network embeddedness (Buskens, 2002; Buskens and Raub, 2002). Three mechanisms accounting for the effects of dyadic and network embeddedness in trust problems have been identified: control, learning, and imitation (Barrera, 2005; Buskens, 2002; Buskens and Raub, 2002). These mechanisms constitute explanations of the trustor's decision whether (or to what extent) to trust the trustee. In the remainder of this section, we briefly introduce these mechanisms and present some selected hypotheses related to each mechanism. This selection is by no means exhaustive; for a more extensive discussion we refer to Buskens (2002) and Barrera (2005).

Control refers to the possibility for the trustor to reward or punish the trustee in the future, depending on whether the trustee honours or abuses trust in the present. Control can operate in two ways: on the one hand, if the trustor has herself the opportunity to punish or reward the trustee by, for example, withdrawing or placing trust in the future, because future interactions are likely, control operates via dyadic embeddedness. On the other hand, if the trustor has the possibility of informing other trustors about the behaviour of the trustee and they might, in turn, decide whether to place trust depending on the trustee's reputation, control operates via network embeddedness. This leads to the following hypotheses:

H1:   Trust of a trustor increases with the expected duration of a series of interactions between this trustor and the trustee in the future.

H2:   Trust of a trustor increases with her[1] possibility of informing other trustors about the behaviour of the trustee.

Learning indicates the mechanism through which information concerning the trustee's behaviour in previous trust problems reaches the trustor via dyadic and network embeddedness. For example, when two actors are having repeated interactions with each other, the trustor can learn to what extent she can trust her partner. If the trustee has been trustworthy in the past, the trustor may more easily place trust. In this case, the mechanism of learning operates through dyadic embeddedness. Just like control, learning can also occur via network embeddedness. When a trustor receives information concerning the behaviour of the trustee in past interactions with other trustors, learning operates via network embeddedness. Hypotheses on learning via dyadic and network embeddedness can be straightforwardly formulated as follows:

H3:   Trust of a trustor increases with the trustee's trustworthiness in past interactions between the same partners.

H4:   Trust of a trustor increases with the amount of positive information that she receives about the behaviour of the trustee in past interactions with other trustors.

Situations in which actors have the potential to obtain information about the reputation of another actor prior to the decision whether to place trust in him are rather common. For example, when completing online transactions, actors can often make use of reputation systems, by means of which a trustor receives information on the trustworthiness of the trustees. However, in many instances, only the information about the behaviour of other trustors is readily available, while information on the trustee's responses in those interactions is virtually impossible to obtain. For example, when looking for a restaurant in an unfamiliar city or neighbourhood, one can easily observe whether the restaurant has many customers, but one is unlikely to ever find out how many of these customers had a stomach ache the day after. It seems inappropriate to argue that trustors can actually learn about the trustworthiness of the trustees from such incomplete information. Nevertheless, it is perfectly plausible that this information on the behaviour of other trustors leads to imitation, in the sense that an individual places trust in a trustee who is trusted by many others. In interactions resembling social dilemmas, imitation could be viewed as a parsimonious way to achieve the optimal decision (cf. Hedström, 1998 on 'rational imitation'), especially in settings where information is scarce. As imitation implies observing what others do, imitation can occur only via network embeddedness, unlike control and learning. An example of a hypothesis concerning the mechanism of imitation looks as follows:

H5:   Trust of a trustor increases with the number of other trustors who ostensibly trust the trustee.

EMPIRICAL STRATEGIES

In his widely recognized programmatic statement 'The quantitative analysis of large-scale data sets and rational action theory: for a sociological alliance' (1996), Goldthorpe argued that rational action theory would benefit from using empirical regularities revealed by large-scale survey research as explananda and, conversely, also that much large-scale survey research would benefit from employing rational action theory as a tool to provide an explanans for those explananda. While the alliance invoked by Goldthorpe might be emerging, we advocate that his conception of 'quantitative analysis of data' should be broadened to include not only survey designs but also experiments and quasi-experimental designs such as vignette studies. Different techniques should be used to test various assumptions and implications of the theoretical models, thus providing a more complete and reliable picture of the phenomenon under investigation (see Falk and Heckman, 2009 for a similar argument). Moreover, such a multimethod approach entails three additional advantages. First, multiple tests of the same hypotheses in diverse settings expand the scope of the theory, by making it applicable in multiple contexts. Second, finding support for the same hypotheses in various settings adds to the robustness of the results. Third, performing multiple tests reduces the problem of measurement validity, which is generally hard to assess in all types of approaches individually.

Accordingly, we have tested hypotheses like those presented above, as well as other more specific ones we do not discuss here, using complementary empirical methods, including laboratory experiments, surveys, and vignette experiments. In the following sections, we discuss the main features of such a multimethod approach, using one example per method. For more extensive reviews of this literature we refer to Barrera (2008), Raub and Buskens (2008), and Buskens and Raub (2010).

Vignette Studies

Distinguishing empirically between control, learning, and imitation effects of embeddedness can be difficult using both laboratory experiments and surveys: in experiments and surveys, actors are engaged in series of interactions in which opportunities for control, learning, and imitation often co-occur. By contrast, in vignette experiments subjects are asked questions about hypothetical real-life situations. A vignette study typically begins with a scenario that provides the 'frame' for the actor's decision. Subsequently, the actor evaluates a series of vignettes in which crucial information is varied. Because the scenarios are hypothetical, vignettes can be used to vary explanatory variables in an independent manner while they are likely to be much more correlated in actual interactions. Accordingly, they can be particularly useful to discriminate between competing explanatory mechanisms (for example, Rossi and Nock, 1982 on vignette experiments; see also the contribution on conjoint analysis by Priem and Weibel, Chapter 20 in this volume).

We designed one vignette study aiming especially at disentangling control, learning, and imitation effects (Barrera and Buskens, 2007). In the scenario, subjects were supposed to let a fellow student – described as 'expert on the stock market' – invest €3000 on their behalf, in exchange for a part of the profit.[2] The vignettes presented our subjects with two alternative investment partners whose characteristics were systematically varied. In particular, we manipulated learning and imitation by telling our subjects that the potential investment partner had previous similar transactions with other students from the same cohort (network embeddedness). However, in some vignettes we stated that these investments had been successful, while in others we omitted this information. This distinction allowed us to test learning and imitation effects empirically closely aligned with our theoretical definitions of the learning and imitation mechanisms. If actors know that previous investments were successful they can learn that their potential partner is trustworthy; if they do not know whether previous investments were successful, they can only imitate others who trusted the potential investment partner. In addition, we tested effects of control by manipulating other characteristics of the two alternative partners. In some vignettes we stated that the potential partner was about to move to a foreign university – thus making future sanctions for abuse of trust unavailable – while in other vignettes the partner was expected to continue his studies at the same university. We tested our hypotheses using a logistic regression in which attributes of the two alternative investment partners were used to predict the subjects' choice. We found empirical support for all three mechanisms. Furthermore, learning effects turned out to be stronger than imitation effects, while the latter appeared to be particularly important when the subjects were uncertain about the partner's ability to make a fruitful investment.

Vignette studies, however, also have disadvantages. First, as the respondents are asked to imagine themselves in a hypothetical scenario, the choices they make related to this scenario do not have any real consequence for the decision makers. This questions the salience of the incentives in driving these choices. Second, as the scenario is hypothetical, more potential sources of unreliability and bias can affect the interpretation of the actors' responses (for example people do not always act in accordance to their stated intentions). Third, similar to laboratory experiments, vignette scenarios can be perceived as rather artificial by the respondents and this might compromise the validity of their decisions.

Laboratory Experiments

Laboratory experiments are a relatively popular empirical strategy within the framework of the social mechanisms approach. A social mechanism, as defined by Hedström (2005: 25–6, emphasis added), '. . . describes a constellation of entities and activities that are organized such that they regularly bring about a particular type of outcome . . . *individuals are the core entities and their actions are the core activities* that bring about the social-level phenomena that one seeks to explain.' Because of this emphasis on the micro level, social-mechanism type of explanations always make explicit assumptions on the individual decisions of the actors involved. While in surveys decisions can be inferred, but hardly ever observed, laboratory experiments permit us to put precisely these assumptions to an empirical test. Therefore, the first and main advantage of laboratory experiments is that, by allowing the observation of actions and decisions of real agents, they provide an adequate test of action-based theoretical models.

Following up on the vignette study described above, we designed an experiment in which the same hypotheses could be tested (Barrera and Buskens, 2009). In this experiment, actors embedded in networks of six people played a repeated Investment Game and exchanged information concerning their own behaviour as well as their partners' behaviour in the game. All networks consisted of four trustors and two trustees, each of the latter playing repeated Investment Games with two trustors. The trustors were variously connected with each other by 'network ties' through which they received information about games played by the other trustors with the same trustee or with a different one. We manipulated network embeddedness by varying the number of network ties available, as well as by varying the content of the information transmitted by these network ties. For example, in some conditions we let trustors know about the decisions of other trustors to whom they were connected as well as about the response of the trustee, while in other conditions trustors were only informed about the decisions of the trustors. As in the vignette study, this manipulation allowed for separate tests of learning and imitation mechanisms, in line with our theoretical definitions of the two mechanisms: learning about the trustworthiness of the trustee is possible when information about his behaviour is available, while actors can only imitate when all they know is whether or to what extent other trustors trusted the trustee. Furthermore, as the total number of games played was known to the subjects beforehand, we were able to test for effects of control via both dyadic and network embeddedness (that is, opportunities for control are available when the number of expected future interactions is high, and they decrease and eventually vanish when the end of the game approaches).

We tested our hypotheses using a random effect model to account for interdependences in our data. We modelled the repeated interactions as a process in which information available at one point in time predicts choices made at the subsequent point in time. Thus, we analysed the trustors' investment decisions as a function of the information that they received about previous games played by other trustors with the same trustee, and/or with a different one. Consistent with previous studies, this experiment provided strong support for the effects of both learning and control via dyadic embeddedness. This implies that own experience and expected duration of the interaction with a given partner are the strongest predictors of trusting behaviour. By contrast, the effects related to network embeddedness were somewhat inconsistent with previous studies. In fact, we found that subjects imitated what other trustors did, whether the information about the behaviour of the trustee was available or not, but there was hardly an additional effect from the behaviour of the trustee when this information was available. We speculated that this anomaly might be due to the complexity of the experiment: it is possible that our subjects were not able to take all the information provided into account when making their decisions. Thus, they may have opted for the 'easiest' option, they just imitated what other trustors did (Barrera and Buskens, 2009). A review of experimental studies on trust can be found in Barrera (2008) as well as in Buskens and Raub (2010).

Laboratory experiments are particularly suitable for testing hypotheses on social mechanisms as they allow us to single out causal mechanisms, eliminating possible confounds. However, the experimental method also has limits. First of all, experiments are often criticized for their scarce generalizability. Generalizing experimental results can be problematic in two ways. First, there is the problem of statistical generalization. In general, statistical analyses on non-experimental data are conducted under the assumption that the observation used for the analyses comes from a random sample of the population to which the results are meant to apply. By contrast, typically, experimental subjects are at best a representative sample of the students' population of the university where the experiment is run, and most often they are not a representative sample at all. However, this is often exaggerated. The aim of a well-designed experiment is to isolate causal factors responsible for the phenomenon observed, by ruling out possible alternative explanations and confounds. Students' samples are used in behavioural experiments under the general assumption that their behaviour sufficiently approximates human behaviour. As long as this assumption can be made, it is not a problem to have a rather homogeneous pool of subjects, in order to facilitate causal attribution to the manipulated factors.

The second way in which generalizability is an issue has to do with a more substantive problem. Insofar as the experimental design aims at isolating possible causal relations, it also makes the interaction occurring in the laboratory extremely abstract and 'decontextualized'. When a given phenomenon is studied in the laboratory, the focal interaction is reduced to its elementary components and then replicated in this stylized form. Arguably, the experimental subjects might not recognize the real interaction that the experiment tries to model in the replica they see in the laboratory, and, most importantly, they might behave differently in the laboratory if the experiment activates different cognitive frames. Then, the problem of generalizability is not a statistical problem, but rather a problem of analytical realism. For the study of trust, the problem especially concerns the model used for the interaction (usually Trust Game or Investment Game) and the respective experimental manipulations. That is, there could be a problem of analytical realism to the extent that subjects do not recognize a problem of trust in the Trust Game or Investment Game. In order to support the generalizability of our experimental work – and in line with the strategy of using complementary research designs outlined above – we tested the same hypotheses using survey data. An example of such a test is discussed in the next section.

Surveys

Effects of social embeddedness on trust are documented in numerous survey studies conducted in a variety of settings and using diverse kinds of data. Some examples of data which have been used to study trust include attitudinal measures applied to national population samples (Simpson and McGrimmons, 2008), interfirm economic transactions (Batenburg et al., 2003; Buskens, 2002: ch. 5), interpersonal trust relationships within professional categories such as managers (Burt and Knez, 1995), intra-organizational trust relationships (Barrera and Van de Bunt, 2009), online economic transactions completed on auction websites using reputation systems (Bolton et al., 2004), and economic relationships between corporate actors, such as R&D alliances (Gulati, 1995). Focusing on different types of actors as well as different forms of interactions, findings based on survey data provide a more general picture of the social mechanisms of trust. Consequently, analytical realism is obviously higher than in experiments and generalizability is less problematic as survey data are usually drawn from well-known populations.

In our own survey on transactions of information technology products (Buskens 2002: ch. 5), we study whether contracts (as a measure for lack of trust since contracts typically reduce incentives for opportunistic behaviour of the trustee and provide some compensation for the trustor if trust is abused) become less extensive with dyadic and network embeddedness of the buyer of the products. We do indeed find learning and control effects related to dyadic embeddedness, but the survey did not provide information to test for imitation effects. In addition, we hardly found effects of network embeddedness. Reasons for this are probably related to more general limitations of cross-sectional survey studies.

Although many surveys offer evidence of the role of embeddedness in promoting trust, it is typically difficult to determine whether these effects are due to control, learning, or imitation effects. For example, surveys measure the existence of a social network between trustors. However, this same network can be used to learn about past behaviour of the trustee, but it can also be used to control the trustee. Survey data do not usually provide enough information to model the link between micro assumptions and macro social conditions appropriately. Therefore, survey data often present a discrepancy between the theoretical models supporting the hypotheses and the empirical tests of these hypotheses. However, as soon as the distance between the theoretical mechanisms and assumptions and the available empirical instruments grow large, the validity of the results and their implications for the theory become questionable.

Furthermore, the use of survey data in research on the social mechanisms of trust suffers from the same limits which are typical of all survey research. First, causal attribution is generally problematic in survey research, especially in cross-sectional surveys. Because all relevant variables are measured simultaneously, causality is usually assumed rather than shown. Generally, a statistical relation between two variables is different from an explanation, because it does not say anything about the actions and interactions that lead these two variables to co-vary (see Hedström, 2005: 20–23 for a discussion of statistical explanation). The causality issue can be remedied using longitudinal data (for example, Barrera and Van de Bunt, 2009). However, collecting suitable longitudinal data to test hypotheses on trust in embedded settings is costly and time consuming. Moreover, it is generally quite difficult for researchers to gain access to appropriate settings where such data can be collected. Consequently the availability of suitable datasets is rather scarce.

Finally, while experiments rely on behavioural measures, surveys often make use of attitudinal measures. Consequently, the same hypotheses are tested using very different operationalizations, depending on the setting where the survey data were collected. Moreover, especially in studies using secondary data, an appropriate variable may not be available and the researcher has to rely on proxies. The use of different operationalizations and proxies for the same theoretical variables increases the risk that different studies testing the same hypotheses yield inconsistent results. However, a single confirmation of a hypothesis always raises the question of whether the finding is robust against changes in the way the hypothesis is tested, which theoretically should not matter. Conversely, if one finds consistent evidence from multiple tests of the same hypothesis using different methods, this provides evidence for the robustness of the relation between the theoretical prediction and the empirical reality.

DISCUSSION

In this chapter, we summarized the main elements of the analytical approach to the study of trust in embedded settings. We introduced a few exemplary hypotheses concerning different social mechanisms, and discussed pros and cons of three different empirical strategies to test these hypotheses: laboratory experiments, survey studies, and vignette experiments. The conclusion of this comparative discussion of alternative empirical strategies is that none of the three alternatives can be said to be entirely superior to the other two for the purpose of testing hypotheses on the social mechanisms of trust. On the contrary, we rather advocate the adoption of a multimethod approach. In the second part of the chapter, we briefly discussed three examples of studies testing similar hypotheses using different techniques. These examples serve to illustrate how complementary empirical tests of the same mechanisms permit a more complete understanding of the effects of social embeddedness on trust.

NOTES

1. For reader friendliness we refer to the trustor using female pronouns and to the trustee using male pronouns.
2. The study was conducted in 2001, in times when such a scenario seemed far more plausible than it would seem in 2011.

REFERENCES

Barrera, D. (2005), *Trust in Embedded Settings*, Veenendaal: Universal Press.
Barrera, D. (2008), 'The social mechanisms of trust', *Sociologica*, **2**, 1–32.

Barrera, D. and V. Buskens (2007), 'Imitation and learning under uncertainty: a vignette experiment', *International Sociology*, **22** (3), 366–95.

Barrera, D. and V. Buskens (2009), 'Third-party effects', in K.S. Cook, C. Snijders, V. Buskens and C. Cheshire (eds), *eTrust: Forming Relations in the Online World*, New York: Russell Sage Foundation, pp. 37–72.

Barrera, D. and G.G. Van de Bunt (2009), 'Learning to trust: network effects through time', *European Sociological Review*, **25** (6), 709–21.

Batenburg, R.S., W. Raub and C. Snijders (2003), 'Contacts and contracts: temporal embeddedness and the contractual behavior of firms', *Sociology of Organizations*, **20**, 35–88.

Bolton, G.E., E. Katok and A. Ockenfels (2004), 'How effective are electronic reputation mechanisms? An experimental investigation', *Management Science*, **50** (11), 1587–602.

Burt, R.S. and M. Knez (1995), 'Kinds of third-parties effects on trust', *Rationality and Society*, **7**, 255–92.

Buskens, V. (2002), *Trust and Social Networks*, Boston, MA: Kluwer.

Buskens, V. and W. Raub (2002), 'Embedded trust: control and learning', *Advances in Group Processes*, **19**, 167–202.

Buskens, V. and W. Raub (2010), 'Rational choice research on social dilemmas: embeddedness effects on trust', forthcoming in R.P.M. Wittek, T.A.B. Snijders and V. Nee (eds), *Handbook of Rational Choice Social Research*.

Camerer, C.F. (2003), *Behavioral Game Theory. Experiments in Strategic Interaction*, New York: Russell Sage Foundation.

Camerer, C.F. and K. Weigelt (1988), 'Experimental tests of a sequential equilibrium reputation model', *Econometrica*, **56** (1), 1–36.

Coleman, J.S. (1990), *Foundations of Social Theory*, Cambridge, MA: Belknap Press of Harvard University Press.

Dasgupta, P. (1988), 'Trust as a commodity', in Diego Gambetta (ed.), *Trust: Making and Breaking Cooperative Relations*, Oxford: Blackwell, pp. 49–72.

Falk, A. and J.J. Heckman (2009), 'Lab experiments are a major source of knowledge in the social sciences', *Science*, **326**, 535–8.

Goldthorpe, J.H. (1996), 'The quantitative analysis of large-scale data sets and rational action theory: for a sociological alliance', *European Sociological Review*, **12** (2), 109–26.

Granovetter, M. (1985), 'Economic action and social structure: the problem of embeddedness', *American Journal of Sociology*, **91** (3), 481–510.

Gulati, R. (1995), 'Does familiarity breed trust? The implications of repeated ties for contractual choice in alliances', *Academy of Management Journal*, **38** (1), 85–112.

Hedström, P. (1998), 'Rational imitation', in P. Hedström and R. Swedberg (eds), *Social Mechanism: An Analytical Approach to Social Theory*, Cambridge: Cambridge University Press, pp. 306–27.

Hedström, P. (2005), *Dissecting the Social. On the Principles of Analytical Sociology*, Cambridge: Cambridge University Press.

Hedström, P. and P. Bearman (eds) (2009), *The Oxford Handbook of Analytical Sociology*, Oxford: Oxford University Press.

Misztal, B.A. (1996), *Trust in Modern Societies*, Cambridge: Polity Press.

Raub, W. and V. Buskens (2008), 'Theory and empirical research in analytical sociology: the case of cooperation in problematic social situations', *Analyse und Kritik*, **30**, 689–722.

Rossi, P.H. and S.L. Nock (eds) (1982), *Measuring Social Judgments: The Factorial Survey Approach*, Beverly Hills, CA: Sage.

Simpson, B. and T. McGrimmon (2008), 'Trust in embedded markets: a multi-method investigation of consumer transactions', *Social Networks*, **30** (1), 1–15.

Annotated Further Reading

Buskens, V. and W. Raub (2010), 'Rational choice research on social dilemmas: embeddedness effects on trust', forthcoming in R.P.M. Wittek, T.A.B. Snijders and V. Nee (eds),

Handbook of Rational Choice Social Research. This chapter surveys the use of rational choice theory and in particular game theory for the analysis of trust problems and embeddedness effects in trust problems.

Goldthorpe, J.H. (2000), *On Sociology. Numbers, Narratives, and the Integration of Research and Theory*, Oxford: Oxford University Press. This book emphasizes the potential of combining rigorous analytic theory building with high-quality empirical research.

Hedström, P. and P. Bearman (eds) (2009), *The Oxford Handbook of Analytical Sociology*, Oxford: Oxford University Press. This volume offers studies on applications of the analytic approach in numerous research areas.

20 Measuring the decision to trust using metric conjoint analysis
Richard L. Priem and Antoinette A. Weibel

INTRODUCTION

Conjoint analysis is a quantitative technique for capturing the utilities, preferences, understandings, perceptions, beliefs, or judgments of decision-makers (Arkes and Hammond, 1986), and ultimately for identifying the relative contributions of attributes and their levels to decision-makers' actions (Hair et al., 1987). Its name is derived from the two words 'considered' and 'jointly' (McCullough, 2002), which together capture its fundamental use characteristic – an individual making a decision (for example addressing a trust situation) based on multiple attributes that must be considered together. Because conjoint analysis examines the decision-making process by asking trustors actually to make decisions, rather than by relying on the theories or processes trustors say they use in retrospective accounts, it provides trust researchers with the ability to capture the 'theories-in-use' (Argyris and Schon, 1974) of trustors, instead of their 'espoused theories'. These 'theories-in-use' represent the underlying cognitive processes that drive a trustor's decision to accept vulnerability in particular trust situations.

Despite the potential of conjoint analysis for examining trustors' decision processes, the technique has seen sparse use in trust research. In the sections that follow, we first discuss why conjoint analysis – a quantitative technique for studying decision making – might be useful for trust researchers. We then explain conjoint methods, classify them in relation to other decision analysis techniques, and provide examples of the relatively few trust-related conjoint studies to date. We conclude by identifying several areas where conjoint studies could contribute to knowledge in trust research.

TRUST AS A DECISION

Trust and decision making are intrinsically linked in most trust research, even though this linkage is seldom acknowledged (for an exception see Kramer, 1999). Mayer et al.'s (1995) influential model, for example, views

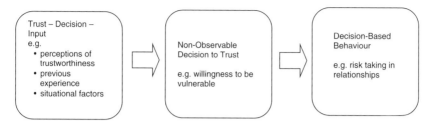

Figure 20.1   A simplified model of the trust decision process

trust as a decision to accept vulnerability to the actions of another party based on a potential trustor's cognitive judgment about another's trust-worthiness. Moreover, researchers often study potential trustors' choice behavior in various trust dilemma contexts. When framed in decision-making terms, a simple trust model would entail: some decision input; a non-observable decision to trust; and a decision-based behavioral mani-festation of trust, as shown in Figure 20.1.

The decision to trust or not to trust can be studied from at least two perspectives: rational choice and behavior. From the rational choice per-spective (Coleman, 1990; Gambetta, 1988; Hardin, 1991) decisions about trust are seen as similar to other risky choices. That is, A will trust B if the expected benefit of trusting is higher than the expected loss (Coleman, 1990). The expected benefit is higher when there are sufficient grounds to believe that it is in the interest of B to honor A's trust. Another lit-erature has studied decision making from a behavioral viewpoint (Cyert and March, 1963; March and Simon, 1958; Simon, 1957), by examining actual rather than normative choices. These studies have shown through experiments, field studies, and simulations that the rational choice theory of expected utility maximization explains only a limited part of observed behavior, because individuals face numerous cognitive (and emotional) constraints when they make decisions (Cohen et al., 1972; March, 1994; Tversky and Kahneman, 1971, 1974). Thus models based on behavio-ral decision-making processes have been put forward. In this tradition, for example, Kramer (2006) conceptualized trust as situated cognition wherein the trustor acts as an 'intuitive social auditor' who bases his deci-sion to trust on heuristics – that is, simple rules – and where trust is under-stood as a learning process. Relational models of trust decisions have also been framed as behavioral decision making. These models incorporate the social side of trust by adding affective factors (McAllister, 1995) or by con-sidering trustors' identity-related needs and the influence of those needs on trust-related cognitions and choice (Tyler, 2003).

When trust is couched in behavioral decision-making terms it becomes context dependent and, thus, 'details matter' (Messick and Kramer, 2001: 89). Beliefs about another's trustworthiness, for example, rely on behavioral cues which are likely to be processed differently in different situations and by different individuals. Yet how behavioral cues are processed depends on individuals' perceptual lenses and on various situation-specific factors. For example Yamagishi and Yamagishi (1994) show that Americans are more likely to apply a default heuristic of trusting than are Japanese people. Moreover, individual predispositions to trust others have been found to affect decision making on trust (Kiffin-Petersen and Cordery, 2003). The decision context also influences the decision to trust. Lewicki and Bunker (1995), for example, explain how the underlying relationship between trustor and trustee affects the weighing and selection of behavioral cues. Other situational factors that possibly affect trust decisions are: levels of risk (Das and Teng, 2001), institutional constraints (Barney and Hansen, 1994) and domain-specific concerns (Lewis and Wiegert, 1985) wherein 'I trust you to do Y', but only Y (Hardin, 2002: 7).

Although a considerable fraction of trust research could be couched in behavioral decision-making terms, trustors' applied decision heuristics and behavioral cue selection have seldom been studied with specific attention to context (see however Messick and Kramer, 2001). In the next section we introduce quantitative techniques that may be particularly useful in obtaining and analyzing the decision criteria of different trustors in a context-sensitive manner. We then provide an overview of metric conjoint analysis – a technique that is likely to be especially useful for future trust research – and we examine the sparse trust-related metric conjoint studies to date. We conclude by identifying opportunities for future research on the decision to trust using quantitative decision analysis methods.

MODELING DECISION PROCESSES

There are two distinct yet complementary approaches to studying the cognitive processes underlying decision making (Arkes and Hammond, 1986; Ford et al., 1989): composition and decomposition methods. Composition methods involve 'building up' a judgment policy based on the decision-maker's contemporaneous description of his/her thinking during the decision process. Decomposition methods are more quantitative and involve statistical modeling. They examine the relationship between the input (for example, the trust problem) and the decision (Abelson and Levi, 1985). By experimentally manipulating the levels of input attributes and observing changes in decision outcomes, researchers draw inferences about the underlying cognitive processes (Svenson, 1979). These techniques 'tear down', or decompose, a series of decisions to identify the underlying beliefs or judgments on which the decisions were based. The focus of decomposition methods is on the judgment itself (that is, the decision content) rather than on characteristics of the process. These methods use judgment tasks (McGrath, 1982) in which a maximum amount of information can be derived from a small number of respondents.

Decomposition methods assume the relevant attributes of the decision are already known and, based on these attributes, seek to examine choice differences for different attribute levels within the stimuli (for example the trust problem). Thus, the selection of variables for decomposition methods must be made a priori based on existing theory, and these methods are most useful in testing existing theory where attributes and their ranges are known in advance. Therefore, while composition methods have their greatest utility in grounded theory building, decomposition methods are most valuable when an established body of theory and empirical evidence already exists, as it does for trust research. There are four main decomposition methods: axiomatic conjoint analysis, nonmetric conjoint analysis, metric conjoint analysis, and policy capturing.

Table 20.1 presents a summary and comparison of methods utilized in decomposition approaches to studying decision making (adapted from Priem and Harrison, 1994).

Metric Conjoint Analysis for Studying the Decision to Trust

In axiomatic and nonmetric conjoint analyses, respondents are asked to rank their preferences for attribute sets representing different combinations of attribute levels. These methods therefore employ an ordinal-scaled dependent variable representing, for example, relative trustworthiness or the likelihood that the respondent would trust a particular trustee.

Metric conjoint analysis, on the other hand, requires respondents to rate attribute sets representing different combinations of attribute levels. It therefore produces an interval-scaled dependent variable (for example, perceived trustworthiness) that is more amenable to inferential statistical tests. This characteristic offers a number of advantages when analyzing decisions such as the decision to trust. By using replications (that is, multiple ratings for the same combination by the same person), for example, metric conjoint analysis makes it possible to test a particular individual's decision model parameter estimates for consistency (that is, test-retest reliability) using a repeated measures analysis of variance (ANOVA). Moreover, metric conjoint also enables the testing of both additive (main

Table 20.1   Decomposition techniques for analysing judgments underlying trust decisions

	Axiomatic conjoint analysis	Nonmetric conjoint analysis	Metric conjoint analysis (functional measurement)	Policy capturing (lens model, social judgment theory)
Essential features of method	Potential Trustor *ranks* likelihood of trusting for all factorial combinations of levels for trust-related variables, X, Y, Z . . .	Potential Trustor *ranks* likelihood of trusting for some or all factorial combinations of levels for trust-related variables, X, Y, Z . . .	Potential Trustor gives two or more replications of *ratings* of trustworthiness for all factorial combinations of levels for trust-related variables, X, Y, Z . . .	Potential Trustor gives *ratings* of trustworthiness for all or some orthogonal or correlated combinations ('profiles') of levels for trust-related variables X, Y, Z, and possibly irrelevant variables Q, R, S
Eventual goal or important result	Linear utility or importance functions for each trust-related variable (u(X), u(Y), u(Z), .) as used in Potential Trustor's judgment rule for when to trust	Weights or 'part-worths' gauging the linear importance of each trust-related variable for each Potential Trustor's judgment rule (that is, implicit theory of when to trust)	Linear (additive) or multilinear (multiplicative) function describing each Potential Trustor's combinatorial judgment rule (implicit theory of when to trust)	Linear function or judgment 'policy' equation relating trustworthiness variables ('cues') to the trust 'criterion'; compares the consistency of Potential Trustor's judgment policy
Number of levels of trust-related variables	Each variable *must* have at least 3 levels; more makes analysis extremely complicated	At least 2; 3 is much better; rarely more than 5	At least 2; 3 allows for limited test of nonlinearlity; no more than 5	At least 2, perhaps many; possible to use random effectives-type levels
Number of combinations of levels of trust-related variables to be judged	Product of number of levels of each trust-related variable	Usually product of number of levels of each trust-related variable. Can be less in	Product of number of levels of each trust-related variable multiplied by # of within-executive	Large number, between 25 and 200; large enough to get stable estimates of regression parameters

Table 20.1 (continued)

	Axiomatic conjoint analysis	Nonmetric conjoint analysis	Metric conjoint analysis (functional measurement)	Policy capturing (lens model, social judgment theory)
		incomplete block designs	executive replications	
Assumed response scale	Ordinal	Ordinal	Interval	Interval
Functional relation between trust-related variables and response	Weighted linear (additive) if axioms hold; otherwise unknown	Assumed to be weighted linear (additive)	Weighted linear (additive) or multilinear (multiplicative); check best fit	Weighted linear (additive); sometimes possible to check nonlinear
Statistical tests	None; misfit to axioms checked with simple tests (for example, monotonicity)	Possible to use within-subject ANOVA to construct quasi-Fs on additive terms	F-tests for all equation terms via ANOVA; power is function of Potential Trustor's reliability and number of replications	F-tests for policy weights in equation; F-tests for configurality of policy; R and R^2 to assess predictability
Definition of trust-related variables (number and content)	All defined or assumed known by the researcher (based on previous theory or evidence)	All defined or assumed known by the researcher (based on previous theory or evidence)	All defined or assumed known by the researcher (based on previous theory or evidence)	All defined or assumed known by the researcher (based on previous theory or evidence)
Functional relations of trust-related (stimulus) variables	X, Y, Z are . . . orthogonal	X, Y, Z are . . . orthogonal	X, Y, Z . . . are orthogonal	X, Y, Z . . . can be orthogonal or correlated, but should be orthogonal to irrelevant variables Q, R, S . . .
Number of trust-related variables in stimulus	Few: usually 2 and always less than 5	Few: 2 to 7	Few: 2 to 5	Moderate, possibly many: 4 to 20

Source: Adapted from Priem and Harrison (1994).

effects) and multilinear (main effects and interactions) decision-making models at the individual level, which allows researchers to compare differences in decision-making models across individuals.

These advantages make metric conjoint analysis a potentially useful method for trust researchers interested in: (1) examining multi-attribute, contingency models of trust; (2) evaluating the same trust decision in differing contexts; and (3) testing differences in approaches to the decision to trust across different potential trustors or across categories of potential trustors. Analytical details about metric conjoint analysis can be found in Louviere (1988). Priem (1992, 1994) provides further description and examples.

Research on the Trust Decision

Several researchers already have begun using quantitative decision analysis to examine the decision to trust. Lapierre (2007), for example, investigated whether subordinates are more willing to show extra-role behaviors to the extent that they perceive their supervisors to be trustworthy. Employing a metric conjoint analysis rating task in a full factorial, $2 \times 2 \times 2$ design, he manipulated in scenarios differing degrees of supervisors' behavioral manifestations of their ability, their benevolence towards subordinates, and their benevolence towards subordinates' peers. Lapierre investigated: (1) which of these behavioral cues most influences trust beliefs and intentions to show extra-role behaviors and (2) whether the separate and joint effects of these cues can be distinguished. He found the benevolence cues to be more important for trust decisions than are ability cues (2007: 286). In addition, there is a moderating effect of benevolence towards subordinates and benevolence towards subordinates' peers on perceived trustworthiness, such that if a supervisor clearly shows benevolence to the subordinate but at the same time neglects the subordinates' peers, the effect of this benevolence on trustworthiness is considerably attenuated (Lapierre, 2007: 287).

Buskens and Weesie (2000) analyzed how the embeddedness of trustors who are prospective buyers of used cars affects their trust decisions, using a vignette study employing a 2^6 fractional factorial design where attribute sets were evaluated via paired comparison ratings. They proposed that temporal embeddedness – represented as past experience in a repeated game situation – and structural embeddedness – represented by reputation effects – would result in higher ratings of intentions for buying a used car from the trustee. Buskens and Weesie found that all embeddedness factors they measured have a positive effect on the trustors' behavioral manifestation of trust (2000: 244). They also found that experience-related embeddedness variables, such as one's own experience with the dealer or the experience of trusted others with the dealer, have a stronger effect on the decision to trust than do control-related embeddedness variables such as the possibility to 'punish' the dealer by withholding future transactions (Buskens and Weesie, 2000: 244).

Schoder and Haenlein (2004) compared the relative importance of different trust sources on a seller's willingness to carry out risky online transactions with a potential buyer online with the help of a full factorial 2x2x2 conjoint experiment where all combinations of levels of the three trust sources were rated simultaneously in a decision tree format (see Priem, 1992, for a similar delivery format). The three different sources of trust were: (1) institutional trust, which signifies that the decision to trust hinges on the regulatory framework in which the seller and buyer are acting; (2) calculative trust, which is determined by the value of the good to be sold; and (3) relational trust, which is built on previous experience. Schoder and Haenlein found that institutional sources for trust are by far the most important trust driver in an online environment, whereas calculative sources of trust are least important (2004: 54).

Finally, Patzelt and Shepherd (2008) used metric conjoint analysis in a 2^5 fractional factorial experiment to examine decisions of whether or not to continue investing in underperforming strategic alliances. Their sample of software and IT industry managers in Bavaria, Germany, rated random subsets of possible level combinations for output, behavioral and social control, and goodwill and competence trust concerning the alliance partner. Patzelt and Shepherd found that the effect of all control types on investment persistence is magnified as goodwill trust increases, and that output and behavioral control effects are similarly magnified with increasing competence trust. Thus, control and trust variables interact in affecting the likelihood of continued investment in underperforming alliances – a judgment policy that could only be revealed via metric conjoint analysis.

None of these trust-related decision-making studies, however, made use of two key benefits of the metric conjoint technique: (1) the ability to use repeated measures and therefore evaluate the consistency of individual respondents' judgment policies; and (2) the ability to compare judgment policies across different individuals, or across categories of individuals, or across different contexts. We next suggest opportunities for future trust researchers who wish to examine these aspects of the decision to offer trust.

DISCUSSION OF RESEARCH OPPORTUNITIES

In outlining opportunities for future research on the decision to trust, we will use as a continuing example Mayer et al.'s (1995) well-known specification that a trustor's judgment of a trustee's trustworthiness is dependent upon the trustor's perceptions of the trustee's ability, benevolence, and integrity. Before reaching a decision in this decision situation, a potential trustor would need to: (1) make judgments about the levels of the trustee's ability, benevolence and integrity; (2) make judgments about direct causal relationships between each of these three variables and trustworthiness; and (3) make a judgment about the interactive effects of ability, benevolence and integrity of the likely trustworthiness of the trustee. These judgments, if consistently applied across multiple decisions for different trustees, would form that potential trustor's trust judgment policy. Although we will use Mayer et al. (1995) as the basis for our subsequent discussion, we do so for decent exposition only; many other theories in trust research could similarly be tested or extended via quantitative decision analysis techniques.

Further Specifying Trust Policies

One way to further Mayer et al.'s (1995) specification of ability, benevolence, and integrity as important factors contributing to the decision to trust would be to determine, for the typical potential trustor, the degree to which each of these variables contributes to perceptions of trustworthiness (that is, the relative strength of each variable's effect) and also the extent to which they interact with one another such that a high level of one variable has an enhanced effect on perceptions of trustworthiness in the presence of a high level of another of these variables. These questions could be answered via a simple 2x2x2 metric conjoint experiment in which all combinations of the three variables at two levels – that is, ability, benevolence, integrity; high or low – are rated by potential trustors as to the likelihood of their trusting a trustee with that combination of attributes. The 2x2x2 design would produce eight possible combinations of trustworthiness attributes for rating. Replication would require 16 combinations in total, which would be presented to respondents in two decision trees with the order of attribute presentation randomly varied across the decision trees. Typically, another 'placebo' task is inserted in between the presentation of the two decision trees to help reduce any carryover from one decision task to the other.

With a sufficient number of respondents, an experiment of this type could indicate the relative contributions of ability, benevolence, and integrity to perceptions of trustworthiness for the typical potential trustor. It could also indicate whether or not various combinations of two of these variables have an interactive effect on perceptions of trustworthiness, or even if high levels of all three jointly affect perceptions of trustworthiness. Findings of this type could enhance our overall understanding of the way these factors influence the decision to trust.

Identifying Individual Differences Among Potential Trustors

Yet it may be that potential trustors are not homogeneous in the judgment policies they employ when making the trust decision. For example, one potential trustor may tend to weight ability most highly when making the decision, while another may consider benevolence or integrity to be the most important factor. A third potential trustor might believe that all three are necessary at high levels before one can offer trust to a trustee.

The same experiment outlined above can be used to analyze whether or not the trust judgment policies of potential trustors are homogeneous, but a few more steps are involved. First, each respondent's trust judgment policy must be tested for consistency across replications (that is, test–retest reliability), and those that are not consistent must be eliminated. Second, using each of the parameter estimates (that is, three main effects, three double interactions, and one triple interaction) from the judgment policies of each respondent who exhibited consistent judgment as input data, the researcher employs cluster analysis to group those respondents who use similar trust judgment policies. The cluster findings could provide considerable insight into the heterogeneity of trust judgment policies used by potential trustors. For example, one group of potential trustors may emphasize the ability main effect with no interactions as their judgment policy. Another group may emphasize integrity. A third group may show an interaction effect between ability and integrity, such that when both are present at high levels the decision to trust is much more likely. Again, findings such as this would allow us to extend our understanding of how potential trustors actually make the decision to trust trustees.

Identifying Differences Across Categories of Potential Trustors

Another way to evaluate possible heterogeneity of trust judgment policies across different groups of potential trustors is to designate theory-based categories a priori instead of letting the data determine the categories as in the cluster approach. For example, one might develop a theory suggesting that supervisors will use different factors in determining the trustworthiness of a subordinate than a subordinate will use in determining the trustworthiness of the supervisor. That is, supervisors may focus more on the subordinate's ability in getting the job done, while subordinates place more emphasis on a supervisor's benevolence. Again using the same simple conjoint experiment, but this time with a sample of supervisors and a separate sample of subordinates, a researcher could compare the judgment policies determined from the supervisor sample versus those shown in the subordinates sample to test the theory. This type of experiment could be performed with many different bases for categorizing potential trustors, including gender, ethnicity, functional experience, and so on, each of which would give added insight into the decision to trust.

Identifying Differences in Trust Policies Across Contexts

Bamberger (2008) recently argued that management theory could be advanced by moving from simply identifying the context within which a distinct phenomenon is analyzed instead of developing theories that incorporate differences in the phenomenon across contexts. He defined 'context theories' as 'those theories that specify how surrounding phenomena or temporal conditions directly influence lower-level phenomena, condition relations between one or more variables at different levels of analysis, or are influenced by the phenomena nested within them' (2008: 841).

Metric conjoint analysis experiments could be useful in testing context theories of the trust decision. For example, one could present the same experiment outlined above to potential trustors, but precede the experiment with a descriptive scenario indicating in more detail the context in which the decision is being made. That is, a researcher could specify one context as climbing Mount Everest and hypothesize that ability would be the most important factor contributing to the decision to trust a mountain-climbing partner. The researcher could then specify another context as, say, a tenure decision, and hypothesize that integrity would be the most important factor contributing to the decision to trust a tenure committee. By employing a within-subjects design where each potential trustor responds to both scenarios, the researcher could determine whether or not an individual trustor will change decision policies based on the decision context, thereby testing one aspect of the context specificity of individuals' trust judgment policies.

Methodological Issues and Insights

There are a number of issues that every researcher faces in conducting a metric conjoint study. Two issues common to all survey studies are the potential for social desirability bias and for lack of realism. These issues can develop from either asking sensitive questions, or biased terminology, or a normatively loaded context, or from using unrealistic ranges or variables for the choices. As researchers, we have frequently incorporated a cognitive pretest that examines for social desirability bias and realism using the same topics with the same type of subjects who will be used in the conjoint study. This allows us to alter the variable names or definitions to minimize social desirability issues.

Another common issue is the number of variables that can be included in a single study. In our experience the tradeoff is between subject fatigue due to too many variables versus the benefits of identifying the strong links among a larger number of variables. This is typically something that should be decided on theoretical grounds. One way we have achieved a balance between subject fatigue and number of variables is through the use of fractional factorial designs that allow examination of more variables while minimizing subject fatigue.

A final issue is whether or not the subjects are sufficiently involved in the task to ensure that they are providing accurate decisions. For metric conjoint studies it is common to use repeated measures designs where two replications of the task are presented to each subject, with the order of presentation varied between the tasks and a leading-away task that minimizes any carryover between the tasks of interest. The repeated measures allows the researcher to test the reliability of each respondent's decision model, so respondents who were non-involved or did not understand the task can be deleted from the analysis. Our experience is that as many as 10 percent of managerial respondents may provide unreliable results in conjoint studies, for a variety of possible reasons. Eliminating such unreliable respondents strengthens confidence in study results.

DISCUSSION

We have introduced in this chapter quantitative decision analysis techniques that may be helpful in analyzing the decision to trust. We paid particular attention to metric conjoint analysis – a technique that is likely to be especially useful for future trust research – and we examined the sparse trust-related metric conjoint studies to date. Although we have identified several opportunities for using metric conjoint analysis future research on the decision to trust, we expect that trust researchers who become familiar with this and other quantitative decision analysis techniques will be inventive in applying these techniques to trust research issues we have not yet even imagined. We hope this will be the case!

REFERENCES

Abelson, R.P. and A. Levi (1985), 'Decision making and decision theory', in G. Lindzay and E. Aronson (eds), *The Handbook of Social Psychology*, 3rd edition, New York: Random House.

Argyris, C. and D. Schon (1974), *Theory in Practice: Increasing Professional Effectiveness*, San Francisco: Jossey Bass.

Arkes, H.R. and K.R. Hammond (eds) (1986), *Judgment and Decision Making: An Interdisciplinary Reader*, Cambridge: Cambridge University Press.

Bamberger, P. (2008), 'Beyond contextualization: using context theories to narrow the micro–macro gap in management research', *Academy of Management Journal*, **51**, 839–46.

Barney, J.B. and M.H. Hansen (1994), 'Trustworthiness as a source of competitive advantage', *Strategic Management Journal*, **15**, 175–90.

Buskens, V. and J. Weesie (2000), 'An experiment on the effects of embeddedness in trust situations', *Rationality and Society*, **12** (2), 227–53.

Cohen, M., J.G. March and J. Olsen (1972), 'A garbage can model of organizational choice', *Administrative Science Quarterly*, **17**, 1–25.

Coleman, J. (ed.) (1990), *The Foundations of Social Theory*, Cambridge, MA: Harvard University Press.

Cyert, R.M. and J.G. March (eds) (1963), *A Behavioral Theory of the Firm*, Englewood Cliffs, NJ: Prentice Hall.

Das, T.K. and B.S. Teng (2001), 'Trust, control, and risk in strategic alliances: an integrated framework', *Organization Studies*, **22** (2), 251–83.

Ford, K., N. Schmitt, S. Schectman, B. Hults and M. Doherty (1989), 'Process tracing methods: contributions, problems, and neglected research questions', *Organizational Behavior and Human Decision Processes*, **43**, 75–118.

Gambetta, D. (1988), *Trust: Making and Breaking Cooperative Relations*, New York: Basil Blackwell.

Hair, J.E., R.E. Anderson and R.L. Tatham (eds) (1987), *Mulitvariate Data Analysis*, New York: Macmillan.

Hardin, R. (1991), 'Trusting persons, trusting institutions', in R.J. Zeckhauser (ed.), *Strategy and Choice*, Cambridge, MA: MIT Press, pp. 185–209.

Hardin, R. (2002), 'Conceptions and explanations of trust', in K. Cook (ed.), *Trust in Society*, New York: Russell Sage, pp. 3–39.

Kiffin-Petersen, S.A. and J.L. Cordery (2003), 'Trust, individualism and job characteristics as predictors of employee preference for teamwork', *International Journal of Human Resource Management*, **14** (1), 93–116.

Kramer, R.M. (1999), 'Trust and distrust in organizations: emerging perspectives, enduring questions', *Annual Review of Psychology*, **50**, 569–98.

Kramer, R.M. (2006), 'Trust as situated cognition: an ecological perspective on trust decisions', in R. Bachmann and A. Zaheer (eds), *Handbook of Trust Research*, Cheltenham, UK and Northampton, MA, USA: Edward Elgar, pp. 68–84.

Lapierre, L.M. (2007), 'Supervisor trustworthiness and subordinates' willingness to provide extra-role efforts', *Journal of Applied Social Psychology*, **37** (2), 272–97.

Lewicki, R.J. and B.B. Bunker (1995), 'Trust in relationships: a model of trust development and decline', in B.B. Bunker and J.Z. Rubin (eds), *Conflict, Cooperation, and Justice*, San Francisco: Jossey Bass, pp. 133–74.

Lewis, D.J. and A. Wiegert (1985), 'Trust as a social reality', *Social Forces*, **63** (4), 967–85.

Louviere, J.L. (ed.) (1988), *Analyzing Decision Making: Metric Conjoint Analysis*, Sage University Paper Series on Quantitative Applications in the Social Sciences, 67, Beverly Hills, CA: Sage.

March, J.G. (ed.) (1994), *A Primer on Decision Making*, New York: Free Press.

March, J.G. and H.A. Simon (eds) (1958), *Organizations*, New York and London: Wiley; Chapman and Hall.

Mayer, R.C., J.H. Davis and F.D. Schoorman (1995), 'An integrative model of organizational trust', *Academy of Management Review*, **20** (3), 709–34.

McAllister, D.J. (1995), 'Affect- and cognition-based trust as foundations for interpersonal cooperation in organizations', *Academy of Management Journal*, **38** (1), 24–59.

McCullough, D. (2002), 'A user's guide to conjoint analysis', *Marketing Research*, **14** (2), 19–24.

McGrath, J.E. (1982), 'Dilemmatics: the study of research choices and dilemmas', in J.E.

McGrath, J. Martin and R.A. Kulka (eds), *Judgment Calls in Research*, Beverly Hills, CA: Sage, pp. 69–102.

Messick, D. and R. Kramer (2001), 'Trust as a form of shallow morality', in K.S. Cook (ed.), *Trust in Society*, New York: Russell Sage Foundation, pp. 89–118.

Patzelt, H. and D.A. Shepherd (2008), 'The decision to persist with underperforming alliances: the role of trust and control', *Journal of Management Studies*, **45**, 1217–43.

Priem, R.L. (1992), 'An application of metric conjoint analysis for the evaluation of top managers' individual strategic decision making process: a research note', *Strategic Management Journal*, **13**, 143–51.

Priem, R.L. (1994), 'Executive judgment, organizational congruence, and firm performance', *Organization Science*, **5**, 421–37.

Priem, R.L. and D.A. Harrison (1994), 'Exploring strategic judgment: methods for testing the assumptions of prescriptive contingency theories', *Strategic Management Journal*, **15**, 311–24.

Schoder, D. and M. Haenlein (2004), 'The relative importance of different trust constructs for sellers in the online world', *Electronic Markets*, **14** (1), 48–57.

Simon, H.A. (ed.) (1957), *Models of Man*, New York: Wiley.

Simons, T. (2002), 'Behavioral integrity: the perceived alignment between managers' words and deeds as a research focus', *Organization Science*, **13** (1), 18–35.

Svenson, O. (1979), 'Process description of decision making', *Organizational Behavior and Human Performance*, **23**, 86–112.

Tversky, A. and D. Kahneman (1971), 'Belief in the law of small numbers', *Psychological Bulletin*, **76** (2), 105–10.

Tversky, A. and D. Kahneman (1974), 'Judgment under uncertainty: heuristics and biases', *Science*, **185** (4157), 1124–31.

Tyler, T.R. (2003), 'Trust within organizations', *Personnel Review*, **32** (5), 556–68.

Yamagishi, T. and M. Yamagishi (1994), 'Trust and commitment in the United-States and Japan', *Motivation and Emotion*, **18** (2), 129–66.

Further Reading

Louviere, J.L. (ed.) (1988), *Analyzing Decision Making: Metric Conjoint Analysis*, Sage University Paper Series on Quantitative Applications in the Social Sciences, 67, Beverly Hills, CA: Sage Publications.

Priem, R.L. (1994), 'Executive judgment, organizational congruence, and firm performance', *Organization Science,* **5**, 421–37.

Priem, R.L. and D.A. Harrison (1994), 'Exploring strategic judgment: methods for testing the assumptions of prescriptive contingency theories', *Strategic Management Journal,* **15**, 311–24.

21 Diary methods in trust research
Rosalind H. Searle

INTRODUCTION

Diary methods present an exciting opportunity for trust researchers to gather detailed, accurate and multi-faceted insights into social behaviour, cognitive and affective states as they occur within their natural settings. The approaches allow events and experiences which shape individuals' perceptions of trust to be richly explored. More importantly for trust scholars, these techniques present the opportunity to develop more comprehensive understandings of the dynamics of trust development, maintenance and repair. Yet despite their potential, to date little research on trust has been conducted using these tools.

One of the most promising applications of this technique is the exploration of major events and their resultant changes and transitions. Such events frequently involve shifts in trust levels between parties. Diary studies could look at how different employees respond to changes such as downsizing, or other major trust breakdowns. There is a paucity of longitudinal study generally in research, but especially in examining trust. We know potentially about the huge impact of trust breakdown on relationships and organisations (Bies and Tripp, 1996; Dirks and Ferrin, 2001; Ferrin et al., 2007; Gillespie and Dietz, 2009; Robinson, 1996; Searle et al., 2011), but we know less about its actual longer-term impact. For example, major life events, such as divorce, can have a substantial and disruptive impact on everyday routines and ongoing moods and cognitions (Caspi et al., 1987; Franklin et al., 1990) but what is the long-term impact on trust? Through obtaining sufficient responses utilising diary methods we could begin to identify patterns and interactions, to explore the situations and conditions which lead to the recorded responses. Diary methods would assist in the systematic examination of the immediate and longer-term effect of trust, which would enable us identify antecedents, processes and consequences of trust. It would give unique insights to fundamental questions, such as whether trust can actually be fully repaired. We could take an organisational level breakdown, such as Enron, and examine what happens to the relationships between subordinates and superiors. Does its impact spill over into other relationships? Does trust really repair, or become more bounded? Through these techniques differences in perceptions of trust and breakdown between respondents could be explored, as well as identifying between-respondent differences in the variability of trust perceptions. By capturing the ongoing changes within respondents' perceptions to key events, such studies could offer insightful and revealing contributions to the field.

   This chapter outlines how the diary method could be utilised in the trust research context. I begin by focusing on three distinct approaches to the method before considering validity issues and some key caveats. Throughout, experiences from a recent study of nurse mentors are highlighted, and potential research questions identified to illustrate how the method could be successfully deployed to further trust studies.

DESCRIPTION OF THE METHOD

The focus of diary methods is on collecting detailed descriptions about the events and experiences that make up respondents' lives. They involve the gathering of ongoing experiences as they occur in situ, focusing on 'structured contemporaneous self-observation' (Reis and Gable, 2000: 190). Data collection may vary in frequency, from those elicited many times a day for an intense duration, such as over a week, to those gathered with less frequency over a longer period, such as many months. These descriptions can include multiple responses to a set scale over a significant time span, such as through a company merger, or used in combination with other methods, such as interviews, to reveal more subtle changes in trust throughout a relationship, such as between a trainee and their mentor. The key advantage for researchers is that these experiences can be collected at, or shortly after, they occur (experience sampling) (Kahneman et al., 2004). As a result, these data can be considered highly accurate points of view of recalled events, offering a unique insight into respondents' worlds, revealing affective, behavioural and cognitive information which relate to both dispositional and situational factors.

   Diary methods can be utilised across different types of study. The choice of which depends chiefly on the type of research question. In designing a study, there are three commonly used recording contingencies, including recording at: set intervals; in response to a researcher's signal; or in response to a specific event occurring. There is insufficient space to discuss these options in detail here. A simple taxonomy differentiates three distinct research approaches (Bolger et al., 2003; see Table 21.1). These include: (i) identification of 'typical' participants, which aggregates data over time; (ii) modelling within-person processes to see how individuals might vary ; and, finally, (iii) modelling a time course to examine what a

Table 21.1 Examples of taxonomy of diary approaches using downsizing example

Format	Recording interval	
	Time-contingent protocols	Event-contingent protocol
Identifying the typical	Weekly recording of trust, well-being and performance by department	Recording of trust, well-being and performance following certain events (information about the redundancies) or interactions (with line manager) by department
Changes over the time course	Recording three times daily: trust, well-being and performance measures for duration of the redundancies, (plus and minus six months) for two distinct groups – survivors vs those laid off.	Recording of trust, well-being and performance only following certain events (information about the redundancies) or interactions (with line manager)
Within-participant processes	Recording twice daily: trust and well-being to see impact of trust repair efforts	Recording of trust, well-being and performance only following certain events (information exchanges) or interactions (with line management)

typical process might be and then explore whether there are differences between participants. These are now discussed in turn.

COMMON STUDY DESIGNS

Identifying the Typical

The simplest type of research question focuses on understanding what typical participants, or typical situations, are like over time. Significantly, while this is a useful technique, it does not take full advantage of the benefits of these methods. Instead, attention merely focuses on generating a summary of what actually happens over time. This simple approach collects data from a range of participants and then simply aggregates them into numerical composites, for distinct departments or levels within the organisations. Researchers determine the frequency and duration over which information is gathered, based on what is appropriate for the question under scrutiny. For example, in a merger context it might be each week for several months. A key concern for those undertaking such research is to ensure sufficient entries are obtained to enable identification of both between-person differences, but also between-person variability (Bolger et al., 2003).

A dilemma for the researcher using this simple design is that potentially valuable information is lost by aggregating these data. At one level, these composites maximise reliability, but where there are large variations between and within person, there may be inaccuracy in the estimation of standard errors and significance levels. These real variances are simply removed. It is therefore important that researchers look closely at their results. Are there discrepancies in the relative frequency of respondents' reporting, or large variations between respondents' recording? For example, in a downsizing situation, one department's manager may be much more considerate in how she informs staff, and thus creates a less significant reduction in organisational trust levels among both those retained and those forced to leave the firm. However, if in the following data collection point this supportive manager is laid off, then retained staff trust levels may fall far more than typical in other departments. Thus, care needs to be taken in the interpretation of these data.

Changes over the Time Course

A second type of question explores change over time and enables more complex multi-level modelling to be performed. Modelling the dynamics of a time course is something trust researchers are just beginning to do and for which a diary approach is perfect. Questions here would include: how does trust develop, or repair occur over time? Using a sampling technique that captures experiences over hours, days, weeks and longer, researchers can begin to look at more complicated ways with analysis that requires the simultaneous examination of between- and within- person effects and their interactions. Such approaches would enable the identification of cycles of trust, rather than merely looking at linear sequences of cause and effect. This approach presents exciting possibilities, allowing empirical examination of what, and how, particular events influence subsequent behaviours, cognitions and affective states.

Identifying different types of sequence and their impact is a central concern. This approach looks at unfolding, affective states, behaviours and cognitions. For example, Margolin, Christen and John's (1996) study of family dynamics collected daily telephone accounts of family conflicts over a two-week period. From this they identified two distinct sequence patterns. They revealed that a defining characteristic of distressed families was the spillover of their conflicts, with each single conflict having an extended duration, creating an ongoing conflictual atmosphere. Such patterns were absent from the other family type.

In considering researching trust and our aforementioned downsizing study, we could compare the role of management style in ameliorating the decline of organisational trust levels. We could then see the impact of trust among retained staff. Through comparing respondents' data from a number of departments, we could explore differences in organisational trust violation and repair. In this way the method provides a useful bridge between experimental studies and field studies. It can be an important tool in identifying mediations. Further, this diary form has higher fidelity than many traditional longitudinal methods, by utilising larger numbers of participants and longer-term repeated measurement. For example, in a recent small-scale study we looked at nurse mentors and their interactions with their students during training placements. From each mentor we gathered well-being data after each formal meeting with their student. They also kept notes from each session and significant things that happened in between. These note diaries formed the basis of interviews held at the start, middle and end of their mentoring experiences. (These notes and in some cases rich pictures were then content analysed by the researchers.) At the final interview we also asked them to complete a propensity to trust scale. From these data, we can explore cycles of trust based on propensity to trust levels.

Within-Person Processes

The final type of question looks at modelling within-person processes. This is arguably where questions concerning processes are among the most challenging, but also the most necessary (Bolger et al., 2003). For example, personal exchange history and expectations are theorised to be important in trust research. Therefore within-person-level studies are fundamentally important. This type of study would enable the identification of antecedents and outcomes of experiences. Through within-person design, processes can be more robustly studied, with the participant acting as their own control. For example, Conway and Briner (2002) used daily diaries to identify the spillover impact of psychological breaches on employees. The types of questions we could examine here would focus on identifying what factors affect personal variability. They might include: how do people differ in their processes of trust development or repair? For example, in our downsizing study, we might look at whether those with a higher propensity to trust are able to recover their trust in the organisation, whereas those with a low propensity to trust may never regain that level of organisational trust. We could examine whether one violation taints subsequent experiences of trust.

RESEARCH VALIDITY AND CAVEATS

In this next section the high reliability and validity of this method is discussed, with reflections on some important caveats, including sampling, transparency and repetition.

Reliability

A central advantage of this approach is that it captures events at, or near to, the time they occur. This increases the reliability of the subsequent recall. Indeed they are often a better technique to use than global survey tools (Reis and Wheeler, 1991), but only if recording occurs at, or close to, the event's occurrence. In part reliability is enhanced because it reduces the likelihood of retrospective bias, in which recall of an event may alter significantly perceptions of what actually occurred. This is particularly important in studying emotive events, such as where trust has broken down. At times respondents' views of the world may have significantly altered and their recollection of what occurred prior to a violation becomes susceptible to 'state-contingent recall' (Bower, 1981). For example, experiencing a trust violation may significantly alter memories, reducing reference to earlier and positive perceptions. Collecting information systematically over time reduces sources of measurement error and allows a more complete picture to emerge. While reliability is an important consideration for those using this approach on a quantitative basis, the technique can also be deployed on a more emergent basis, as in the nurse study, adopting a more phenomenological approach to examining these data.

Certain types of data, including affect and attitudinal retrospections, are very susceptible to capturing the mood at the time of the report, rather than time of occurrence (Blaney, 1986). For example, those studying a physical phenomenon, such as perceptions of pain, have found that participants subjectively aggregate their experiences, placing much more weight on more recent or extreme levels (Stone et al., 2000). For trust researchers, gaining an accurate account of the sequence of events and shifts in perceptions may be critical to understanding exactly how trust is altered by breaches. These methods would address whether trust changes and impacts are different when altered through slow erosions or through a major event. Was there a tipping point caused by the cumulative actions of others, or a single person? Other retrospective-based methods, such as interview or questionnaire, tend to aggregate events, resulting in a faulty reconstruction of what actually occurred, altering the prominence of key actors or events. The diary method allows for the immediate capture of these events and their impact as they unfold, boosting its reliability. Let us now discuss some caveats.

Sampling

One critique of diary methods concerns the nature of the sample. Few methods require such dedication and commitment from participants. We have all tried to keep diaries at different points in our lives, but how many have succeeded beyond a few weeks or months? The process places a burden on participants which can significantly influence their willingness to become involved. As a result, convenience samples are often a major source, with participants who cannot be bothered simply dropping out due to the high workload involved. Convenience sample can be biased, making it unrepresentative of the general population and so may impede the wider application of the findings. Indeed we used snowballing to access participants in our mentor study, and were aware that we might not access those who were more reluctant about having this role. However, a benefit of potentially skewed populations is that they often have higher retention rates than those found in other studies. Recruitment involves only those interested in the topic and who are willing to complete the diaries. For example, Conway and Briner (2002) in their study of breaches of the psychological contract had a sample of 45 employees, who completed daily diaries over a ten-day period, producing 450 data points, or Totterdell et al.'s (2006) weekly study of psychological strain, which contained 64 participants over a six-month period, resulted in 1,164 responses. Each case varied in the frequency of data recording, but they indicate that, with the correct recruitment and ongoing contact throughout the study, satisfactory samples can be achieved.

Connected to the issue of retention are the decisions taken concerning the duration and recording frequency of data gathering. This aspect can have a direct and critical impact on recruitment and retention. Over-researched participants can be destructive to data collection, or simply drop out of the study as it goes on.

Researchers need to be clear about the focus of their study. Studies which involve a lucid and pertinent issue and where participants feel involved as a co-investigator can be helpful. Indeed in our recent mentor research we enhanced the study's attractiveness to participants by showing that it could count towards a nurse's continuing professional development (CPD) hours. We developed the study to focus on important or significant events occurring over a finite period, which helped participants to see their relevance. A further approach which reduces the burden on participants and still results in the necessary data being collected, is to vary the level of self-report required, for example only some items required high-frequency reporting (see Reis and Wheeler, 1991 for details of the Rochester Interaction Record (RIR) approach) and the remainder are recorded far less frequently.

Transparency

A central debate in trust research is the issue of 'psychological reactance', in which participants' experience or behaviour is altered as a result of being involved in the study (Brehm, 1966). This is particularly relevant where the term 'trust' is used in the study. Trust – often implicit within a relationship – may rarely emerge as a consideration until it is challenged. Studies where trust is explicitly mentioned can potentially sensitise, change, or even distort, participants' perceptions by suddenly making them aware of it. In diary studies evidence is limited that validity is reduced through reactance (Bolger et al., 2003), however, trust may be an exception. Researchers therefore face a dilemma in striking a balance between divulging the objective of the study in order to assist participants' understanding of what content and level of detail is required, against not identifying the real focus because it may subsequently skew the responses provided. One way around this problem can be to avoid use of the word trust until the end of the study. For example, in our mentor study we did not collect 'propensity to trust' (Costa and McCrae, 1992) data until towards the end. We then computed their results and utilised them in a final debrief, talking through emergent changes and the associated diary entries. However, this may not be practical if the central research question concerns dynamics of trust and gathers data on trust measures through a Likert-type scale.

Diary method can alter further respondents' conceptualisations of a particular domain in two ways. First, through collapsing and entraining their own perceptions to fit those provided by the researcher (Bolger et al., 2003), or second, through the actual process of completing the diary, sensitising and altering their insight and understanding into the construct. Overall care must be taken if choosing to utilise a repeating scale.

It is clear from the type of questions I have been suggesting that the diary method could be used to explore sensitive topics. We know less about the impact of diary method in vulnerable contexts, such as those where trust has been damaged. In conditions of broken trust, a diary tool, particularly one which utilises repeated sampling and collection through fixed-format questionnaires, could create a destabilising vortex effect with responses to a previous scale still having an impact on responses within the current sampling window. Researchers therefore must pay great attention to ethical dimensions of their work and anticipate unforeseen impacts on participants.

Repetition and its Impact

As noted earlier, a critical consideration within any repetitive design study, but particularly where the same instrument is repeatedly presented, is to ensure that each record is actually capturing pertinent data for *that* event. Researchers must be sensitive to participants habituating their responses to particular types of recording, such as repeated scales and either becoming less reactive, or skimming and omitting sections (Bolger et al., 2003). One way to reduce the impact is through simply prompting participants to complete their entries in a mindful way, focusing only on this particular event or occurrence. Alternatively, varying the choice of items or scale can break up the monotony of the task. In our recent mentor study we also found that reminding respondents that we will be asking them about their responses in the interviews helped keep them focused on accurately recording events (plus it also allowed us to verify responses). Thirdly, using a more open response style leaves interpretation to the respondent, helping reduce the boredom associated with the completion of the same question over and over again. Indeed many diary researchers have had their studies sabotaged through respondents becoming fed up with the task and simply making up their responses. Having some supplementary process such as subsequent interviews can be a useful mechanism for corroborating entries, as well as providing further clarification and insight into the context surrounding key entries – for example, where a response dramatically changes. Utilising open responses can also be important for publication purposes, with independent coders identifying and agreeing robust categories of response. Therefore different methods can be combined to supplement and enhance the quality of the recordings made, improving the sophistication of these data.

A final and very important stage in the development of diary studies is the use of piloting. As diary studies ask a great deal of input from participants, piloting is one mechanism of ensuring their effectiveness is maximised. Often these studies seem straightforward to naive researchers, but piloting is useful in ensuring that they do work the way that they were intended, capturing events as they unfurl and eliciting the right quality and quantity of data at each entry. For example, pilots can reveal unforeseen issues, such as how different work schedules might conflict with recording protocols, or what shift-workers should do when their 'morning' recording actually becomes a 'night' one, and vice versa. In addition, context-related problems may be found, such as noisy environments in which the beeper used to signal time for a recording cannot be heard, or where there is no internet access in a study utilising online recording methods.

Practical Support

There can be some anxiety about the size of the sample recruited. In our nurse study we used snowballing technique in three different contexts and recruited only 12 participants. However, through using a mixed methods approach we were able to gather a plethora of written, verbal and scale-level data. An important consideration is how you ensure that your participants remain actively engaged.

Before commencing any study it can be of great use to hold a familiarisation event. It is an important means both of further personal contact with participants, but also of ensuring they know how to use the tools. We provided information on the duration, frequency and type of events we wanted recorded, plus the level of detail required. Such events are vital to ensure that your instructions are being adhered to, helping researchers identify and resolve any adverse issues that may have a significant and deleterious impact before participants return to their work.

A further support from these sessions is to devise take-away supplementary materials for participants. This can help in preventing overeager participants from overdoing their records, and remind everyone about the preferred level and content. Online data collection can be a real advantage in helping to spot this type of behaviour early, but it is not always appropriate. In our study we decided to use paper-based collection as internet access was very restricted in an NHS context (see Green et al., 2006 for a discussion of the merits of paper versus online data collection).

At times someone may drop out, especially around briefings. The briefing can bring home just the level of commitment required, although when the individual knows about the requirement, they often feel some onus to help identify another potential participant for you. In addition to these one-off events, maintaining regular, but unobtrusive contact with participants is very helpful in ensuring ongoing involvement in any study. In our research, the impact of doing a full-time job, plus their student mentoring, meant that many participants became really busy. Ongoing contact helped prompt them. These types of reminders are, however, a delicate balance and there needs to be some sensitive gauging of the appropriate level, which may vary with individuals.

One useful strategy to ensure ongoing contact is through supplementary interviews. Some studies utilise a final debriefing interview. In our mentor research, we had three collection points spaced throughout, and their diaries became an in-depth aide memoire. This provided opportunities to thank participants again, but also to clarify, check and confirm the validity of entries being made. Such contact can alert researchers to entries which might have been deliberately altered. Where trust has been unexpectedly broken, attempts at distortion or change might be critical. In addition, being able to talk to an outsider may have a cathartic effect; this self-reflexive process can have a substantial positive physical and mental impact (Suedfeld and Pennebaker, 1997). Many of our mentors commented how helpful it had been to reflect on and consider their current practices.

In starting to analyse data obtained from diaries, it is often necessary to centre results (Reis and Gable, 2000). Our data consisted of well-being measures and the diary accounts. We collected baseline working measures and also levels for each stage through their mentoring. We centred the data for each of these distinct stages at a between-subject level, letting us identify outliers. (Thanks to our research questions we could use this to prompt us to go back to that individual's in-depth diary and interviews.) We looked at the high propensity to trust and low propensity to trust mentors and compared their aggregated scores. In this way these data could be examined for the different stages, with changes in well-being scores alerting us to distinct issues. Though this was a small sample, such an approach is typical.

When focusing on day-to-day variations, it can be useful to centre data around each respondent's mean, but when comparing across respondents, centring should be around the sample's mean. It is important in interpretation and writing up your research that you note what has been done; where centring has been utilised, the interpretation of the results concerns deviations from the corresponding means.

DISCUSSION

The diary method presents trust researchers with exciting opportunities to collect detailed, accurate and multi-faceted insights into an array of social behaviour, cognitive and affective states as they occur within their natural settings. Such studies have a pivotal role in supplementing experimental data from trust-based games to allow research to examine whether there are similar outcomes to trust dilemmas in the workplace. These techniques may have a central part in the identification of further mediators and moderators of trust. Even with small sample sizes, such approaches allow the events and experiences which help shape individuals' perceptions of their world, and of trust to be explored richly. Further advances in technology herald some stimulating new online tools. In addition, diary methods offer a significant resource to utilise in exploring the dynamics of trust development and its repair. They provide highly accurate records of events as they unfold, offering invaluable insights. Although underutilised generally, they have many advantages for those interested in trust.

REFERENCES

Bies, R. and T. Tripp (1996), 'Beyond distrust: "getting even" and the need for revenge', in R. Kramer and T. Tyler (eds), *Trust in Organizations: Frontiers of Theory and Research*, Thousand Oaks, CA: Sage, pp. 246–60.

Blaney, P.H. (1986), 'Affect and memory: a review', *Psychological Bulletin*, **99** (2), 229–46.

Bolger, N., A. Davis and E. Rafaeli (2003), 'Diary methods: capturing life as it is lived', *Annual Review of Psychology*, **54** (1), 579–616.

Bower, G. (1981), 'Mood and memory', *American Psychologist*, **36**, 129–48.

Brehm, J.W. (1966), *A Theory of Psychological Reactance*, New York: Academic Press.

Caspi, A., N. Bolger and J. Eckenrode (1987), 'Linking person and context in the daily stress process', *Journal of Personality and Social Psychology*, **52** (1), 184–95.

Conway, N. and R.B. Briner (2002), 'A daily diary study of affective responses to psychological contract breach and exceeded promises', *Journal of Organizational Behavior*, **23** (3), 287–302.

Costa, P.T. and R.R. McCrae (1992), *NEO PI-R*, Florida: Psychological Assessment Resources.

Dirks, K.T. and D.L. Ferrin (2001), 'The role of trust in organizational settings', *Organization Science*, **12** (4), 450–67.

Ferrin, D.L., P.H. Kim, C.D. Cooper and K.T. Dirks (2007), 'Silence speaks volumes: the effectiveness of reticence in comparison to apology and denial for responding to integrity- and competence-based trust violations', *Journal of Applied Psychology*, **92** (4), 893–908.

Franklin, K.M., R. Janoff-Bulman and J.E. Roberts (1990), 'Long-term impact of parental divorce on optimism and trust: changes in general assumptions or narrow beliefs?', *Journal of Personality and Social Psychology*, **59** (4), 743–55.

Gillespie, N. and G. Dietz (2009), 'Trust repair after an organization-level failure', *Academy of Management Review*, **34** (1), 127–45.

Green, A., E. Rafaeli, N. Bolger, P. Shrout and H. Reis (2006), 'Paper or plastic? Data equivalence in paper and electronic diaries', *Psychological Methods*, **11** (1), 87–105.

Kahneman, D., A.B. Krueger, D.A. Schkade, N. Schwarz and A.A. Stone (2004), 'A survey method for characterizing daily life experience: the day reconstruction method', *Science*, **306** (5702), 1776–80.

Margolin, G., A. Christensen and R.S. John (1996), 'The continuance and spillover of everyday tensions in distressed and nondistressed families', *Journal of Family Psychology*, **10**, 304–21.

Reis, H.T. and S.L. Gable (2000), 'Event-sampling and other methods for studying everyday experience', in H.T. Reis and C.M. Judd (eds), *Handbook of Research Methods in Social and Personality*, Cambridge: Cambridge University Press, pp. 190–222.

Reis, H.T. and L. Wheeler (1991), *Studying Social Interaction with the Rochester Interaction Record*, New York: Academic Press.

Robinson, S.L. (1996), 'Trust and breach of the psychological contract', *Administrative Science Quarterly*, **41**, 574–99.

Searle, R., A. Weibel and D.N. Den Hartog (2011), 'Employee trust in organizational contexts', in G.P. Hodgkinson and J.K. Ford (eds), *International Review of Industrial and Organizational Psychology*, Chichester: Wiley, pp. 143–91.

Sonnentag, S., C. Binnewies and E. Mojza (2008), '"Did you have a nice evening?" A day-level study on recovery experiences, sleep, and affect', *Journal of Applied Psychology*, **93** (3), 674–83.

Stone, A., J. Broderick, A. Kaell, P. Deles Paul and L. Porter (2000), 'Does the peakend phenomenon observed in laboratory pain studies apply to real-world pain in rheumatoid arthritics?', *Journal of Pain*, **1**, 212–17.

Suedfeld, P. and J. Pennebaker (1997), 'Health outcomes and cognitive aspects of recalled negative life events', *Psychosomatic Medicine*, **59**, 172–7.

Totterdell, P., S. Wood and T. Wall (2006), 'An intra-individual test of the demands-control model: a weekly diary study of psychological strain in portfolio workers', *Journal of Occupational and Organizational Psychology*, **79** (1), 63–84.

Annotated Further Reading

Among the references listed above, there are some useful texts in this field that provide more comprehensive insights, especially into technology. These include Reis and Gable (2000) and Bolger et al. (2003). Sonnentag and colleagues (e.g. Sonnentag et al., 2008) always develop interesting applications.

22 Measuring implicit trust and automatic attitude activation
Calvin Burns and Stacey Conchie

INTRODUCTION

When researchers measure trust, they often use direct (explicit) measures such as questionnaire surveys. This chapter considers the use of indirect (implicit) measures of trust, which rely on reaction times. These measures are less susceptible to the effects of response biases and are more likely to be indicative of spontaneous behaviours.

Although the concept of trust appears in a variety of senses in the social sciences, it is widely regarded as 'a psychological state comprising the intention to accept vulnerability based upon positive expectations of the intentions or behaviour of another' (Rousseau et al., 1998). Many authors have shown that certain attitudes and perceptions about an individual can lead to trust in that individual (for a review of the factors of trustworthiness, see Mayer et al., 1995). Trust can then result from the activation of a trust-related attitude for the individual to be trusted. We will review some of the literature on automatic attitude activation and argue that the use of indirect or implicit measures can yield new insights into the nature of trust, specifically implicit trust.

Trust is an important variable to consider, especially in research in organisational contexts. Most questionnaire studies about organisational culture/climate include items about trust. In studies such as this, participants explicitly consider and state their attitude about trust towards an individual (for example, I trust my supervisor). However, survey instruments may lead to overestimates of trust because they can give rise to response biases such as self-presentation and social desirability. Researchers have argued that questionnaire scores not only reflect respondents' attitudes but also the deliberate and conscious manipulation of responses to regulate their impression on others (Fazio and Olson, 2003). Thus, organisational survey data about trust may be based on respondents' attempts to convey that they are trusting individuals by stating that they trust their work colleagues more than they actually do.

In an attempt to minimise response biases associated with questionnaire measures, researchers have developed techniques that measure attitudes indirectly, or implicitly. Instead of asking for direct verbal reports, implicit measures rely on the automatic activation of attitudes. For example, if we say 'salt' you might automatically think of 'pepper'. If you do, then you likely have a pre-conscious association between salt and pepper stored in memory. Now, if we can measure the time it takes you to automatically think of 'pepper' after we say 'salt', then we have a measure of the strength of this pre-conscious association; the quicker the time, the stronger the association. The same rationale is applied to measuring trust implicitly. If we say 'supervisor' and we measure the time it takes you to classify some trust-related aspect of your supervisor, then we have an index of the strength of your pre-conscious association between your supervisor and trust. Thus, implicit trust is a pre-conscious association between an individual (or other attitude-object) and trust-related aspects of that individual which can be activated automatically from memory, and is not affected by response biases which result from consciously evaluating and stating one's attitude about that individual.

Automatic activation of implicit trust for an individual should produce a psychological state of willingness to take risk with that individual (the widely accepted conception of trust). However, activation of implicit trust is more likely to influence spontaneous behaviours (or behaviours that an individual does not try to control consciously) than deliberated-upon behaviours (see the section on Validity and Caveats, below). This has implications for predicting and explaining behaviours under stress or conditions of high mental workload when people may not have the cognitive resources to consider an individual's trustworthiness explicitly.

Up to this point, we have established that implicit measures can give us another important way of assessing trust. We will now describe the method we used for measuring implicit trust, and then comment on our personal experience of using this method. We conclude by considering the implications of implicit measures of trust in terms of their predictive validity, and some caveats.

DESCRIPTION OF THE METHOD

A number of methods exist for measuring implicit attitudes (see Fazio and Olson, 2003 for a review). The most common method is the Implicit Association Test or IAT (Greenwald et al., 1998). Another well-known but more straightforward technique is Fazio et al.'s (1995) Bona Fide Pipeline. This section shall describe the general procedure used by Burns et al. (2006) to measure implicit trust, which is based on the Bona Fide Pipeline. For a detailed description of this procedure (which requires a more in-depth knowledge of the issues associated with implicit cognition, see Burns et al., 2006).

The equipment needed to conduct the Bona Fide Pipeline consists of a laptop computer, some software (we used SuperLab), and a four-button response box. Participants should first be made familiar with the equipment and then told that they will complete tasks in three phases: a baseline phase, a priming phase, and a recognition memory test.

Baseline Phase

The first phase involves presenting target words (words indicative of trust or distrust) very quickly on the computer screen one at a time. The participant's task is to press a key on the response box labelled 'trust' or a key labelled 'distrust' as quickly as possible to indicate their judgment of the word. The purpose of this phase is to obtain baseline reaction times for the target words. There are 10 target words in total: five words indicative of trust and five words indicative of distrust. The five trust target words are: caring, confide, dependable, honest, and loyal. The five distrust target words are: backstabber, dishonest, liar, traitor, and unreliable (see Burns et al., 2006 for how these target words were developed).

Participants classify each target word twice. Each word is presented once per block, which consists of the randomised presentation of all 10 target words. Participants can take a break between these two blocks and are encouraged to do so. During data analysis, the average reaction time for a target word is calculated. This serves as the participant's baseline reaction time for that target word, which is used to determine the strength of implicit trust.

Priming Phase

The second phase is a priming task. This is the experimental manipulation which measures the extent to which an attitude-object (for example, supervisor) activates and is associated with implicit trust. Participants are told that they still have to judge the meaning of target words, but now they also have to remember different primes (job titles such as 'supervisor') that flash very quickly before each target word. There are 10 different primes. Participants are told that it is important for them to pay attention to the primes because they have to complete a recognition memory test in the next phase.

Each pairing of a prime and target word constitutes a trial. There are 20 randomised trials in each block. Over five blocks, each prime is followed by the five trust target words, and the five distrust target words. These pairings are shown in Table 22.1. Participants are encouraged to take a short

Table 22.1   Primes and pairs of target words presented in the priming phase

Prime	Block				
	1	2	3	4	5
Workmates	Caring Traitor	Honest Liar	Loyal Dishonest	Dependable Backstabber	Confide Unreliable
Supervisor	Honest Liar	Loyal Dishonest	Dependable Backstabber	Confide Unreliable	Caring Traitor
Plant Leadership	Loyal Dishonest	Dependable Backstabber	Confide Unreliable	Caring Traitor	Honest Liar
Contract Company	Dependable Backstabber	Truthful Deceitful	Honour Twofaced	Count on Sly	Be sure of Devious
Shell	Confide Unreliable	Honour Twofaced	Reliable Double dealing	Honest Liar	Count on Sly
Safety Rep	Honour Twofaced	Reliable Double dealing	Truthful Deceitful	Loyal Dishonest	Dependable Backstabber
Maintenance Staff	Reliable Double dealing	Confide Unreliable	Be sure of Devious	Honour Twofaced	Loyal Dishonest
Gas Plant Services	Truthful Deceitful	Be sure of Devious	Count on Sly	Reliable Double dealing	Honour Twofaced
Formal Methods Sheets	Be sure of Devious	Count on Sly	Caring Traitor	Truthful Deceitful	Reliable Double dealing
Permit to Work	Count on Sly	Caring Traitor	Honest Liar	Be sure of Devious	Truthful Deceitful

Source: Adapted from Burns et al. (2006).

break between blocks so that they do not get fatigued and can react as quickly as possible during the next block. Thus, in this phase, participants have to learn job titles and still judge the meaning of the target words.

The rationale behind the priming task is as follows. Suppose, for example, that a participant has implicit trust for his/her workmates stored in memory. Presenting the prime 'workmates' very quickly on the computer screen should automatically activate implicit trust. If the target word that is subsequently presented is also trust related (for example, 'loyal'), then that participant should be able to classify that target word relatively quickly (that is, quicker than the baseline reaction time for 'loyal' from phase one). In this case, responding has been facilitated, which is indicative of implicit trust.

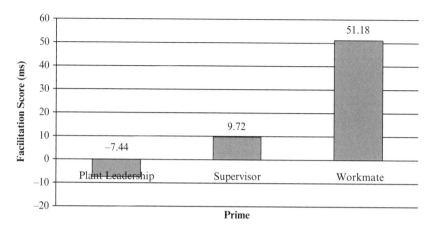

Source: Adapted from Burns et al. (2006)

Figure 22.1 UK gas plant workers' implicit trust

To quantify this, a facilitation score is calculated. This is done by subtracting this (quicker) reaction time from the baseline reaction time for 'loyal'. The facilitation scores for each prime for the five trust target words are then averaged together and the same is done for the five facilitation scores for the distrust target words. These mean trust and distrust facilitation scores are taken as an index of implicit trust and implicit distrust for that prime (see Figure 22.1).

Recognition Memory Test

The third phase is the recognition memory test that participants had been led to expect during the previous phase. The purpose of this phase is to determine whether participants had followed instructions to pay attention to the primes in the previous task. This is important because paying attention to a prime is necessary to activate implicit trust automatically. Thus, this phase consists of the random presentation of the primes used during the priming task along with an equal number of new fillers that were not presented in the previous task. Participants are instructed to press the key on the response box labelled 'Yes' if they thought the prime/filler was presented in the previous task, and to press the key labelled 'No' if they thought the prime/filler had not been presented earlier. A detection score is then calculated as per Fazio et al. (1995) to check that participants had paid attention to the primes.

PERSONAL EXPERIENCE OF MEASURING IMPLICIT TRUST

Burns et al. (2006) measured implicit trust (as per the method above) at a UK gas plant. Trust is the foundation of an effective safety culture (Reason, 1997) and they used implicit as well as explicit (questionnaire) measures to offer a more complete assessment of trust at that particular gas plant, and to investigate the role of trust in safety behaviours.

Burns et al.'s (2006) study was the first and to date the only published study to measure implicit trust. We tested participants individually in a private room at the workplace. A researcher was in the room to welcome participants, familiarise them with the laptop computer and response box, explain the procedure, and to answer any questions they might have had. On average, it took participants 14 minutes to complete the Bona Fide Pipeline. The average testing session lasted 25 minutes, during which participants also completed a short questionnaire about trust at work, and were debriefed.

Most participants reported that they enjoyed completing the Bona Fide Pipeline. Some participants likened it to playing a computer game. However, some older participants were sceptical about using a computer. Reassuring these participants about their anonymity and that their data would be treated confidentially, and reminding them that they were free to withdraw from the testing session at any time seemed to assuage any fear or sceptism they may have been experiencing as no one chose to withdraw from the study.

Gaining organisational access to conduct the Bona Fide Pipeline proved surprisingly unproblematic. The organisation is committed to improving its safety culture and the plant manager (who granted research access) was very supportive of research that might yield new insights into this. Given operational demands, it was slightly more difficult to get line managers to agree to give worker participants 30 minutes each away from the job to take part in the study. However, in the end 53 frontline workers (approximately 50 per cent of the workforce) took part.

Burns et al. (2006) found that workers expressed implicit trust for their workmates but not for their supervisor or senior managers. These data are presented in Figure 22.1. The bars represent the overall mean trust facilitation score. A positive score is indicative of implicit trust as the prime facilitated responding. Conversely, a negative score is indicative of a lack of implicit trust as the prime did not facilitate responding. It should be noted that Burns et al. (2006) also reported mean distrust facilitation scores but for the purposes of this chapter, these data are not considered.

An important issue when using this method is to make sure that participants do not lose their concentration during any of the tasks. The reaction times that are measured are in milliseconds (thousandths of a second). So, if a participant experiences a momentary lapse of attention (even as small as 100 milliseconds, one tenth of a second) on a trial in the priming phase, the resulting mean facilitation score would be artificially decreased. This would increase the standard error of the mean for the facilitation score, making it more difficult to detect differences in implicit trust between different attitude-objects (for example between workmates and supervisor). So, when using this method, it is important to make sure that participants take a short break between blocks during the priming phase so that they can maintain their attention on the task and respond as quickly as possible. Burns et al. (2006) reported large standard errors of the mean but still found significantly greater implicit trust for workmates as compared to supervisors and senior managers.

RESEARCH VALIDITY AND CAVEATS

This section considers the implications of implicit measures of trust in terms of their predictive validity and some caveats.

Predictive Validity

The predictive validity of implicit trust can in part be established by examining the relationship between explicit (questionnaire) and implicit measures of trust. Burns et al. (2006) conducted correlation analyses between their questionnaire items about trust for workmates, supervisor, and the plant leadership, and the respective facilitation scores. They found no relationship between these explicit and implicit measures of trust. These results are consistent with findings reported in the prejudice literature (Fazio et al., 1995; Greenwald et al., 1998) and the predictions made by the MODE model (Motivation and Opportunity as Determinants of whether the attitude-to-behaviour process is primarily spontaneous or deliberative in nature).

Fazio and Olson (2003) used the MODE model to explain the predictive validity of explicit and implicit measures. They stated that, 'when motivation and/or opportunity [to deliberate] are low, behaviour is expected to be largely a function of the automatically activated attitude, and hence, the implicit measure should prove predictive. When motivation and opportunity [to deliberate] are high, the explicit measure should be more predictive – presumably because the explicit measure will have been influenced by these same motivational forces' (2003: 305). Thus, the MODE model predicts that implicit trust should influence behaviour in situations of time pressure, heavy mental workload or other kinds of mental stress. So, in order to offer a more complete assessment of trust in a particular context, implicit as well as explicit measures should be used.

Caveats

We have already pointed out that the Bona Fide Pipeline measures reaction times in the order of milliseconds, and that it is important for participants to pay attention to the task and respond as quickly as possible for the most accurate results. Another issue about the use of reaction times has to do with how they should be interpreted. Reaction times are measured on a continuous scale and as such there are no absolute end points like those on a Likert-type scale on a questionnaire. A facilitation score that is significantly greater than zero (that is, baseline reaction time from phase one) should be regarded as being indicative of implicit trust because the prime facilitated responding. However, it is unclear just how strong this implicit trust might be. In order to interpret Burns et al.'s (2006) findings further, we are using the Bona Fide Pipeline to gather implicit trust data for common social figures (Burns and Conchie, in preparation). These attitude-objects are presumably trusted social figures such as 'doctor' and 'priest', presumably neutral figures such as 'postman' and 'police officer' and presumably distrusted figures such as 'politician', 'MP' (Member of Parliament). These data are being collected independently of any field studies so as not to make work-related figures such as 'supervisor' more salient and inadvertently skew the findings. When complete, this study will offer markers for comparison for Burns et al.'s findings and future studies on implicit trust.

One last issue about using the Bona Fide Pipeline concerns test–retest reliability. Fazio and Olson (2003) found that the test–retest reliability for various priming measures ranged from very low to moderate levels. They argued that too few trials in the priming phase lead to inadequate and unstable estimates of implicit attitudes. Burns et al. (2006) used five trials for each prime in the calculation of the mean trust facilitation score. However, where a participant made a mistake (that is, responded to a trust target word by pressing the distrust key or vice versa), those trials were removed, and so trust facilitation scores for some primes were based only on three or four trials.

For our study of implicit trust in common social figures, we are using 10 trials for each prime to determine the mean trust facilitation score and 10 trials for each prime to determine the mean distrust facilitation score (Burns and Conchie, in preparation). We are aiming to establish the test–retest reliability of this version of the Bona Fide Pipeline as well as Burns et al.'s (2006) version as it is currently unknown.

Another advantage of our revised version of the Bona Fide Pipeline is that it may yield a more valid measure of implicit trust as it is based on responses from 10 priming trials instead of five. Similarly, this may also yield lower standard errors of the mean for the facilitation scores as the trials are broken up into 10 blocks instead of five, giving participants fewer trials to complete during each block and more opportunities to rest between blocks; this should prevent them from becoming fatigued, so they can respond more quickly and accurately. A potential disadvantage to the revised version is that in order to keep the average completion time to about 14 minutes, it can only measure implicit trust for five different attitude-objects instead of 10, as it only uses five different primes.

DISCUSSION

This chapter has shown that implicit measures such as the Bona Fide Pipeline can offer another important way of assessing trust. Implicit attitudes have mainly been measured as part of studies about prejudice. Applied research like the role of implicit attitudes in employment discrimination is starting to emerge (Ziegert and Hanges, 2005) but these studies are rare. The study by Burns et al. (2006) appears to be the only study that uses implicit measures to assess trust.

Although there is a need to continue developing and refining implicit measures of trust, they can offer important insights into spontaneous trust behaviours. From our experience of using implicit measures in an organisational setting, managers were receptive to granting research access despite the fact that the Bona Fide Pipeline takes longer to complete than most standard questionnaires. Employee participants also reported that they enjoyed the computerised tasks. However, implicit measures should not be used to the exclusion of explicit measures. In order to offer the most complete assessment of trust in a particular context, implicit as well as explicit measures of trust should be used.

REFERENCES

Burns, C. and S. Conchie (in preparation), 'Implicit trust for common social figures'.
Burns, C., K. Mearns and P. McGeorge (2006), 'Explicit and implicit trust within safety culture', *Risk Analysis*, **26**, 1139–50.
Fazio, R.H. and M.A. Olson (2003), 'Implicit measures in social cognition research: their meaning and use', *Annual Review of Psychology*, **54**, 297–327.

Fazio, R.H., J.R. Jackson, B.C. Dunton and C.J. Williams (1995), 'Variability in automatic activation as an unobtrusive measure of racial attitudes: a bona fide pipeline?' *Journal of Personality and Social Psychology*, **69** (6), 1013–27.

Greenwald, A.G., D.E. McGhee and J.L.K. Schwartz (1998), 'Measuring individual differences in implicit cognition: the implicit association test', *Journal of Personality and Social Psychology*, **74**, 1464–80.

Mayer, R.C., J.H. Davis and F.D. Schoorman (1995), 'An integrative model of organizational trust', *Academy of Management Review*, **20** (3), 709–34.

Reason, J. (1997), *Managing the Risks of Organizational Accidents*, Aldershot: Ashgate.

Rousseau, D.M., S.B. Sitkin, R.S. Burt and C. Camerer (1998) 'Not so different after all: a cross-discipline view of trust', *Academy of Management Review*, **23** (3), 393–404.

Ziegert, J.C. and P.J. Hanges (2005), 'Employment discrimination: the role of implicit attitudes, motivation, and a climate for racial bias', *Journal of Applied Psychology*, **90** (3), 553–62.

Further Reading

Burns, C., K. Mearns and P. McGeorge (2006), 'Explicit and implicit trust within safety culture', *Risk Analysis*, **26**, 1139–50.

Fazio, R.H. and M.A. Olson (2003), 'Implicit measures in social cognition research: their meaning and use', *Annual Review of Psychology*, **54**, 297–327.

23 A voice is worth a thousand words: the implications of the micro-coding of social signals in speech for trust research

Benjamin Waber, Michele Williams,
John S. Carroll and Alex 'Sandy' Pentland

INTRODUCTION

Self-report measures of trust reflect an important and often highly reliable tool for researchers interested in trust (Mayer and Davis, 1999). However, self-report measures require subjects to stop and think about how much they trust others or are trusted by others. Researchers are not able to use these methods when subjects cannot stop to fill out surveys in real time. In our setting, medical conversations or handoffs, one member of the pair must quickly receive critical information about a patient's current medical condition and then immediately begin caring for that patient. The rushed and technical nature of these conversations also makes qualitative research difficult because most of the social signals embedded in these conversations are non-verbal. During a transition in care, such as those we observed, medical personnel rarely stopped to relay social information verbally, making transcripts of their conversations useless for retrieving social content. Although video recording and coding of non-verbal behaviour such as eye contact is an option, it is more invasive than audio recording.

The social signals embedded in the non-linguistic elements of conversation reflect a source of relational information that has received little research attention from trust scholars (Curhan and Pentland, 2007; Pentland, 2004). Thus in this chapter we seek to understand how the social signals embedded in non-linguistic elements of conversations are related to interpersonal trust. Non-linguistic elements of conversations include voiced utterances, which are vowel sounds like /o/, and unvoiced utterances, which are everything else such as bursts from the lips like /p/ and fricatives like /s/. They also include features of one's voice such as emphasis. Emphasis, for example, is determined by both the loudness of your voice and its pitch, that is, how high like a soprano or low like a baritone your voice sounds. The non-linguistic elements of a conversation exclude 'content'; that is, the information or meaning contained in the words or sentences you utter.

Specifically, our research team studied the social side of technical communication in a major hospital setting. Although effective communication during transitions in care is known to be essential for the continuity of patient care in hospitals, we only have a partial understanding of the interpersonal communication behaviours that health care providers can use to enhance both the accurate transfer of clinical information and the maintenance of interpersonal trust.

Our research group faced the challenge of understanding and measuring the non-linguistic elements of technical medical conversations. Because these conversations focused on patients' medical conditions, our transcripts provided little insight into the relational elements of the conversation. However, relational aspects of these conversations were present in the non-linguistic elements of the participants' speech, such as activity level and emphasis. These elements reflect aspects of people's engagement in the conversation and their relational responsiveness to one another. We argue that non-linguistic elements of the participants' speech not only influence the transfer of technical information, but also affect participants' experience of trust during these interactions. In this chapter, we will describe the challenges and benefits of using computers to code the non-linguistic elements of conversations and present results from a pilot study.

DESCRIPTION OF THE METHOD

In this chapter, we investigate the use of computer coding of non-linguistic aspects of speaking patterns such as emphasis and activity level. Humans and to a certain extent all mammals have evolved to pick up on 'social signals'. That is, they interpret the non-verbal behaviour of others, such as non-linguistic elements of speech (Pentland, 2008). Even watching a foreign film when you do not understand the language, you can still pick up the gist of what is occurring: which characters are interested in the conversation, who is positioning themselves in a dominant role, and so on. Similarly, you can infer what your dog or your baby is feeling, not from what they say, but the way that they vocalize or move.

Psychologists recently began to take an interest in these signals, particularly after the ground-breaking research by Ambady and colleagues (2002). Subjects in this study were asked to listen to 20 seconds of a doctor–patient conversation and then judge whether or not the patient would sue the doctor for malpractice. They found that subjects that listened to the audio with the content (that is, audible words) filtered out did as well as subjects who heard the content.

Despite this research, coding the non-linguistic elements of conversations from audio and video recordings typically presents the challenge of agreement among multiple human raters. In addition, certain features of speech such as speaking speed simply cannot be coded without computational aids. Thus, in this chapter, we investigate the use of computer coding of non-linguistic aspects of speaking patterns such as emphasis.

Sumit Basu and Alex Pentland at the MIT Media Lab began developing methods in 2001 to segment human speech and extract useful features automatically (Basu, 2002; Pentland, 2004). Although coding the non-linguistic elements of conversations from audio and video recordings presents challenges, Pentland (2004) constructed measures for four types of vocal social signalling: activity level, engagement, emphasis, and mirroring. These four measures were extrapolated from a broad reading of the voice analysis and social science literature.

Activity level refers to how long a person is speaking, combined with how much emphasis is present in their speech. It is computed by breaking up speech into speaking and non-speaking segments and computing the voiced segments to determine emphasis. Engagement refers to how much each person is influencing the pace of the conversation, and it is determined by examining how the average pace of a conversation for an individual is changed in the current conversation.

Emphasis as described earlier combined information about the loudness and pitch of one voice and reflects the amount of deviation in these values from their mean. Socially, emphasis indicates the importance that the speaker puts on an interaction (Curhan and Pentland, 2007). Finally, mirroring, which may signal empathy, is defined as the amount of short interjections uttered by both conversational participants (for example: 'OK? OK!') (Curhan and Pentland, 2007). (See Appendix for a technical description of these measures.)

By modelling the way humans produce speech, Pentland and colleagues were able to achieve unprecedented accuracy in speech segmentation and created new, compelling models of conversational dominance. Pentland and colleagues are now working to establish the general validity and nomological networks of these measures.

Recently, Pentland's group applied these techniques in experimental settings. One study examined the voice features of two people involved in a salary negotiation. By calculating four simple voice features, such as activity level, conversational engagement, prosodic emphasis, and vocal mirroring, the authors were able to predict 30 per cent of the variance in the final salaries (that is, $R^2 = 0.30$ in the regression equation, Curhan and Pentland, 2007). Although not measured in this study, it stands to reason that because vocal features reflect one's interest in one's conversational partner, they would not only influence the substantive outcome of a negotiation but also the relational outcome; for example, the trust and relationship quality established during a negotiation.

Madan et al. (2004) showed the generality of these features by performing a similar experiment in a speed dating scenario. In this experiment, pairs of one man and one woman sat at separate tables and talked for five minutes with the purpose of determining whether or not they should go out on a date. After five minutes the males changed tables and talked to a different female. At the end of the exercise, each person rated their interest in dating the people they talked to. Collecting the same features as those mentioned above, the authors were able to predict 40 per cent of the variance in responses (that is, $R^2 = 0.44$ in the regression equation). Although not measured, trust is likely to be an important component of people's interest in dating one another and thus predicted by vocal features.

Our research seeks to establish the link between vocal features of a conversation and interpersonal trust. This line of study has the potential to enable future research using vocal features as: (1) a proxy for trust or relationship quality, (2) an antecedent of trust building, and (3) a moderator of positive and negative vocal content (the meaning of a conversation) on trust.

In this chapter, we focus on the non-linguistic feature of emphasis (pitch and volume), which had a consistent relationship with both trust and information transfer.

PERSONAL EXPERIENCE OF MICRO-CODING OF SPEECH

Trust facilitates information sharing and knowledge transfer (Currall and Judge, 1995; Levin and Cross, 2004). Trust enhances self-disclosure and allows individuals to ask questions without the fear of being taken advantage of (Levin and Cross, 2004). However, little is known about the relationship between trust and non-linguistic speech behaviour. We argue that the non-linguistic components of speech carry the relational content of technical conversations and also influence the effectiveness of speech. For instance, emphasis (a combined measure of pitch and volume) indicates the importance that the speaker puts on an interaction (Curhan and Pentland, 2007) and also focuses listener attention on specific content or information that the speaker believes is most important. We argue that trust increases the use of relational speech features and that relational speech features, in turn, should enhance both the transfer of technical information and subsequent trust.

In our study of medical transitions in care, we studied nurses from a large urban hospital. These nurses were engaged in transferring the information required for the ongoing care of actual patients. We recorded the specific constrained interaction situations in which one outgoing nurse transferred the medical information associated with a patient to an incoming nurse who would then care for the patient during the upcoming shift. Our data was dyadic by handoff. Using a sample of 29 nurses in 45 unique dyads and a fixed effects model, we used computer coding of speaker dyads to investigate the impact of non-linguistic features of communication on the transfer of technical information and interpersonal trust. The raw audio files from the interactions were fed into a computer program, which then performed voicing analysis and speaker identification. Next higher-level features such as loudness and pitch were computed and used to create the activity, engagement, emphasis, and mirroring features.

We found that emphasis (variations in pitch and volume) that partners used in their speech mattered. Emphasis, which reflects emotional engagement in a conversation, was significantly associated with the technical adequacy of the information transfer as coded by an independent nursing expert, but it was not related to the trust experienced during the transfer as reported by the dyad partners. In an additional, individual-level analysis, however, a nurse's trust in his or her colleagues measured several weeks prior to the observed transition in care[1] was significantly related to the variation in emphasis used by that same outgoing nurse during the observed transition. Thus, our preliminary findings suggest that trust may form a context that influences the use of non-linguistic elements of conversation, elements which in turn are related to the accuracy of information transfer.

RESEARCH VALIDITY AND CAVEATS: CHALLENGES FOR RECORDING AND CODING TRUSTFUL CONVERSATIONS

Recent methods for voice analysis have been developed through computationally modelling the speech production process (that is, how air is compressed in the vocal cords and modified by the tongue), as well as extensive training of the data processing software on large datasets to determine appropriate settings for determining speaking/non-speaking and voiced/unvoiced thresholds. These methods are also robust to noise and microphone distance. In particular, under outdoor settings researchers have correctly labelled 98.3 per cent of the voicing information as well as 99.3

per cent of the speaking information (Basu, 2002). Here voicing information can be thought of loosely as vowel sounds, or voiced utterances, and unvoiced utterances, which are everything else including bursts from the lips such as /p/ and fricatives such as /s/.

However, recording voice data is challenging in a dynamic setting such as medical transitions in care, where dyads are talking in a crowded room. For instance, our data collection consisted of direct observation and audio taping that took place in the nurses' lounge of a 30-bed medical surgical unit of a large urban teaching hospital. The room was approximately 12 by 12 feet square with a large round table in the middle. The room also had a refrigerator, microwave, toaster oven, and various cabinets. Depending on how many nurses were going off and on shift, the room would have from four to ten nurses, who would all be speaking in dyads at the same time.

A difficult problem with such unconstrained contexts is detecting who is interacting with whom. Recently, conversations have been detected and isolated with reasonable success (Choudhury, 2004). Even when conversation detection is accurate, however, the corresponding audio features lose some of their predictive power in unconstrained settings (Wu et al., 2008). This is most probably due to the fact that the topics of conversations can vary widely in these situations, making it more difficult to isolate speech patterns related to work versus purely social conversations.

In our setting, not only did each participant in the conversation need to wear a recording device, but in addition, the placement of each device had to ensure that both voices in the conversation were not equidistant from any one recording device. In our pilot study, we found that only 45 out of 70 of the recordings (unique and repeating dyads) had sufficient quality for the computer to extract vocal features easily. The remaining recordings required human intervention to process them accurately. Significant human intervention was also necessary for pre-processing the recordings in order to extract features from the audio data.

DISCUSSION: IMPLICATIONS FOR TRUST RESEARCH

Our pilot data suggests a link between trust and non-linguistic features of speech that, in turn, enhance the transfer of technical information. In our medical setting, this enhanced information transfer has implications for patient safety. For example, communication breakdowns were considered to be the primary root cause of over 60 per cent of the sentinel events in a national sample of preventable errors in hospitals.[2] At our research site, communication breakdowns were identified as a contributing factor in 31 per cent of the asserted malpractice claims. Thus, because effective communication has implications for safety, the relationship among trust, non-linguistic features of speech, and effective communication may be important for a variety of high-reliability organizations.

We were surprised that the non-linguistic features of speech were not significantly related to our measures of trust during the observed transition in care, but only to trust measured several weeks prior to the observed transition. However, we believe that the survey that nurses filled out after their interaction may have been compromised by the fact the outgoing nurses were rushing to go home and incoming nurses were rushing to see their patients. Another 'real-time' measure of relationship quality such as the physical proximity between dyad partners during the interaction may help reveal the more relational implications of the non-linguistic coding. Alternatively, it may also be the case that trust in this situation is related to competence (that is, the quality of the information provided by the outgoing nurse as assessed by the incoming nurse over the course of the next shift). In this case, a time-delayed measure of trust may reveal the hypothesized link between non-linguistic elements of speech and trust.

Our study contributes to trust research by suggesting that trust influences effective communication through a non-linguistic path. Although substantial research on trust suggests that trust facilitates communication and information sharing (Currall and Judge, 1995), there is little if any work suggesting that trust improves communication by facilitating non-linguistic elements of speech that, in turn, enhance information transfer.

We did not find a significant correlation between vocal features and trust during the observed transition in care, although we did find a significant correlation between vocal features and trust measured several weeks earlier. We therefore believe that the significance of vocal features for trust is still untapped. For instance, vocal features may only be important for trust in new relationships or after a trust violation. In these contexts, such features may signal genuine interest and engagement in the relationship. Because of their potential signalling value, vocal features may play an important role in trust repair. For instance, they may moderate the impact of trust repair strategies such as apologies and accounts on subsequent levels of trust.

The benefits of the social signalling methods for predicting persuasion, interest, and handoff success are compelling. Wider application of this computer technique to trust research is demanded, not only due to this success but also because of the relative ease with which these features can be extracted, especially when compared to manual coding. In the future we hope that additional sensors, such as accelerometers, infra-red transceivers and the like will be used by researchers to develop even richer datasets.

Armed with these new analytical tools, we are sure that future research will yield many unprecedented and useful results.

NOTES

1. Trust had been measured earlier as the psychological safety of the outgoing nurse (that is, willingness to trust or make oneself vulnerable to the other nurses on the unit, see Edmondson, 1999).
2. Joint Commission on Accreditation of Healthcare Organisations, Root causes of sentinel events, 2004, www.jointcommission.org/.

REFERENCES

Ambady, N., D. LaPlante, T. Nguyen, R. Rosenthal, N. Chaumenton and W. Levinson (2002), 'Surgeons' tone of voice: a clue to malpractice history', *Surgery*, **132** (1), 5–9.

Bailenson, J. and N. Yee (2005), 'Digital chameleons: automatic assimilation of nonverbal gestures in immersive virtual environments', *Psychological Science*, **16** (10), 814–19.

Bailenson, J.N., S. Iyengar and N. Yee (2005), 'Facial identity capture and presidential candidate preference', paper presented at the 55th Annual Conference of the International Communication Association.

Basu, S. (2002), 'Conversational scene analysis', PhD thesis, Cambridge, MA: MIT Media Laboratory.

Chartrand, T.L. and J.A. Bargh (1999), 'The chameleon effect: the perception-behaviour link and social interaction', *Journal of Personality and Social Psychology*, **76**, 893–910.

Choudhury, T. (2004), 'Sensing and modelling human networks', PhD thesis, Cambridge, MA: MIT Media Laboratory.

Curhan, J. and A. Pentland (2007), 'Thin slices of negotiation: predicting outcomes from conversational dynamics within the first 5 minutes', *Journal of Applied Psychology*, **92** (3), 802–11.

Currall, S.C. and T.A. Judge, (1995), 'Measuring trust between organizational boundary role persons', *Organizational Behavior and Human Decision Processes*, **64**, 151–70.

Edmondson, A. (1999), 'Psychological safety and learning behavior in work teams', *Administrative Science Quarterly*, **44** (2), 350–83.

Jaffe, J., B. Beebe, S. Feldstein, C.L. Crown and M. Jasnow (2001), 'Rhythms of dialogue in early infancy', *Monographs of the Society for Research in Child Development*, **66** (2).

Levin, D.Z. and R. Cross (2004), 'The strength of weak ties you can trust: the mediating role of trust in effective knowledge transfer', *Management Science*, **50** (11), 1477–90.

Madan, A., R. Caneel and A. Pentland (2004), 'Voices of attraction', technical report, Cambridge, MA: MIT Media Laboratory.

Mayer, R.C. and J.H. Davis (1999), 'The effect of the performance appraisal system on trust for management: a field quasi-experiment', *Journal of Applied Psychology*, **84**, 123–36.

Olguin, D., B. Waber, T. Kim, A. Mohan, K. Ara and A. Pentland (2009), 'Sensible organizations: technology and methodology for automatically measuring organizational behavior', *IEEE Transactions on Systems, Man, and Cybernetics Part B*, **39** (1), 43–55.

Pentland, A. (2004), *Social Dynamics: Signals and Behavior*, Chichester: ICDL, IEEE Press.

Pentland, A. (2008), *Honest Signals*, Cambridge, MA: MIT Press.

Rabiner, L.R. (1989), 'A tutorial on hidden markov models and selected applications in speech recognition', *Proceedings of the IEEE*, **39** (1), 43–55.

Stoltzman, W.T. (2006), 'Toward a social signaling framework: activity and emphasis in speech', master's thesis, Cambridge, MA: MIT Media Laboratory.

Wu, L., B.N. Waber, S. Aral, E. Brynjolfsson and A. Pentland (2008), 'Mining face-to-face interaction networks using sociometric badges: predicting productivity in an IT configuration task', paper presented at ICIS 2008, Paris, France.

Further Reading

Basu, S. (2002), 'Conversational scene analysis', PhD thesis, Cambridge, MA: MIT Media Laboratory.
Curhan, J. and A. Pentland (2007), 'Thin slices of negotiation: predicting outcomes from conversational dynamics within the first 5 minutes', *Journal of Applied Psychology*, **92** (3) 802–11.
Pentland, A. (2008), *Honest Signals*, Cambridge, MA: MIT Press.

APPENDIX

Measures of non-linguistic vocal signalling

Activity level	Calculation of the activity measure begins by using a two-level Hidden Markov Model (HMM)[1] to segment the speech stream of each person into voiced and non-voiced segments, and then group the voiced segments into speaking vs. non-speaking (Basu, 2002). Conversational activity level is measured by the z-scored percentage of speaking time plus the frequency of voiced segments.
Engagement	Engagement is measured by the z-scored influence each person has on the other's turn taking. Intuitively, when someone is trying to drive the conversation, they are more engaged than their conversational partner. When two people are interacting, their individual turn-taking dynamics influence each other and can be modelled as a Markov process (Jaffe et al., 2001). By watching people interact over long periods of time, we can determine what their normal interaction patterns are and see how they are influenced by the person they are currently interacting with. To measure these influences we model their individual turn-taking by an HMM and measure the coupling of these two dynamic systems to estimate the influence each has on the others' turn-taking dynamics (Choudhury, 2004). Our method is similar to the classic method of Jaffe et al. (2001), but with a simpler parameterization that permits the direction of influence to be calculated and permits analysis of conversations involving many participants.
Emphasis	Emphasis is measured by the variation in prosodic emphasis. For each voiced segment we extract the mean energy, frequency of the fundamental format, and the spectral entropy. Averaging over longer time periods provides estimates of the mean-scaled standard deviation of the energy, formant frequency and spectral entropy. The z-scored sum of these standard deviations is taken as a measure of speaker stress; such stress can be either purposeful (e.g., prosodic emphasis) or unintentional (e.g., physiological stress caused by discomfort).

Measures of non-linguistic vocal signalling

Mirroring	Mirroring behaviour, in which the prosody of one participant is 'mirrored' by the other, is considered to signal empathy, and has been shown to influence the outcome of a negotiation positively (Chartrand and Bargh, 1999). It has even been manipulated in the past in virtual reality experiments to influence the trustworthiness of avatars (Bailenson and Yee, 2005). While we cannot measure mirroring directly using automated methods, we can look for mirroring-like behaviour by detecting short interjections ('uh-huh') and a quick exchange of words ('OK?', 'OK!'). The z-scored frequency of these short utterance exchanges is taken as a measure of mirroring. In our data these short utterance exchanges were also periods of tension release.[2]

Notes:
[1] An HMM is a statistical model that consists of a series of states, each of which is only dependent upon the previous state. Each state has a certain probability of outputting different symbols. After the model parameters have been chosen (number of states, possible state transitions, possible outputs), the Baum–Welch algorithm is used on a training set of data to find the optimal values of state transition and output probabilities based on the initial starting conditions of the model, which consists of initial state transition and output probabilities. A more detailed description of HMMs can be found in Rabiner (1989).

[2] When extracting time-dependent features such as mirroring and interruptions, time synchronization of the recorded data is essential. While under certain circumstances this may be done automatically, the most accurate method still relies on human intervention, introducing something of a time burden on the researchers, although this requires much less time than manual coding. Using combined sensor packages helps alleviate some of these issues. The recent development of Sociometric Badges pairs a microphone with a radio, clock, and other sensors to allow for the automatic synchronization of data by using the actual time transmitted by base stations when logging data (Olguin et al., 2009). Another method is to use easily recognizable unique sounds on the audio track to aid automatic synchronization. Loud hand claps are particularly useful, since they are easy to generate and leave a distinct frequency signature in the audio data.

24 It takes a community to make a difference: evaluating quality procedures and practices in trust research

Katinka M. Bijlsma-Frankema and Denise M. Rousseau[1]

Empirical science is a collective quest for answers to questions directed to the resistant character of the given empirical world under study. One has to respect the obdurate character of that empirical world – this is indeed the cardinal principle of empirical science. Empirical science pursues its quest by devising images of the empirical world under study and by testing these images through exacting scrutiny of the empirical world. (Blumer, 1969: 21)

INTRODUCTION

Trust is a long-standing topic in the social and organizational sciences (Kramer and Tyler, 1996; Mayo, 1933). The wealth of research and commonality of understandings regarding what trust is and how it works implies a mature research domain (cf. Rousseau et al., 1998). Yet, the 'proof' of trust's maturity is less than evident in the quality, accumulation, and convergence of its research findings and their interpretation.

The goal of this chapter is to prompt more systematic attention to the quality and accumulation of evidence and understandings regarding trust. This goal is motivated by the recent attention paid to the gap between organization sciences and management practice, and the plea for greater quality connections between research and practice. To accomplish this goal, we evaluate how principles and procedures promoting research quality apply to the actual practices of trust scholars. The quotation by Herbert Blumer which serves as this chapter's epigraphy highlights two of the key challenges: (1) a continuous focus on scrutinizing the relation between the empirical world and the theoretical representation of that world and (2) the collective, not individual, production of science.

Scholars and practitioners increasingly recognize that concerted actions within a scientific community are necessary to promote high-quality research that informs practice (Cohen, 2007; Rousseau, 2007). Better promotion of research quality and use requires socially complex supports.

259

These include, among others, shared understandings (for example, the centrality of trust to society's organizations and institutions), scholarly findings that inform institutional legitimacy criteria (for example, underscoring the role of public trust in institutions), and quality connections of scholars with both practitioners and the general public. No mere sum of separate individual efforts, no matter how well motivated, can meet the challenge these value shifts pose. Bridging the gap between organizational sciences and practice calls for a collective endeavour.

To come to grips with the nature of this challenge, we first examine research procedures and practices as applied in trust research. We assess them in terms of four scientific ideals derived from Goudsblom (1977), Thorngate (1976), and Weick (2006). Goudsblom identified several critical ideals in science, including accuracy (validity, precision), generality, theoretical systematic (parsimony, explanatory power, accumulation of understandings), and relevance to society. The first two mirror the key quality criteria others have specified for theoretical explanations (Weick, 2006: quoting Thorngate, 1976): (1) accuracy (consensually valid representation of the actor's world); (2) generality; and (3) simplicity. To evaluate the procedures the field of trust research uses, we incorporate the criteria of Goudsblom, Thorngate and Weick into a four-part framework, using points 1–3 above along with (4) theoretically systematic (parsimony, explanatory power, accumulation) to represent the quality criteria for scientific theory and evidence. Our evaluation will be guided by this question: is the present body of evidence and its theoretical understandings the product of optimal procedures and practices? And if not, how can we improve the procedures and practices to build higher-quality evidence and theoretical understandings? We focus first on accuracy and generality as essential conditions in representing the empirical world. Subsequently, we will explore the implications of our recommendations in attaining the remaining criteria.

ACCURACY

The first criterion we use to evaluate procedures and practices is accuracy, which encompasses validity and precision of measurement. The primary forms of validity are 'construct validity and predictive validity' (Nunnally, 1967).

Construct validity addresses whether a study's constructs measure what is intended, for example, produce observations consistent with the theoretical properties of each construct. It indicates whether the postulated relations between the constructs provide a valid representation of the empirical world. In his early methodology book, Kerlinger (1969: 449) argued that construct validity is about how well measures of constructs and hypothesized relations between them represent the theoretical constructs or concepts and postulated relations between them: 'The significant point about construct validity, which sets it apart from other types of validity, is its preoccupation with theory, theoretical constructs [. . .] Construct validation in measurement contrasts sharply with empirical approaches which define the validity of a measure purely by its success in predicting a criterion.' We follow Kerlinger (1969) in distinguishing between the theory-directed matter of construct validity and the more empirical matter of predictive validity.

Construct validity is an evidentiary requirement for all scientific constructs and agreement on valid constructs is a prerequisite of cumulative theory development. Several procedures exist to address construct validity. Analysing the content of the construct and comparing it with the items used to measure it is one way to establish an aspect of construct validity, content validity.

Content validity concerns the question of whether the indicators or items chosen to assess a construct are representative of the domain (Nunnally, 1967), and is largely a matter of judgment. Researcher triangulation can promote this form of validity. Next, other parties can be included in the process and procedures can be refined to heighten the construct validity. Panels of researchers or field experts can be used to judge the fit between constructs and measures. A sample of respondents from the field to be studied, moreover, can be asked to react to the items of the measure while completing the survey, or they can be interviewed in a non-directive mode to discover the meanings the constructs have in their perspective. More technical approaches assess the psychometric qualities of the measure, for example, tests of convergent and discriminant validity, via factor analysis or multicollinearity statistics, establishing whether the empirical measures are sufficiently distinct.

Given the practices regarding construct validity in the field of trust research, it is disappointing to note that the theory directedness of construct validation, as stressed by Kerlinger (1969), has become less visible in scholarly practice, particularly in quantitative studies. Presentations at conferences seldom allude to the meaning of concepts and why the measures chosen are considered valid given these meanings. Journal articles are not different in this respect, including those in highly ranked publications, where reviews often focus on whether conventional practices (that is, as used in previously published studies) are followed, less so whether these are actually theoretically appropriate. Instead, considerable attention is given in both survey studies and reviews to technical devices legitimating measures (for example alpha and multicollinearity tests). These tests have little to do with determining whether the meaning of the construct is adequately captured. In qualitative studies, the situation is not much better. Validity of constructs used to capture the phenomena studied is often assumed as a product of the qualitative method chosen, but construct validity is not often demonstrated in a systematic manner, as, for instance, is proposed by proponents of grounded theory (Glaser and Strauss, 1967).

Since researchers often fail to report what they may have done to validate their constructs in a theory-directed way, public discussion of the validity of constructs is not common. Another consequence of this lack of public discussion impacts theory building. If construct validity is rarely discussed for established constructs, treating relations between concepts in a theoretically thorough mode will suffer, too. Construct validity is a stepping stone to the thorough understanding of conceptual relations.

Trust research lacks a critical and rich debate about construct validity. Such a public discussion constitutes an important next step to what appears to be the existing consensus regarding the trust concept as a willingness to be vulnerable to another party's intentions and actions (Mayer et al., 1995; Rousseau et al., 1998). Although trust scholars widely accept this definition, we seldom allude to how vulnerability is expressed in the relations they observe. How, for instance is this vulnerability shaped within team member–manager relations, or in organizational member–organization relations? Do core vulnerabilities differ across trust relations with different referents? These matters are important for measuring trust validly, but the silence surrounding them is deafening.

We contend that to establish that trust is a real and meaningful phenomenon, purported and variegated observations of trust in the organization are needed to demonstrate consistency with its conceptualization as a willingness to be vulnerable. Another matter is how the willingness to accept vulnerability and positive expectations are related. Positive expectations may have little meaning if a bad outcome from one's vulnerability to another is unlikely. We are aware of virtually no research that takes into account the perceived or actual level of adverse consequences at risk under conditions of trust. Consider how difficult it would be to understand conflict management if no information existed on the potential for conflict in the circumstance studied. Potential conflict is essential for the phenomenon of conflict management to be meaningfully observed. So too is the presence of risk and vulnerability to the meaningful observation of trust.

Concomitantly, the meaningfulness of trust as a phenomenon in its own right requires that its characteristics be distinct from other similar phenomena. These include liking a person or being satisfied with an organization. This discriminant validity necessitates a thorough scrutiny of the construct's content and meaning, and how these differ from other constructs. This analysis of construct distinctiveness is also largely missing from the public debate on trust research. Trust is a phenomenon of ubiquitous concern. It overlaps and is easily confused with other interpersonal or organizational dimensions. The concepts of trustworthiness (Mayer et al., 1995) and trust, for instance, are often used in an undifferentiated way, as if the constructs have a common meaning. Nonetheless, their definitions differ. Other concepts in need of clarification in relation to trust are social capital and identification, given the lack of agreement on their boundaries and conceptual networks. Discussions regarding these validity matters are essential to create consensus on construct validity. At present, the matter of validity is confined to narrow technical considerations and largely ignores trust's fundamental conceptual issues.

Predictive validity refers to the extent to which a study properly demonstrates a causal relationship between a presumed cause and effect. Predictive validity is actually an amalgam of features that an informative body of evidence requires (Rousseau et al., 2008). *Co-variation* means that indicators of cause and effect are interrelated. It must however be noted that significance tests are statistical in nature, and that sample size co-varies with the chance of a significant relation. *Temporal precedence* means that studies are designed such that the 'cause' precedes the 'effect' in time.

The next criterion is a contentious one. *Effect size* is a measure of the strength of the observed relationship between two variables (Hedges and Olkin, 1985). In research on causal relationships, a statistically significant effect is a key indicator. It is less apparent whether its size per se is important given the host of factors that can constrain it, including the observed variance in variables (Fichman, 1999). Moreover, some effects can be so easily induced that their size is less important than the fact that they are relatively pervasive (for example, in-group/out-group effects; Prentice and Miller, 1992). However, effect sizes are the common currency of *meta-analyses* summarizing findings across quantitative studies (Hedges and Olkin, 1985). That aggregated effect size is not zero is meta-analysis' essential information. Meta-analyses, moreover, provide accumulation of evidence and by mapping the evidence enable us to see on which relations robust insights have been gained and where more studies are needed.

The last feature of predictive validity, *non-spuriousness*, means that no plausible alternative explanations exist for the variables' observed co-variation. This matter has a two-fold character. On the one hand, spuriousness can be a matter of poor measurement, which brings us back to the matter of construct validity, because measurement quality is important to reducing spuriousness. Poor measurement quality creates false explanations for observed co-variation where measures are unreliable or invalid, for instance when two variables correlate because they lack discriminant validity. Measures become unreliable when they contain substantial error, as when respondents have difficulty answering complicated questions, or when they do not measure what they are supposed to measure, due to low construct validity, as in the case of a general intelligence test that taps cultural knowledge but not mental abilities per se. On the other hand, spuriousness is also a theoretical matter. Theoretical thinking in terms of alternative explanations can identify non-spurious ones, as well as discern third variables that can act as mediators. More systematic and concerted attention to alternative explanations of relations between phenomena under investigation can promote the theoretical capacity of a community of scholars to distinguish spurious relations from non-spurious ones. Non-spuriousness should be a matter of ongoing concern in any community of researchers, because excluding alternative explanations is a way to build robust theoretical insights. Yet, public exchanges regarding this matter in the domain of trust are infrequent.

We conclude that common practices in the field of trust research mirror many less than laudable practices evident in the wider field of organization and management research. These poor but common practices have reduced attention to validity to narrow consideration of technical devices. In doing so the original focus on theory's link to the empirical world has largely been lost. As the matter of non-spuriousness shows, technical devices alone cannot solve this problem effectively.

VALIDITY: AN ALTERNATIVE APPROACH

Informed by Herbert Blumer's work, we seek to recapture a broader conception of validity. Blumer (1969), a symbolic interactionist, advocated attention to whether the image of the world that social scientists study adequately represents the empirical world. According to Blumer, reality exists in the empirical world, not in so-called 'empirical' methods used to study it. The procedures employed in scientific inquiry should be assessed in terms of whether they respect the nature of that empirical world. Every phase of the research process must address the adequacy of this representation. This process begins with a critical examination of the researcher's image of the empirical world. This image influences the selection of problems, the means used in getting the data, and the kind of relationships sought among them: 'The problems set for study need to be critically studied to see whether they are genuine problems in the empirical world; the data chosen need to be inspected to see if in fact they have in the empirical world the character given to them in the study' (Blumer, 1969: 22). Blumer warns us of the tendency for researchers to create a separate world, with constructs of their own making, and relations between constructs and problems regarding constructs which bear insufficient resemblance to the empirical world. In Blumer's view, researchers must be aware of this self-constructed character of the research world, because it can lead to invalid statements about the empirical world.

Signals that the constructed world of researchers may not bear sufficient resemblance to the empirical world to be valid can be often found in research findings of other domains. Research showing that altruistic behaviour is rather common among humans, for instance, can challenge research that models problems of choice purely in rational, calculative terms. Another example is that the problem formulation of why working-class pupils are less intelligent than middle-class pupils has been contested by studies that showed a 'Pygmalion effect' in school classrooms in which differential class-related expectations of teachers play a key part in student performance differences (Rosenthal and Jacobson, 1965).

Blumer's treatment of validity is far broader than we observe in current approaches to validity in trust research. His argument for continuous attention to validity as a matter of representation in every phase of the research process warns against the narrowing of construct validity to mere technical concerns or other taken-for-granted devices. His plea coincides with Weick's (2006) recent exploration of two modes of scientific validation, verification and falsification, in other words rhetorics of verification and/or falsification (Weick, 2006). These rhetorics constitute hard-to-change and pervasive vocabularies. Weick (2006) argues that, as scholars, we are more caught up in a rhetoric of verification than we realize, due to a tendency to see selectively what we believe and to ignore falsifying information. As vocabularies, Weick argues, rhetorics are tools for coping with rather than validly representing the empirical world. Instead of allowing selective perception and limited vocabularies, Weick asserts the need for a rhetoric of falsification. The rhetoric of verification fosters mindlessness in the research process. Mindlessness is evident in both the taken-for-grantedness of dominant constructs and the routine imposition of pre-existing categories onto our observations. In contrast, the rhetoric of falsification furthers mindfulness. Mindfulness is evident in the active questioning of the categories and constructs we use and how we use them. Citing Kabat-Zinn, Weick points at 'just how quickly we put our experiences into tidy and unexamined conceptual boxes . . . how reluctant we are to examine those conceptual boxes and how much is discovered when we do examine those boxes' (Weick, 2006: 1727). Instead of servile reliance upon dominant conceptualizations, we need diversity in categories to promote reflection. Following this diversity, undertaking syntheses can improve conceptual quality.

Changing rhetoric requires collective effort of the part of the community that developed it. In the rhetoric of falsification, doubt is built in. Examination of procedures, practices and vocabularies is part and parcel of the research process, used to build understanding of the empirical world and confidence in these understandings. According to Weick, 'simultaneous believing and doubting is the signature of a wise act' (2006: 1730). Blumer could not agree more.

Now the question is whether incorporating the approaches of Blumer and Weick in our daily research practices as trust scholars would add to the quality of our evidence and our understanding. What would we do differently in research processes and can net benefits be expected? Note that Blumer's approach redirects our attention to construct validity as Kerlinger describes, as a matter of how adequately theoretical concepts and relations between concepts represent the empirical world. Two questions arise from this manner of representation: the first question is the familiar construct validity question of whether the constructs are reflected in information the study obtains. Blumer, however, proffers another question: whether the theoretical constructs in use and their relations represent the empirical world as it is. Although the first question is about valid deduction of operational measures from constructs, the second question is about valid induction of abstract constructs from the empirical world. If applications of research to the world of practice (that is, evidence-based management) are taken seriously, this question must be answered.

Both types of validity can be promoted by scholarly debate on constructs and their empirical referents, including attention to these matters in review procedures, journal articles, and presentations. The second matter, however, cannot be adequately solved without an inquiry into the nature of the empirical world and the meanings given to phenomena in that world, to be compared with the theoretical concepts designed to grasp the essence of these phenomena and the meaning people give them. This kind of inquiry asks for inductive, qualitative approaches such as grounded theory (Glaser and Strauss, 1967) or analytical induction (Silverman, 2001).

Trust researchers relying on quantitative methods often only pay lip service to the notion that such inductive research approaches can be useful. Inductive methods are seldom represented as being indispensable to define concepts, and to build understandings of relations between concepts and models that in turn can be tested in deductive designs. This to us seems odd. In the field of trust research, wide agreement exists that trust is in the eye of the beholder, as are almost all individual-level correlates of trust. Given this agreement, great interest might be expected in how people experience trust, what in their eyes are relevant antecedents and consequences and why these are relevant, because these are the ingredients of how people perceive and interpret the situations they are in. In a similar vein, Kramer has advocated a study of 'naive' theories of trust, which are based on 'mental accounts' of people in the population under study. Kramer (1996: 238) observed that: 'A survey of extant theory and research on trust evokes another critique. It quickly becomes evident from even a casual inspection of the larger sociological and psychological literature on trust, that there is a pressing need for more naïve theories about trust.' Naive theories, we contend, are rich sources of inspiration and provide testing grounds for theory building and argumentation.

Mental accounts can bring understanding of the nature of a problem in the empirical world, about the meaning of constructs and the nature of relations between these constructs as respondents perceive them; all very important matters in evaluating the validity of theoretical constructs and proposed relations between them. This could be a breakthrough regarding the gap between research and practice as well. If researchers would pay more attention to how phenomena appear in the organizational field they study, the usefulness of their results for practice will increase. For instance, the dynamic nature of phenomena in daily organizational life argues against the static nature of cross-sectional research. If this validity matter would be taken up in the vein of Blumer, researchers would more often use longitudinal and dynamic research designs, providing practitioners with insights regarding the developmental character of the phenomena they deal with daily.

Blumer's ideas enable us to recognize that two validity matters are far from salient in the community of trust scholars, too. The first is to examine researchers' prior pictures of the empirical world critically, because the choice of problems and measures is partly dependent on these representations. This recommendation fits in nicely with the argument of Weick (2006), that a rhetoric of verification is to be avoided and doubt to be built in to maintain an operational rhetoric of falsification. When researchers repeatedly use the same research design, the same scales, and ask the same kind of research questions, these repetitions indicate a taken-for-grantedness characteristic of a creativity diminishing rhetoric of verification. We contend that developing and maintaining the rhetoric of falsification is a community task among trust researchers. Such a norm could be promoted by more critical scholarly debates on validity. Another means is prioritizing mindful theorizing and research designing. A telling example of the current counterproductive state of practice is a highly rated journal that recently desk-rejected a paper because not all hypotheses were supported by the data! (Raise your hand if this has happened to you!)

Another way to reduce the field's rhetoric of verification is to hold meetings, with the aim of pitting recent developments against each other. These meetings might thus identify competing or contentious questions for future research, and stimulate the formation of research teams to address them. Promising insights can arise when doubt holds a central place in the research process.

A second validity issue flowing from Blumer's approach is the relationship that research problems have with real-world problems. This matter is seldom addressed as a serious validity concern in research publications. Studying mental accounts can help to solve this validity matter as well. Mental accounts can bring understanding of the nature of a problem in the empirical world, about the meaning of concepts which figure in the problem formulation and the nature of relations as respondents perceive them, all very important matters in evaluating the validity of a problem statement, a research design, or measures used. So far, there are very few publications reporting having conducted qualitative research or having used the results of qualitative work of others to inform the problem formulation chosen in a study. Yet, if the validity of problem formulation would receive more attention and could be established as an important validity matter, a breakthrough in the validation of research endeavours could result. Resolution of the recently identified gap between organization research and management practice (Rynes et al., 2007) would especially benefit from the recognition that validity matters include the relation between how problems are formulated in the empirical world and in scholarly studies.

A key link between problem formulation and practice is how well the particular conditions of a study correspond to circumstances of its finding's potential use. Establishing this link may entail conducting reviews giving emphasis to societal relevance and the conditions under which findings might be applied. As an example, medical research employs the concept of treatment compliance to refer to the extent to which all conditions are represented that are required to induce a particular cause to occur or a treatment to be applied. 'Treatment' non-compliance is a common factor when the effects observed in medical research are inconsistent across patients and settings. Were all practices specified in the protocol followed? How well-trained, skilled or competent were those responsible for implementation?

Compliance matters in organizational research because of variations in organizational processes and management practices. For instance, widespread variation exists in how organizations implement routines (for example, performance appraisal) or interventions (such as training, quality programmes). A study providing information regarding differences in implementation, and the sensitivity of outcomes to it, has considerable evidentiary value. Research that ignores potential variation in required supports is far less useful and has less potential to generate generalizable insights.

GENERALITY

The second criterion, generality, refers to the extent to which a result holds across populations, settings, procedures, and times. Some results are idiosyncratic to particular research contexts and do not occur outside them, for instance answers to a situation-specific survey item (Fischhoff, 1991; Sudman et al., 1996). Most experimental settings never occur naturally, providing instead special 'pure' conditions. A study has evidentiary value when it provides information (qualitative or quantitative) regarding the conditions under which a treatment or phenomenon is generalizable. Robust causal relationships, such as certain effects of trust and in-group/out-group relationships, may be relatively stable across contexts (for example, Brewer, 1979; Fichman, 2003), suggesting widespread, even universal validity. Others such as effects of leadership style on follower behaviour may be context-dependent (for example, Porter and McLaughlin, 2006) due to interpretive differences and situational demands. In the case of trust, propensity to trust varies across cultures. It also varies within cultures in response to situational demands. A person with a high propensity to trust may trust a doctor to perform surgery but not necessarily in another domain, such as investments or real estate.

Context can severely limit generality by altering the meanings people attach to the phenomena studied. Paternalism, for example, can be viewed as devaluing individuals in the United States, and as familial and supportive in Mexico. Such shifts in meaning are commonly noted with respect to location (for instance, industry or country) and time frame (for example, pre-internet, cf. Rousseau and Fried, 2000). In the case of location, national culture for example is known to influence how trust is socially constructed. Such is the case where directive leadership produces greater trust and other positive responses in countries valuing authority than in more egalitarian nations (see House et al., 2004). In the case of time frame, historical forces can influence trust, as witnessed by the evolution of employee–employer relationships since the beginning of the industrial revolution (Miles and Creed, 1995). Employer inclination to promote a trusting relationship with workers also coincides with the shifting dynamics between capital and labour (Barley and Kunda, 1992). In interpreting studies of employee–employer relationships the time frame the research involves must be taken into account, considering that trust levels between labour and management can change over time (Miles and Creed, 1995).

Generality is largely a matter of judgment based on information that a set of studies provide about participants, treatments, circumstances, and settings; all details that research reports may not fully or systematically disclose (Rousseau and Fried, 2000). A critical aspect of generality is related to deeper consideration of context. *Contextualization* refers to empirical evidence regarding how context influences the phenomenon under study. It augments understanding of generality by identifying the limits of a phenomenon or cause–effect relationship, by providing information regarding why it is limited. One important form of evidence to identify contextual supports – that is, co-occurring conditions not part of the phenomenon itself, which influence its occurrence or consequences. Such is the case where effects of high-involvement work systems depend on organizational supports such as workforce training and appropriate rewards (cf. MacDuffie, 1995). In the context of trust, prevailing levels of societal trust and the extent it exists broadly between social classes or limited within them can affect the implementation of organizational practices. In other words, trust itself can be a contextual support to other phenomena. Although buddy or peer ratings have been used in the American military, the British declined to use them during World War II as a source of assessments of potential officer candidates. According to Eric Trist (Cutcher-Gerschenfeld, 1982a), despite the need for more officer candidates, senior military officers, drawn from Britain's elite, mistrusted the opinions of soldiers, drawn largely from the poorer segment of society. An absence of contextual support, as in the example of buddy ratings, is indicated when a setting is inhospitable to a new management practice or other intervention.

Generality is also threatened when only findings from published studies are considered, since this increases the likelihood that the findings are the product of verification rhetorics. A purpose of traditional literature reviews is to identify whether findings are stable across researchers, methods, measures, and times to provide a firm foundation for advancing knowledge (Webster and Watson, 2002). However, identifying the stability of findings requires that relevant unpublished as well as published studies be reviewed, in order to overcome the bias of journals towards publishing significant findings. Statistical meta-analyses that make a special effort to overcome the 'file drawer problem' provide more generalizable results than reviews limited to published materials (Schmidt and Hunter, 1990). Drawing on our recommendations regarding validity matters, a few points can be added. If construct validity is given more attention in scholarly exchanges, the chance of agreement on meanings of constructs and the valid measurement of same can grow, greatly enhancing the comparability of findings, and confidence in their generality. The balance of explorative qualitative studies with exploitative quantitative studies is a more fruitful base for generality judgments than quantitative studies alone. Construct validity analyses can produce insights regarding a construct's generality (or its antipode, context boundedness).

If followed, we contend that Blumer's conception of validity, with its emphasis on the temporal and process dynamics of the empirical world, would alter the focus of our search for generality. If more dynamic models were developed and tested, we would have to model our quest for generality accordingly, which may mean forgoing linear or static cross-sectional modelling. More useful ways to model involve dynamic processes that lend themselves to formulating general statements about how they are related. The form of the relationships studied may entail more cyclical forms. A statement put to a generality test could be, for instance, 'avoidance of interaction and perceived value-incongruence are mutually reinforcing phenomena', suggesting a cycle of reinforcement at work, in which the independent and dependent variable interchange their positions.

Efforts to assess generality contribute to the quality of our evidence and theory building, but even more so if we make this a common endeavour. Through closer attention to the full array of research relevant to a particular phenomenon, as a community of scholars we are more likely to 'close areas where a plethora of research exists, and uncover(s) areas where research is needed' (Webster and Watson, 2002: xiii).

SIMPLICITY

Thorngate (1976), who coined the term 'simplicity' as a quality of theoretical explanations in terms of accessibility, argues that with the introduction of this criterion, next to accuracy and generality, a problem of incompatibility arises, because no explanation can be simultaneously general, accurate and simple. According to Weick (2006: 1732), generality tends to drive out accuracy. He argues that an explanation 'stripped of context, situation, configuration, relational meaning and particulars . . . has some combination of generality and simplicity, but lacks accuracy. General-simple explanations fail to move us because they misrepresent the world of involved actors.' If a theory's representation is accurate, then it is either general-accurate (and not simple) or simple-accurate (but not general).

In Weick's view, the problem appears to be a tension between general-accurate explanations and simple-accurate explanations. According to Boisot (1995), abstraction serves the purpose of generalizing information or explanations, while abstraction as a principle works against simplicity (accessibility), observable in abstractions such as mathematical equations or economic models. For practitioners, for instance, comprehensibility may be lost completely, however general the explanation is. One way of dealing with this tension is to develop a two-level approach to theory development. At the upper level, abstract, general explanations are developed, which due to their generality are not very simple (accessible). In iteration with the general, abstract explanation, concrete examples of this explanation could be gathered in different contexts. These examples are accurate-simple (accessible) explanations. In this way the general-accurate explanation, which holds across contexts, is validated with a range of concrete manifestations. In this framework, no choice need be made between general-accurate and simple-accurate explanations. Instead, these are developed together into a coherent set of general and simple explanations regarding phenomena.

Thorngate argued that simplicity heightens accessibility. Accessibility can, however, be promoted in several other ways. One is using the problem definitions people in the organizations studied are using. If they see dynamic processes but we model statics, we may not help accessibility. Relevance to society, the fourth ideal Goudsblom (1977) proposed, is material to simplicity (accessibility). Simplicity, in turn is relevant to promoting the uptake of evidence by practitioners and the general public (Rousseau and Boudreau, 2011).

THEORETICAL SYSTEMATICS

Theoretical systematics are indispensable to building good theory. Goudsblom describes theoretical systematic as a combination of non-eclectic accumulation of theoretical ideas and striving for an optimal combination of explanatory power and parsimony. Parsimony and explanatory power, when salient within a research field, can help maintain mindfulness of the community of researchers. Parsimony enhances simplicity, but it is also a strong driver of mindfulness, a parsimonious model requires that careful choices be made. Explanatory power, which most researchers relate to percentages of explained variance only, refers in this context to the explanatory power of the theoretical argumentation, which encompasses its generality. Theory can produce eye-opening explanations of phenomena for both researchers and practitioners.

Accumulation of insights is a powerful tool in building high-quality theory, but this tool can only be sharpened if a community of scholars purposefully pursues accumulation. Only in synthesizing an accumulated body of studies can the full meaning and quality of evidence be interpreted. Threats to validity can be overcome when accumulated studies using diverse research designs and measures yield comparable findings. In the field of trust research, accumulation of studies can be found, especially in the tradition of researchers following the Mayer et al. (1995) model. Unfortunately these studies show little variation in research design. Most employ survey studies and experiments. Outside this tradition, accumulation is weak and mostly confined to groups of authors who frequently work together. In the field as a whole, interaction between inductive (qualitative) and deductive (quantitative) studies is low, and often even completely absent. This lack of methodological interaction inhibits the construct validity and theory development the trust field needs to achieve the theoretical systematic ideal.

DISCUSSION

We have discussed several means of furthering the accumulation of theoretical understandings in trust research. We stressed that a community is needed to enact the proposals we made. Our challenge is to become a community that carries out a collective conversation about what we know and its limits, where we more systematically reflect on our methods and findings to question whether we have adequately tested theory and adequately developed better-specified theory in response. Next to community-building initiatives, the quality of trust theory would benefit from more active synthesizing of existing research and theory.

The field of trust research can be represented as a three-layer space, in which each layer is in close interaction with the other two. At the bottom there is the empirical world and researchers and practitioners, who are closely in touch with that world. This layer is the source of validation of theoretical constructs, hypotheses, and problem formulations, as intended by Blumer. The top layer is where theoretical ideas are developed, forged together into more encompassing or higher-order theory. The middle layer is where theoretical models are operationally measured and tested. Its relation to the theory space is the familiar matter of construct validity. The middle layer provides the theory layer with evidence about the value, viability and generality of its theoretical ideas. Its relation to the bottom layer of the empirical world is another matter of validity, as proposed by Blumer, and the empirical world is the source of data for the tests conducted in the middle space. The middle layer not only secures the validity of constructs, measures, and hypotheses; it also provides the order, accumulation, and synthesis of empirical research that in turn act as input to theoretical work at the top layer. The middle layer comprises the many individual studies that beg for synthesis. Synthesis can involve meta-analyses, systematic reviews and thematic sessions at conferences. Other synthesizing activities include meetings to discuss the state of the art of theory and research. When addressing specific topics, these can be a powerful mechanism to jump-start communal thinking about synthesis. Meetings that challenge vested theoretical ideas in a mindful way can also promote theory building as a core activity of the community. The gaps and blind spots that are identified can be purposefully addressed by planning future research in a more concerted mode.

The good news is that the change to a more communal approach need not happen overnight. It starts with small steps. Any step in the right direction enables a more cumulative next step. We can do it!

NOTE

1. The authors wish to thank Sim Sitkin for helpful ideas contributing to the writing of this chapter. Both authors shared equally in its writing.

REFERENCES

Barley, S.R. and G. Kunda (1992), 'Design and devotion: surges of rational and normative ideologies of control in managerial discourse', *Administrative Science Quarterly*, **37**, 1–30.
Blumer, H. (1969), *Symbolic Interactionism: Perspective and Method*, Englewood Cliffs, NJ: Prentice Hall.
Boisot, M.H. (1995), *Information Space. A Framework for Learning in Organizations, Institutions and Culture*, London and New York: Routledge.
Brewer, M. (1979), 'In-group bias in the minimal intergroup situation: a cognitive-motivational analysis', *Psychological Bulletin*, **84**, 307–24.
Cohen, D.J. (2007), 'The very separate worlds of academic and practitioner publications in human resource management: reasons for the divide and concrete solutions for bridging the gap', *Academy of Management Journal*, **50**, 1013–19.
Cutcher-Gershenfeld, J. (1982a), Oral history interview with Eric Trist, Toronto, Ontario.
Cutcher-Gershenfeld, J. (1982b), Personal communication with Denise Rousseau, Chicago, 19 September 2007.
Fichman, M. (1999), 'Variance explained: why size does not (always) matter', *Research on Organizational Behavior*, **21**, 295–331.
Fichman, M. (2003), 'Straining towards trust: some constraints on studying trust in organizations', *Journal of Organizational Behavior*, **24**, 133–57.
Fischhoff, B. (1991), 'Value elicitation: is there anything in there?', *American Psychologist*, **46**, 835–47.
Glaser, B.G. and A.L. Strauss (1967), *The Discovery of Grounded Theory: Strategies for Qualitative Research*, Chicago: Aldine.
Goudsblom, J. (1977), *Sociology in the Balance: A Critical Essay*, Oxford: Basil Blackwell.
Hedges, L.V. and I. Olkin (1985), *Statistical Methods for Meta-analysis*, San Diego, CA: Academic Press.

House, R.J., P.J. Hanges, M.J. Javidan, P.W. Dorfman and V. Gupta (2004), *Culture, Leadership and Organization*, London: Sage.

Kerlinger, F.N. (1969), *Foundations of Behavioral Research*, London: Holt, Rinehart and Winston.

Kramer, R.M. (1996), 'Divergent realities and convergent disappointments in hierarchical relations: trust and the intuitive auditor at work', in R.M. Kramer and T.R. Tyler, *Trust in Organizations: Frontiers of Theory and Research*, London: Sage, pp. 216–45.

Kramer, R.M. and T.R. Tyler (1996), *Trust in Organizations: Frontiers of Theory and Research*, London: Sage.

MacDuffie, J.P. (1995), 'Human resource bundles and manufacturing performance: organizational logic and flexible production systems in the world auto industry', *Industrial and Labor Relations Review*, **48**, 197–221.

Mayer, R.C., J.H. Davis and D.F. Schoorman (1995), 'An integrative model of organizational trust', *Academy of Management Review*, **20**, 709–34.

Mayo, E. (1933), *The Human Problems of Industrial Civilization*, New York: Macmillan.

Miles, R.E. and W.E.D. Creed (1995), 'Organization forms and managerial philosophies: a descriptive and analytical review', *Research in Organizational Behavior*, **17**, 333–72.

Nunnally, J.C. (1967), *Psychometric Theory*, New York: McGraw-Hill.

Porter, L.W. and G.B. McLaughlin (2006), 'Leadership and the organizational context: like the weather?', *Leadership Quarterly*, **17**, 559–76.

Prentice, D.A. and D.T. Miller (1992), 'When small effects are impressive', *Psychological Bulletin*, **112**, 160–64.

Rosenthal, R. and L. Jacobson (1965), *Pygmalion in the Classroom: Teacher and Pupil's Intellectual Development*, New York: Holt, Rhinehart, Winston.

Rousseau, D.M. (2007), 'A sticky, leveraging and scalable strategy for high-quality connections between organizational practice and science', *Academy of Management Journal*, **50**, 1037–42.

Rousseau, D.M. and J.W. Boudreau (2011), 'Sticky evidence: research findings practitioners find useful', in S.A. Morhrman, E.E. Lawler and Associates (eds), *Useful Research: Advancing Theory and Practice*, San Francisco: Berrett Koehler, pp. 269–88.

Rousseau, D.M. and Y. Fried (2000), 'Location, location, location: contextualizing organizational behavior', *Journal of Organizational Behavior*, **22**, 1–15.

Rousseau, D.M., J. Manning and D. Denyer (2008), 'Evidence in management and organizational science: assembling the field's full weight of scientific knowledge through syntheses', *Advanced Institute of Management Research Paper 67*, www.evidencebased-management. com/. . ./ROUSSEAU-Evidence_2_15_08-11.pdf.

Rousseau, D., S. Sitkin, R. Burt and C. Camerer (1998), 'Not so different after all: a cross-discipline view of trust', *Academy of Management Review*, **23**(3), 393–404.

Rynes, S.L., T.L. Giluk and K.G. Brown (2007), 'The very separate worlds of academic and practitioner periodicals in human resource management: implications for evidence-based management', *Academy of Management Journal*, **50**, 987–1008.

Schmidt, F.L. and J. Hunter (1990), *Methods of Meta-analysis: Correcting Error and Bias in Research Finding*, Thousand Oaks, CA: Sage.

Silverman, D. (2001), *Interpreting Qualitative Data: Methods for Analysing Talk, Text, and Interaction*, 2nd edition, London and Thousand Oaks, CA: Sage.

Sudman, S., N.M. Bradburn and N. Schwartz (1996), *Thinking about Answers: The Application of Cognitive Psychology to Survey Methodology*, San Francisco: Jossey-Bass.

Thorngate, W. (1976), 'Possible limits on a science of social behavior', in L.H. Strickland, F.E. Abound and K.J. Gergen (eds), *Social Psychology in Transition*, New York: Plenum, pp. 121–39.

Webster, J. and R.T. Watson (2002), 'Analyzing the past to prepare for the future: writing a literature review', *MIS Quarterly*, **26** (2), xiii–xxiii.

Weick, K.E. (2006), 'Faith, evidence, and action: better guesses in an unknowable world', *Organization Studies*, **27** (11), 1723–36.

Further Reading

Ericsson, K.A. and H.A. Simon (1993), *Protocol analysis: Verbal Reports as Data*, revised edition, Cambridge, MA: MIT Press.
Webster, J. and R.T. Watson (2002), 'Analyzing the past to prepare for the future: writing a literature review', *MIS Quarterly*, **26** (2), xiii–xxiii.
Whitley, R. (2000), *The Intellectual and Social Organization of the Sciences*, 2nd edition, Oxford: Oxford University Press.

Name index

Abelson, R. 214
Abma, T. 141
Acitelli, L. 192
Alex, Nadezhda 50–60
Alvesson, M. 102, 150, 151, 152, 153,
    154, 156
Ambady, N. 250
Andersson, B. 170
Andrews, M. 141
Argyris, C. 212
Arkes, H. 212, 214
Arksey, H. 110, 166
Ashleigh, Melanie J. 138–48
Atkinson, P. 142

Bacharach, M. 19, 20, 25
Bachmann, Reinhard 2, 6, 54, 130–37
Baier, A. 3
Bailenson, J. 258
Bamberger, P. 222
Barber, B. 25, 169
Bargh, J. 258
Barley, S. 269
Barney, J. 214
Barrera, Davide 199–211
Barthes, R. 141
Basu, S. 251, 254, 257
Batenburg, R. 207
Bearman, P. 199
Bebbington, A. 91
Bell, E. 102, 106
Bem, D. 190
Bendor, J. 20
Berg, E. 192
Berg, J. 32
Beugelsdijk, S. 80
Bies, R. 62, 226
Bigley, G. 176
Bijlsma-Frankema, Katinka 259–76
Bitner, M. 162
Blackburn, R. 86, 88
Blackburn, S. 152
Blaney, P. 231

Bligh, Michelle C. 189–98
Blumberg, Boris F. 61–71
Blumer, H. 259, 264–5, 266, 267, 268,
    271, 273
Bohnet, I. 74
Boisot, M. 271
Bolger, N. 227, 229, 230, 233, 234
Bolton, G. 207
Bonito, J. 192
Bottom, W. 35
Boudreau, J. 272
Bourdieu, P. 70
Bower, G. 231
Breban, S. 41
Breeman, Gerard 149–60
Brehm, J. 76, 233
Brewer, M. 20, 269
Brichoux, D. 41
Briner, R. 230, 232
Brinkmann, S. 110, 168
Brinsfield, Chad 29–39
Brislin, R. 105, 162
Brockner, J. 25–6
Bromiley, P. 37, 158, 180
Brown, B. 32
Brownlie, J. 6
Bryman, A. 102, 106, 114, 125
Bunker, B. 6, 29, 35, 138, 214
Burns, Calvin 239–48
Burt, R. 64, 70, 207
Buskens, Vincent 199–211, 218–19
Butler, E. 192
Butler, J. 165, 176
Butterfield, R. 192

Camerer, C. 32, 200
Campbell, J. 76
Campbell, L. 192
Canary, D. 192
Capra, C. 74
Carroll, J.M. 170
Carroll, John S. 249–58
Caspi, A. 226

Subject index